Ridiculous
Miracles

Ridiculous Miracles

God Can Take an Ordinary Person
and Do Extraordinary Things

Dr. Clarice Fluitt

Ridiculous Miracles © 2014 Clarice Fluitt

Unless otherwise noted, Scripture quotations are from the King James Version of the Bible (Public Domain). In some instances they are author's paraphrases.

Scripture quotations marked (AMP) taken from the Amplified® Bible, Copyright © 1954, 1958, 1962, 1964, 1965, 1987 by The Lockman Foundation. Used by permission." (www.Lockman.org)

Scripture quotation marked (NKJV) taken from the New King James Version®. Copyright © 1982 by Thomas Nelson, Inc. Used by permission. All rights reserved.

ISBN: 978-0-9903694-1-7

Publisher: Clarice Fluitt Enterprises, LLC
P O Box 15111
Monroe, LA 71207
www.claricefluitt.com
www.claricefluitt.org

Cover Design by: Emery Thibodeaux
Corinne Sanzone

Dedication

To FRIEND: When I was five years old, a Man dressed in a white robe and a large gold belt came down a golden staircase from heaven, walked over to me while I was making mud pies under a gum ball tree, smiled, and asked what I was doing. I replied, "Making stuff out of dirt." He laughed and said He had done that before. I asked Him His name. He said, "Call Me Friend." That was my first encounter with Jesus. He has been my faithful and best friend all of my life.

To my uncle Seville and aunt Bessie Banks who, one week after I met Friend, took me to church for the first time. Uncle Seville picked me up and ran down the aisle praying out loud, "Lord, bless this little girl and use her for your glory." He also dedicated me to the Lord. To the people from his congregation who also prayed and marked me to be set apart to do the works of God. No one will ever know how their act of obedience impacted my life.

Acknowledgments

Every act of gratitude is a refinement to our soul.

I have been extremely blessed to have had so many excellent and enriching friendships that have served to inform and transform my life. Among these great treasures are my brilliant staff that faithfully plow through every challenge; Dr. Tandie Mazule, my Executive Assistant, and Dr. Evon Peet, my Administrative Assistant, who both spent many hours, days, and nights proofreading and editing this work. Their vision, compilation, and formatting for this book are what made it possible. A big thank you to Carol Martinez for her help with the interior design. Only eternity will reveal how your callings and election have changed the world. You are champions.

I cannot begin to thank all those who have been a positive influence to me through the years, but each and every one contributed to my understanding of the power that is released when we choose to appropriate the fullness of *Ridiculous Miracles* in our lives.

To my precious parents Clyde and Audie Brown for their love, encouragement and Christian training. I learned about miracles from my wonderful parents Clyde and Audie Brown.

Mom's life was full of miracles from five years old. She was my greatest inspiration. Dad's love and endorsement established my confidence and security. There are not enough adjectives for me to describe my love and appreciation for Mom and Dad.

To George, my faithful husband and soul mate. I am blessed to have shared so many wonderful years and memories with you. You have been my champion and confidant. We have experienced a life of miracles to the glory of God. Thank you for your love and infinite patience that encourages and endorses God's call upon my life.

To my children who have lived in the midst of miracles, Debra, Becky, Cathy, Trey and Julie. You are all the strong arrows in my quiver.

Endorsements

I loved reading this book! From the very first chapter I was captivated by the tumultuous testimony. I was kept hanging on to every word as though I was on the greatest roller coaster ride of my life! It's been said that a testimony is simply pain that has been reassigned. Dr. Clarice's life story is one of advancing over adversity; instead of getting bitter, she just got better! I have continuously sought to find resources that both deepen my faith and challenge me to rise into my God-appointed destiny. This is one such book. It will bless your socks off and remind you that courage, determination, and unwavering faith will propel you into a life of ridiculous miracles and unlimited blessings!

JOSHUA MILLS
HEALING EVANGELIST, AUTHOR,
RECORDING ARTIST
NEW WINE INTERNATIONAL, INC.

Among all the qualities I look for in a Life Strategist and Personal Advisor, of utmost importance is the quality of intuition. The merging of strategic fundamentals and intuition become manifest in a keen ear to hear what the client is saying, and an inner ear to hear what needs to be said. At the top of my list of those possessing these combined skills is Dr. Clarice Fluitt. She has a unique ability to see the finished blueprint of a person's life while accurately reading the next step they need to take. Time and again she has demonstrated this ability with me personally. As you continue moving toward your own life quest, I wholeheartedly endorse Dr. Clarice and encourage you to engage her assistance on your life's journey. You can anticipate a life changing experience.

DR. LANCE WALLNAU
AUTHOR, LEADERSHIP MENTOR
AND GROWTH STRAGEGIST
THE LANCE LEARNING GROUP

Table of Contents

Foreword

JOAN HUNTER

*J*am a woman who has lived in a family of miracle workers and am well acquainted with a life of miracles, but this book, *Ridiculous Miracles,* is one of the most inspiring and exciting books that I have ever read! Dr. Fluitt's incredible testimonies are of the most awesome miracles. They will ignite your faith to a totally new realm. Get ready to have your faith and love elevated to new heights in Christ.

It is my experience that many Christians become settlers and grow content to simply admire those who are the pioneers of the faith. Thank God there are those who are willing to pay the necessary price to explore and conquer new territories. They have chosen to fully identify with the Word of God and have tapped into the resurrection power of Jesus. These are the champions of the faith that are forever pressing deeper into the promises of God.

Some Christians follow the lead of others in life and ministry. They are content to emulate those they admire. Thank God some have been willing to pioneer for others. Thank God some have been willing to pay the price necessary to lead the body of Christ into greater levels of fruitfulness and glory. Some have been willing to go outside the camp and so identify with Christ that they are able to tap into the healing and resurrection power of Jesus for the sake of the whole body of Christ.

Dr. Clarice Fluitt is one such individual. She is a proven prophetic voice who continuously leads thousands into their full potential in Christ Jesus. Her ministry is accompanied by miracles, healings, and even the raising of the dead. She has a uniquely humorous and personable approach to life and ministry that is compelling to all ages and walks of life. I heartily recommend that you buy and read *Ridiculous Miracles*. These powerful testimonies will encourage you to overcome all your challenges and teach you to trust God for His supernatural grace and power.

JOAN HUNTER
AUTHOR/HEALING EVANGELIST
JOAN HUNTER MINISTRIES

Part One

The Greater

the change,

the greater

the reward

Introduction

Who I Am and Why I Am Writing this Book

There is a Scripture found in 1 Thessalonians 5:12 that instructs us to "know those who labor among you." With this thought in mind, I want to share my story and trust that it will serve to inform, inspire, and strengthen you and your walk of faith with our Omnipotent and All Knowing God.

Despise Not the Day of Small Beginnings.
(Zechariah 4:10)

I believe that the prayers of my dying maternal grandmother after she had given birth to her fifth child have served to release redemption to her beloved bloodline. My mom related to me that her father and all five of the children were around their dying mother's bed. All that her mother would say or pray was, "Oh God, take care of my babies. The Word of God holds promises that to me and my household and to as many as You would call." Those were her last words.

My maternal grandmother's name was Lonie. She was only 24 years old when she slipped into eternity leaving five small children ages newborn to seven and her grieving husband. It was the winter of 1929 and the great depression had devastated the United States. The economy was desperate and employment was impossible. My grandfather James, who I affectionately called Papa Jim, buried his wife, and without employment, a horse, mule, wagon, phone, or food was faced with feeding and caring for his helpless clan.

> To the degree we experience limitation, frustration, and humiliation we can also experience exaltation without pride.

I am convinced that to the degree we experience limitation, frustration, and humiliation we can also experience exaltation without pride. We could all learn obedience through the things we suffer. I have learned not to waste my sorrows on regrets, revenge, or bitterness. I choose to believe God is always good. God has a plan.

Papa Jim and his children lived in a remote rural area. There were no neighbors or relatives to help him. It was a time in our American history of great struggles for everyone. In an attempt to gather food for the family, Papa Jim, who was only 26 years old, left the household in the charge of Aunt Mildred who was seven and Mom Audie, who was five. He returned with two rabbits and began to prepare food for the family. He accidentally left his loaded shotgun lying on a chair. One of the children knocked it over. The gun discharged and shot off Mom's foot. Once again, no doctor, phone, or transportation. Three days later the welfare department came, took all the children, and placed them in a Baptist orphanage. My mom had lost her mother, her foot, and her family in less than two weeks!

THE ANSWER TO A MOTHER'S PRAYER
A nickel and an orange

Mom related to me that she was in the orphanage at Christmastime. She had never seen a Christmas tree or heard about Jesus. She had never received any kind of a gift and was referred to as "the little crippled girl" instead of being addressed by her given name Audie.

A preacher named "Daddy Flowers" was visiting the orphanage and brought fresh fruit and a nickel for each of the children as a Christmas present. All the children were brought into a large room with a beautiful Christmas tree decorated with lights and glass ornaments. Daddy Flowers took notice of my mom. He said, "Little crippled girl, come here." Mom told me she was in total awe of the Christmas tree as she made her way to the front of the room. Daddy Flowers lovingly placed Mom on his lap and asked her if she knew what the Christmas tree meant and whose birthday they were celebrating. Mom simply shook her head no.

Daddy Flowers explained to her that there was a loving God that wanted her to know Him and spend forever in heaven with Him without being in pain, or being lonely or rejected. He told her that God had sent His Son from heaven to earth to save everyone who believed that He was God's Son. The reason for the beautiful Christmas tree was to remind everyone that God gave His greatest gift to us when He sent His son Jesus. He explained that, at this time each year, we remember Jesus' birthday and give gifts to each other in His memory.

Mom was so amazed at this story that she gathered her courage and asked Daddy Flowers what she had to do to go to heaven. He said, "I will give you a nickel and an orange and you can ask Jesus to come into your heart." That was the day that my mom received her first orange, her first nickel, and her first love, the Lord Jesus Christ.

She later graduated at the top of her class and became a very successful executive secretary for a large food brokerage company. She was a woman of amazing faith and love who modeled what it meant to be a champion, an overcomer, and a lover of God's Word. All of her siblings received Christ and were taught and trained at the Baptist Children's Home. The devil had meant evil but God meant good! Our tragedies can become our triumphs, especially when prayers are being sent from a dying mother and received by a loving God. All this information is to boast in the faithfulness of God.

MY MATERNAL GRANDMOTHER'S PRAYERS

Back to the future

You will need to understand Mom's story before you can appreciate mine. Mother was a product of poverty and all its horror; a broken home, medical neglect, and a national time of depression. No real hope. But at age five she met Jesus and entered a life of overcoming victories.

My mother got married at a very young age to my father, Clyde Brown. I was born in April of 1940. Mom had a terrible time with her pregnancy. At the time of her delivery the doctors discovered that she had developed multiple tumors in her womb. During the delivery she began to hemorrhage. After my birth, the doctors performed a complete hysterectomy. Her crippled foot over the years of neglect caused her leg to begin to wither. The doctors discovered that Mom had developed gangrene in her right femur, and that her leg must be amputated immediately!

Then, World War II was declared December 8, 1941.

For the next two years, Mom was very sick. Dad was doing all he could to care for her during her recovery. A time of world war had begun on every front and my father was deployed to Germany. My mom and I had to move in with my father's parents. After Mom's recovery, she returned to work. Due to a lack of transportation where my grandparents lived, Mom had to move in with her sister in order to be close to her place of employment. I was left to live with my grandparents who were already overcrowded with their three young children in a small two bedroom home.

REMEMBER MY MATERNAL GRANDMOTHER'S PRAYER

At five years of age, while still living with my paternal grandparents, I was playing under a gumball tree when, for the first time in my life, I heard beautiful music. The heavens opened and a golden staircase dropped down to earth. A Man dressed in a white robe and a large gold belt came down the golden staircase and walked over to me. I asked Him how He came out of the sky. He smiled and asked me what I was doing? I replied, "Making

> Friend pointed to the staircase and told me that someday I would bring thousands of people up those stairs. He then placed His hand on my shoulder and said, "You will never be lonely again."

stuff out of dirt." He laughed and said He had done that before. I asked Him His name. He said, "Call Me Friend."

He pointed to the staircase and told me that someday I would bring thousands of people up those stairs. He placed His hand on my shoulder and said, "You will never be lonely again." He smiled and walked away. That was my first encounter with Jesus. He has been my faithful friend all of my life. I am grateful for God's amazing grace to transcend all the impossible and hopeless circumstances of life. No one is too far from God's love. I know God loves helpless children.

I have proclaimed God's Word, power, and love around the world. I have seen the dead raised, limbs grow back, third degree burns healed, fortunes restored, and much more. But, nothing has ever moved my heart like knowing God loves the little children and watches over the prayers of passion.

My first sermon was about the truth that nothing is impossible with God. My advice for all who aspire to serve God is to learn to hear His voice. Never start a work without a Word from God. In times of great adversity, stand and do not faint. I have never seen the righteous forsaken nor His seed begging for bread.

The week after I met "Friend" my Grandfather's brother Uncle Seville came to my grandparents' home and told them he wanted

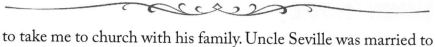

to take me to church with his family. Uncle Seville was married to a very devout Pentecostal lady named Bessie. I was only five years old and did not really know either of them.

I had never been to church but it did not take me very long to realize that church was very exciting. The people were singing, shouting and dancing. Uncle Seville picked me up and ran down the aisle praying out loud, "Lord, bless this little girl and use her for your glory." At that point, he dedicated me to the Lord while the prayers and intercession of the whole congregation marked me to be set apart for God. Everyone gathered around and laid hands on me, singing and shouting. I made up a song and started singing with them. I can remember that the words of my song were about a farmer who had a little shovel, dug a hole, planted a little seed, and a great big crop grew and grew. It was just a simple childish song and was the first song I ever sang.

When my maternal grandfather passed away years later, I sang his favorite song, "I Come to the Garden Alone," at his funeral. This time it was a real song. Uncle Seville was at the funeral and was very kind. He said, "I knew you were going to be a singer." My uncle's faith in me came to pass through my formal training in opera. Many years later when Uncle Seville was 100 years old he said to me, "Lonie, I went and got Audie's baby girl Clarice and dedicated her to the Lord. I want you to know she is going to be fine," then, he walked away never realizing who he was talking to. He thought I was my maternal grandmother Lonie and was reassuring her that her dying prayers for all her bloodline were being answered. Uncle Seville passed away that evening.

My first sermon was about the truth that nothing is impossible with God. My advice for all who aspire to serve God is to learn to hear His voice. Never start a work without a Word from God. In times of great adversity, stand and do not faint. I have never seen the righteous forsaken nor His seed begging for bread.

Prayers are powerful!

GOD IS SOVEREIGN

We are all at war. Everything that is wrong is against all that is righteous. To understand what war means can help equip us to navigate through conflict, strife and confusion. War is defined by Webster as an open armed conflict between any active hostility, contention or struggle; to battle for dominion, freedom and peace.

Ephesians 6:12 instructs the saints that the war we are in is not against flesh and blood or mere physical opponents but is against the devil and his world rulers of this present darkness; against the spirit forces of wickedness in the supernatural realm. We are instructed that our weapons of mass destruction are not carnal but mighty through God and can pull down all the destructive forces of satan! We have the Name of Jesus, the Word of God, the Blood of the Lamb, and the full armor of God.

When we begin our journey in Christ, we will learn to believe the Word of God if we really want to realize the benefits of our salvation. Job says, "He who observes lying vanities *(that is anything apart from the Word of God)* will forsake his own mercy." This revelation has served to build in me an ever-increasing faith towards God's ability to cause me to win in every situation. "Thanks be to God, who always causes me to win!" (1 Corinthians 15:57)

Chapter 1

The Journey

World War II's official timeline was from 1939 – 1945; six years and one day. The Japanese bombed Pearl Harbor on December 7, 1941. President Roosevelt declared war on December 8, 1941. Approximately sixteen million Americans went to war. Approximately four hundred thousand died.

I was born in 1940 and when I was two years old my father joined the army and was sent to Germany. He was discharged in September of 1946. Dad was gone for four years and was only a vague memory in my six-year old mind. I was starting the first grade and for the first time in my life my mother, dad, and I were all living as a family in the same home. The chaotic effects of a world war left millions of people to rebuild, reunite, and realize that the devastating effects of war could not continue to have the power to keep us as spiritual Prisoners of War. It was a new day for restoration. A time to forgive, forget and face the future in faith.

When I was 12 years old, my parents bought a new home two doors down from the Temple Baptist Church. Mama would smile and say, "We are Baptist born, and Baptist bred, and when we die, we'll be Baptist dead."

The church was the core of all of our social activities. On Monday night we had a cottage prayer meeting, on Tuesday a church visitation, on Wednesday a church prayer meeting, on Thursday choir practice, on Friday the Royal Ambassadors for boys, Girls Auxiliary, and Baptist Training Union for teens, on Saturday a fellowship dinner, and on Sunday both morning and evening services. I learned how to go to church!

I went to a Baptist Summer Camp meeting in June of 1953. I was 13 years old and had just received water baptism a few weeks earlier. All the campers were enjoying a time to go swimming. I was in the middle of everything, just a naive teenager without an agenda. Suddenly I became a bit disoriented and asked the camp counselor permission to go to my bunk house and lay down. She said, "Sure."

I was alone in the bunk house and did not understand what was happening to me. When I climbed to the top bunk, I lay down and shut my eyes. There was no outside or emotional stimulus to activate what happened next.

I shut my eyes and realized I was no longer in my bunk. I opened my eyes to see a place and a people that I had never seen before. I heard a voice speak to me and say, "I am preparing you to be a deliverer for My people." I then saw an undetermined number of black faces that were crying and calling my name and saying, "Clarice, come help us! Come help us!" The faces would be clear and then fade away, but each face and voice was sincere and compelling. I asked, "Who are these people, and where am I, and how can I help them? I'm just a young girl."

The response was, "This is a vision for another season. You are in Africa and the faces you see represent those who will be saved in one of the world's greatest reformations that will begin in Africa and sweep the world. Rest in Me, and when the time is near, I will send for you."

Immediately I was back on my bunk crying my eyes out. All I had ever heard about Africa was that there were man-eating beasts, all the natives were naked, and cannibals were everywhere. I had seen

I heard a Voice speak to me and say, "I am preparing you to be a deliverer of My people."

enough Tarzan movies to know everything about Africa. I had also watched King Kong several times. I did NOT want to go to Africa!

Forty years later, in 1993, I went to South Africa for the first time. It was amazingly beautiful, the people were very educated, beautifully dressed, and not anything like I had seen in the movies. I felt like I had come home. God had placed this nation and its wonderful citizens in my heart. I will write more about my African adventures in a later chapter.

The events following the next seven years were those of saving faith in Jesus, but I longed for more. This created a discontent that led me to begin to investigate other denominations. At 16 years of age, I felt led to become Methodist. I am now very sure that the drawing to leave my Baptist heritage was inspired by the fact that the Methodist Church I joined had the most handsome youth leader.

At 18, I had matured and my wisdom and great understanding of the deeper things of life brought me to the decision to become a Presbyterian. I should mention that I could not help but notice that most of the Presbyterians were rich. I am sure this was all pre-destined.

At 19, I was in college. My major was in speech and drama with a minor in music. An Episcopal priest heard me sing and offered to pay me to sing at the Episcopal Church. So, long story short, I became a full-fledged Episcopalian and was into the bells and beanies. I knew I was definitely on the right track.

At 20, I met George, the love of my life, who was a most devout Catholic. We got married and I became a convert (again) this time to the Catholic faith.

In 1971, George and I were introduced to the Charismatic renewal in the Catholic Church. We both received the baptism of the Holy Spirit and our lives were dramatically changed. George later became a very successful realtor and land developer. His desire was to make millions of dollars, and my desire was to spend it.

After the many years of searching for the purpose and power of my faith, I became very aware that it really does not matter what your denomination is; but, it is essential that you have a true born again personal experience with Jesus Christ as your Savior.

THE FINGER OF GOD

As a child growing up in a small southern town, one of my dreams was that someday my prince would come and we would live happily ever after, whatever that meant. I was young and impressionable and the powerful children's stories of Cinderella, Sleeping Beauty, Snow White, and many others, had helped to establish a seedbed of sprouting fantasies in my mind. Nothing about this mysterious prince was based on fact; just childlike faith and fictional fairy tales.

My story begins in the late summer of 1953. I had recently completed the sixth grade and for the first time in my life was a real teenager. I was preparing to enter Junior High School, and at this time, both Junior and Senior High students were in the same school building. I was so excited and my thoughts of being among the "high school crowd" were filled with anticipation and nervous uncertainty. I was only 13 years old and life was in session.

To make things even more exciting that summer my parents bought a new home in a new neighborhood with neighbors I knew nothing about. It was my opportunity for discovery. Would I find other young teens with similar circumstances? Being an only child, I had no siblings to instruct me on how to decorate my new room in a teenage fashion, or help prepare me for the "coming of age" journey I was about to embark on. Everything was overwhelmingly new to me.

Fortunately, the family next door had three daughters and we quickly became friends. One of the daughters was named Carolyn and I was drawn to her confidence and poise. She was eighteen years old, had her own car, and was absolutely beautiful. With her long, thick, curly hair, a brilliant smile, no pimples, and a real body, she was the image of the storybook princess that every prince would be looking for. The one thing Carolyn and I had in common was our long hair, that is, until my mom decided to have it permed. It is a sad story because my long hair was seriously over processed and burned. It had to be cut very short and I felt like a clipped pet poodle. The little self-confidence I had was shattered and sinking to an all-time low. Carolyn was not fazed at all by my disappointment. She wisely taught me how to wear pretty barrettes and flowers to enhance my challenged hairdo and also encouraged me by saying that I was still cute.

Carolyn also became my life coach on how to behave in high school, how to dress, to decorate my room, and how to be cool. In exchange for the "privilege" of being in her presence, she commandeered me to become her assistant. I was thrilled to learn about her exciting life and worked hard to embrace her advice and knowledge. She was enjoying having me do her chores and errands. We had an agreeable deal. I was a very good student, and our friendship grew as I learned to live my dreams through Carolyn's enlightening stories.

I noticed that Carolyn wore a large, masculine looking ring on a silver chain around her neck. I did not know why, so I asked. She laughed and explained that the ring was a sign to others that she was dating somebody who she considered to be a serious boyfriend. Wow, what a great idea. I wondered how I would ever learn all this important information.

Carolyn had decorated her bedroom with all manner of high school memorabilia. The focal point of her room was a large cork bulletin board filled with pictures of many boys. As I studied the pictures, I wondered if any of them were her prince charming.

I knew for certain that I did not have a prince charming, so I gathered my courage and asked Carolyn for a picture of one of her boys. She asked me which one I wanted. I carefully selected a picture of a handsome young man with a deer rifle and a backpack. She agreed to give it to me. She told me that his

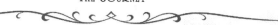

name was Marbury and he lived in Denver, Colorado. Marbury was her first boyfriend when she was in the ninth grade but he had moved to Colorado. He sent her this picture but she had not heard from him since. With great delight, I took Marbury home, made a small cork bulletin board like Carolyn's, and pinned his picture on it. I hid the bulletin board in my closet pretending he was my secret love and that someday I would marry him.

Later I went to the five and ten cents store (like a dollar store) and bought a ring, but I did not know where to get a chain. My mom had a chain on the bath tub drain stopper. I detached the chain from the stopper, put the ring on it, and wore it around my neck. I was so proud, until I realized that the cheap chain made my neck turn green. Nevertheless, I had my own prince. I was learning how to be a big girl and was imitating Carolyn to the best of my understanding. When I went to school and the other girls would ask whose ring I was wearing, I would tell them about this young man named Marbury that I was going with who lived in Colorado and that someday we would be married. For two years I wore the ring and told the same story.

So far I had learned that we all must dream dreams but also be careful what we hear and who we listen to because words and thoughts will shape our dreams. Words and thoughts are powerful. When I became a Christian and attended Sunday school I learned that if I really believed, then someday a great King would come on a white horse and take me to His perfect Kingdom where I would be happy forever. It was true that someday my prince would come! That dream was embedded into my conscious and subconscious being. I lived out the hope each day as I wore that ring that someday my prince would come. It was a comforting sign for my adolescent emotions.

The Scripture tells us that dreams are important. Solomon, the wisest king, once said, "Without a vision you perish and without a progressive vision you become careless." (Proverbs 29:18)

Eleanor Roosevelt said it this way, "The future belongs to those who believe in the beauty of their dreams and visions."

> Dreams are important: "Without a vision you perish and without a progressive vision you become careless."
> Proverbs 29:18

We are instructed by the Apostle Paul to call the things which do not exist as though they did. (Romans 4:17)

While I had never actually met Marbury, he had become real to me by faith. I eventually realized that I had only enjoyed a beautiful childhood fantasy. The time had come to move on with my life and embrace a new chapter and a fresh dream. Now I realized that Marbury had only been a figment of an innocent teenage girl's overactive imagination.

I enrolled into the local university after graduating from high school and while there met and became engaged to a fine young man named George. It was in December of 1959 and our speech club was hosting a Christmas party. I was class president, so I had to attend. My fiancé could not attend because he was the leader of a dance band that was playing elsewhere. Suddenly, there was a tall handsome stranger who walked into the party with great confidence and self-assurance. All the female eyes followed him as he crossed the floor.

The girl sitting next to me said, "That is the new student. Isn't he handsome? I'm going to ask him to dance." With those words, she floated across the floor and engaged the stranger in a dance. She really could not dance on his level. He stopped abruptly and presumed to give her lessons, beginning with a basic box step. How embarrassing. Surprised and taken back by his boldness, I began to criticize him to my friends. I insisted that, "I wouldn't dance with him if he was the last man on the face of the earth."

Finishing the dance, he stepped back and glanced around the room. He looked in my direction. And then, as though I was a mystical magnet, he came over to my table and asked me to dance. I was shocked and before I knew it, I squeaked out a timid little, "Yes." He never spoke a word throughout the dance. He swirled and turned and never missed a beat. I had decided that if he danced up the wall, I was going to follow him. He was NOT going to give me lessons. At the conclusion of the dance I found myself in a very compromising dip in the middle of the room. The music had stopped and everyone was watching, but he continued to hold this position where my head was almost touching the floor. "What's your name?" he asked. Still timid, I quietly responded, "Clarice Brown." "Clarice Brown," he said, "my name is George and someday I'm going to marry you." I was not prepared for his proclamation and awkwardly I insisted, "Let me up. I'm engaged to be married to another George in June." He let me up, spun me around, and walked away smiling. I returned quickly to the safety of my friends. "I think he's crazy," I commented, but the power of his words had my head spinning and he was so handsome.

The following night at 7:00 p.m. the phone rang at my home. It was him. "Hello. This is George. I just called to tell you that I love you and someday I'm going to marry you!" I told my mom that this man was crazy, and must be some kind of stalker. That was in December. He called every night for several months and it was always with the same message. Yet every night, there I was at 7:00 p.m., anxiously waiting to answer his crazy call.

In March an interesting situation arose when my drama teacher, Dr. Brian, assigned me a part in a one act play as a requirement of my school work. The play was to be presented spontaneously and without a rehearsal at a local upscale restaurant. The play only featured two people, a man and a woman; that's all I knew. I arrived at the restaurant and to my surprise I learned that it was George #2 playing the male part. The name of the play was, "The Finger of God." The play went very well, but I was beginning to wonder what was going on with this unusual relationship. What was I feeling when I was with him, and when I was not? Feelings that I did not want to explore were growing toward this man.

Later in April, while at the university one afternoon, I had a serious disagreement with my fiancé, George #1. I was so frustrated with his condescending attitude that I angrily walked away from him. Looking up, the first person I saw was that persistent handsome stalker George #2 sitting on the bench. I looked at him and boldly, maybe defiantly, asked if he would like to go to the movies. He anxiously said yes and we went out that evening.

I was surprised with this George #2. He was kind, thoughtful, a perfect gentleman and very interesting. "Tell me about yourself," I said. "Well," he responded, "I was born about thirty miles from here in Columbia, Louisiana. My father is a paymaster accountant and we travel all over the country. I am a transfer student from Denver University and I came back to Monroe to help take care of my grandmother. My full name is George Marbury Fluitt."

I was startled and astonished. "Marbury?" I asked. "Yes," he answered, it's our family name." Marbury? The name ran through my mind over and over again. I wondered what the possibility might be that this was the same Marbury from my picture. Then, not being able to stand the suspense, I asked him if he had ever known a girl named Carolyn. "Carolyn was my first girlfriend when I was in the ninth grade and living in Monroe," he replied. "When my family moved to Colorado I sent her my picture but we didn't keep in contact." With utter amazement I began to tell him the story of his picture and the fact that I had been in love with him since I was thirteen years old. I related how I had faithfully told everyone that someday I was going to marry Marbury. We tearfully put our arms around each other and right there he asked me to marry him! We were married on December 26, 1960, and have been together since then.

How amazing is the finger of God? Indeed, my prince did come. Even after 50 plus years of marriage and five children, my prince proudly tells anyone who will listen, "This is my bride the Lord sent me." He remains my number one advocate and encourager.

It took seven years for my dream to be fulfilled.

Beloved, hold onto your dreams. There are things you have believed for but you may have grown weary and lost hope. Believe God; confess His Word for with God all things are possible. Believe for your marriage, your children, your health and your prosperity, for the promises of God are yes and amen. Faith comes by hearing about God's goodness.

> For the vision is yet for an appointed time; But at the end it will speak, and it will not lie. Though it tarries, wait for it; Because it will surely come, It will not tarry.
>
> *-Habakkuk 2:3 (NKJV)*

Chapter 2

I Need to Meet the God
who Works Miracles

This amazing story was a forerunner to the astounding miracles that God privileged us to experience.

A blood-chilling scream of a small child in terrible pain alerted the entire household. Our family was visiting in my parent's home. Our three young daughters were happily playing with their toys in the hallway. My mom and dad, my husband George, and I all ran toward the agonizing cries to find our three year old daughter Cathy lying on the floor of the hall closet covered with blood. Our other two children, Debra and Becky, were screaming, "We didn't do it! We didn't do it!"

George picked Cathy up and realized the blood was coming from her hand. I grabbed a wet towel and wrapped it around

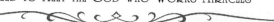

her finger. Cathy had caught her hand in the hinge of the closet door and her little pinky finger had been severed at the first joint. George, trying to be composed, said, "Call the hospital." I called our doctor to meet us because there was no doctor in the hospital's emergency room at that time of night.

George was in the car holding Cathy trying to console her in her agony. He was weeping and began to pray. He said, "Oh God, please take away her pain. I'll do anything. I'll serve You all my life!" Immediately, Cathy stopped crying and said, "Daddy, do you have chewing gum?"

I rushed to the car not knowing what to expect. There, little Cathy was, holding up her hand still wrapped in a blood soaked towel. She had a big, sweet smile on her face. "Hi Mommy. I don't hurt anymore!" I was amazed. With tears streaming down George's face, he told me that he had prayed and promised God he would serve Him if God would take away Cathy's pain. He looked at me and said, "You must give your life to God, too, and we will serve Him together."

I had been reared as a Baptist, became a Methodist, then a Presbyterian, then an Episcopalian, and married a Catholic who was more Catholic than the Pope. At this immature stage in my life, I was convinced that there was no supernatural power in any church and being a church member was like joining a civic organization that required your annual dues and regular attendance. As a young child, I had an amazing encounter with Christ, but religion had left me confused and somewhat cynical.

From deep within my soul I responded, "I'm so glad that Cathy is not crying and not in pain but I need more than that. I need to meet the God who works miracles, raises the dead, and opens blind eyes. Then, I will commit to that kind of God!"

George was driving as fast as he could to the hospital. I was holding Cathy, and she was chewing gum. George said, "Are you asking God for a miracle?" "Yes!" was my immediate response. "I need God to grow a new bone, fingernail, and complete finger." George was amazed and shocked at my response.

From deep within my soul I responded: "I need to meet the God who works miracles, raises the dead, and opens blind eyes!"

We arrived at the hospital and, as we entered the emergency room, another couple with a little boy Cathy's age came in. He was screaming and inconsolable. Cathy was still chewing gum and smiling while she kept her hand lifted up with the blood soaked towel still in place. The little boy had accidently severed his little pinky finger in the hinge of a closet door; identical circumstances. As we sat waiting for the doctor, we were amazed at what our child was experiencing with the same severed finger, same type of accident, same hospital, but not the same reaction.

The doctor arrived and carefully unwrapped Cathy's hand to evaluate her condition. After observing her hand, he asked, "Where is the finger?" It had never occurred to either of us to bring the severed finger to the hospital. I phoned my dad, "Daddy, the doctor needs Cathy's little finger." My dad replied, "Oh honey, we pulled it out of the hinge of the door and threw it in the trash. It is covered with cabbage leaves and coffee grounds." I said, "Get it out now and put it in a cup of ice and bring it to the emergency room right away!" He agreed, and while we waited, the little boy in the other room continued to scream.

Daddy came running into the emergency room with the remains of Cathy's finger in an "I Can't Believe It's Not Butter" container filled with ice and the mutilated remains of what had once been a beautiful, perfectly formed finger.

The doctor carefully examined the wounded finger and the mangled remaining piece of finger. Somehow, Cathy had caught her finger in the door hinge and instinctively pulled back. She had severed the bone and stripped the remaining tip of her finger and nail bed from the bone.

The doctor said the finger had been disconnected too long and it would be too painful to try and reconnect. He said, "We will bandage it, let it heal, and then at a later time she can have a plastic surgeon just reshape and round off the finger; but she will never have a fingernail."

I cannot explain what came over me. I am usually compliant and reasonable but, without understanding, I responded to the doctor, "I want you to sew that finger back on my baby!" He began to try and reason with me that, because the finger was so mutilated, it would not be a wise medical decision.

All I could say was, "I am her mother and I want you to sew it back on." Ultimately he said, "I will attempt to reconnect the finger but I believe your daughter is in shock and I will not administer any drugs while I attempt to reattach the finger." Cathy was peacefully lying on the hard surgical table. The unfamiliar surroundings and bright lights coupled with the drama of the night all pointed to another painful challenge; but, I knew in my heart that this was the thing to do.

I gently caressed her sweet trusting face and told her that the doctor was going to fix her finger. I said, "Cathy, it is important for you to be very still and very quiet." She looked up at her daddy and said, "Daddy, you have pretty eyes," and went to sleep. She never moved while the doctor performed the challenging surgery. He wrapped it securely and told me that the chances for gangrene were very great and that he had no faith the finger would heal.

It had been a long stressful night but I had my baby and she had all of her fingers. Three days later I went back to the doctor to examine our progress. When he unwrapped the finger, he gasped, "Oh my God, it is black. The blood supply is not functional. We must take off the dead flesh so the finger can heal." I was outraged and refused to comply. He dismissed me and said he was off the case and not responsible.

I brought Cathy home and began to call everyone I thought could offer a prayer to ask God for a finger miracle. I acted on what I knew. I was consumed with taking care of Cathy. I had secured her hand to her chest so she would not bump or jar it in any way. I carried her everywhere I went.

After another week, the finger was black and withered. George came home from work and said to me, "You have become too focused on Cathy and both of you need a break from one another. I have called my mother and she is coming over to babysit. I am taking you out to dinner." I resisted, but to no avail.

My mother-in-law, Allie, arrived with great confidence that she was more than able to skillfully take care of Cathy, Debra, and Becky. I repeatedly instructed her to be sure Cathy did not fall or bump her hand. Allie assured me that she knew what to do and that I needed to trust her judgment and seniority.

We went to dinner and, while we were gone, Allie fed and prepared the children for bed. She decided to bathe Cathy. She carefully secured Cathy's hand to the towel rack so she could not get her hand wet. She took the shower sprayer and, while Cathy stood up in the tub, carefully bathed her. Then the phone rang. Allie said to three-year old Cathy, "Grandmother is going to answer the phone and I will be right back." Somehow, Cathy got loose from the towel rack and sat down in the tub, bandage and all.

When Allie returned, Cathy was splashing in the tub and the bandage was floating in the water. Allie picked up the bandage and inside was Cathy's finger. Allie cried out loud, "Oh Cathy, your little finger came off and your mother is going to kill me." Cathy sat up, held up both hands with five whole fingers on each hand and said, "Look, Grandmother. I have a new finger." God had given us our miracle. Cathy had a new fully functioning finger, with a new bone and new nail bed.

> Cathy held up both hands with five whole fingers on each hand and said, "Look, Grandmother. I have a new finger."

You cannot imagine my joy, amazement, and realization when this happened. I had said if there was a God that could and would work signs and wonders, I would surrender my life, gifts, talents, and serve Him now and forever. I did, I have, and I will.

All of this happened two years before George and I received the life changing experience of the baptism of the Holy Spirit. Since 1971, we have been in full time ministry. Cathy became a very skilled and anointed registered nurse. God continues to use her on a daily basis helping and healing all she meets. She is quick to show her miracle finger and share her amazing story. Cathy and her husband Roger have two beautiful daughters.

With God, all things are possible.

Chapter 3

Baptism of the Holy Spirit

"You shall receive power after the Holy Spirit comes upon you." *(Acts 1:8)*

*E*verything in our lives drastically changed after we received the empowering baptism of the Holy Spirit. Time will not allow a complete retelling of my story, but my desire is to give you an authentic and transparent accounting of my amazing journey filled with signs, wonders, and miracles. My intent is to encourage and exhort you to personally believe and activate the supernatural realms of divine activity with the Holy Spirit. You can become an extension of God's love, power, and words. As believers, we are all called to be royal ambassadors of Jesus Christ in this earth and throughout eternity.

As I share the essence of my story, I ask you to remember that it covers most of my life. I am following the Biblical pattern as I write and you will learn about the challenges, victories, and amazing grace and mercy of our Heavenly Father.

Several months before we received the baptism of the Holy Spirit, I began to hear music. I was sure it was a radio or a singing toy of one of our children. Our home was a two story six bedroom house. I had just given birth to my fifth child, a precious little girl named Julianna Marie who we called Julie. Getting all my young children ready and willing for bed was a major accomplishment. When the end of my day finally came so that I could go to bed, I knew what awaited me. Every two hours I would have to get up and change the baby, feed, rock and burp her, and pray that she would sleep for another two hours. This routine would last seven days and nights for several months. God bless young parents.

I would be so tired and when I would lie down I would hear the most beautiful music. It would sound near, then far, but it so blessed and refreshed me. I was too tired to explore where it was coming from so I just enjoyed it. This continued every night from January to July of 1971.

On July 13, 1971, in Ruston, Louisiana, at the Holiday Inn, a handsome and enthusiastic guitar playing and singing Mr. Personality Baptist preacher named Dave Fisher was traveling with a brilliant and very proper Franciscan priest named Father Duane Stanzel. They were on an apostolic assignment to minister together about the Catholic Charismatic renewal. Pope John III had prayed for a new Pentecost and these two drastically different men had been chosen to travel together and teach about the baptism of the Holy Spirit with the evidence of speaking in an unknown tongue. George and I had attended the meeting out of

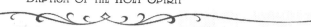

curiosity. Although I had been Baptist, Methodist, Presbyterian, Episcopalian, and Catholic, none of these experiences had equipped me for what I was about to see and hear.

George was a cradle Catholic and he only came to the meeting to investigate why a true Catholic priest from the one true Holy Roman Catholic Church would even minister with a Baptist! We know better today. Praise the Lord.

The evening was amazing. I have some wonderful CD recordings that tell this story in detail. I promise you when you listen to them you will laugh, cry, shout, and laugh some more.

After the meeting, the priest quickly approached George and said, "Dave and I are supposed to come home with you." I was not thrilled, but you should know that, at that time in George's life, whatever a Catholic priest would tell him he would know he had heard from God.

Many things happened on that 30 mile journey home that not only changed our lives forever, but the thousands of lives that would come to know God because of this divine ecumenical meeting.

This dynamic duo of Father Duane Stanzel and Dave Fisher came to our home. It was 2:00 a.m. I quickly prepared their rooms while tending to our curious children who were awake and wanted to know who was in our house. I cannot explain how the atmosphere in the house changed. We all had a feeling of great expectations.

As our two holy men were going up the stairs, Father Stanzel stopped, smiled, and said to me, "Clarice, have you ever heard the Scripture that the Lord your God that's in the midst of you will take joy over you with singing?" I responded, "No, sir." He said,

"God's angels have been rejoicing over you and your family with great joy. The Father has revealed to the angels His plans for your life. Have you been hearing heavenly sounds?" I was amazed. No one knew about the music except George and I. This was a great endorsement of God's sovereign plans unfolding in our lives. I quietly said, "Yes, sir, and sweet dreams."

My head was spinning with a million questions. I was too excited to sleep. I was up early preparing breakfast. Father Stanzel came into the kitchen and gently said to me, "My dear, Dave and I will not be eating today. We will remain in our rooms to fast and pray for the meeting tonight." I said, "Oh, I didn't know you were going to a meeting." He smiled and said, "The meeting will be here at 7:00 p.m." With that, he left and went to his room.

I asked George, "Did you know about a meeting to be here at our home tonight?" He was shocked and said, "I did not know anything about a meeting."

As the day was closing, George became quite concerned that there would not be anyone at the meeting. He went throughout the neighborhood knocking on doors and inviting anyone and everyone to come and meet the Baptist preacher and Catholic priest at 7:00 p.m. I prepared refreshments and we waited. We had done all that we knew to do.

At 6:45 p.m. I heard the gentlemen coming down the stairs. Father Stanzel kept saying, "Isn't it wonderful!" As they entered our den, Dave took his guitar and began to play and sing praise songs. Amazingly, at 7:00 p.m. our home was filled with neighbors we had never met. The power of God manifested in such a magnificent way. The people were healed, filled, delivered, prophesying, and speaking in tongues. It was a Holy Ghost celebration and revelation party!

The priest and preacher left the following day and told us we were now the parents to this newborn baby community. I immediately knew what it meant to care for a new baby. God equipped, and over 10,000 people came through our home during the next three years receiving salvation, the baptism of the Holy Spirit, deliverance, and great healings. The people in our prayer community were increasing in wisdom and knowledge. They were being equipped to rule and reign in God's Kingdom.

The initial meeting with Father Duane and Dave Fisher produced the Charismatic renewal in Northeast Louisiana that led to the Ark of Covenant prayer community that led to The Lord's Chapel Church that led to the founding and establishing of the Eagles Nest World Prayer and Training Center, and on and on and on.

Incredible miracles were an everyday occurrence. On several occasions when we prayed, it would actually rain on us inside the two story home. Anointing oil would form and flow down our doors. Beautiful doves nested on our roof. Nuns, priests, governors, drug addicts, students, prostitutes, preachers, and those of every race and creed would find their way to our home. God always manifested His power and love.

> Incredible miracles were an everyday occurrence. It rained on us inside our home. Anointing oil flowed down our doors. Beautiful doves nested on our roof.

How could anything be better? As the Bible says, Oh, how lovely it is when the brethren dwell together in love and unity.

We lived across the street from a very large Jewish Synagogue. The Rabbi became so interested in what was happening in our home that he came to visit George. They spent time together talking and praying. The power of God convicted the Rabbi that Jesus is the true Messiah and he became a born again believer.

Chapter 4

Charged Up, Changed, and Totally Healed

THE KATHRYN KUHLMAN STORY

When I was a child, I was diagnosed with tuberculosis, asthma, and severe skin allergies. My body would sting and itch while large unsightly welts that looked like I had either been burned or beaten would appear and last for hours. This was painful and humiliating. The tuberculosis was in remission after I turned twelve years old, but the asthma and allergies were consistent reminders of all the things I could not do. I adjusted to these limitations with medication and carefully avoided the things that would trigger an asthma or allergy attack.

I was a Christian but I had never been taught that healing was a part of my salvation. My challenged health continued to follow me even after I married and had my children. My husband was very kind and understanding. He helped me with my injections and saw to it that I received medical care; but, the sickness ruled our lives and I became addicted to a very powerful steroid nasal spray. I developed a painful and unpredictable hemorrhaging nasal passage. I had a prolific nose bleed three or four times a day.

After we received the baptism of the Holy Spirit, I began to hear about healing. I learned that there was a lady named Kathryn Kuhlman who prayed for the sick and they were healed. While reading a Christian publication, I learned that Ms. Kuhlman was going to be in Dallas, Texas, the following month. I cannot explain the hope, faith, desire and many other emotions and devotions that caused a knowing within me that I needed to go to Dallas and be in those meetings.

When George came home, I showed him the article and asked him to take me to the meetings. He was kind and knew very well the severe suffering that I would experience without warning. He said, "Honey, you know, there are a lot of false ministers in the world and I don't even know if God uses women in a healing capacity; but, if it is really important to you, we will go and check her out." We arrived in Dallas and went to the Statler Hilton ready to attend a traditional church service. That did not happen; tradition was nowhere to be found.

A Kathryn Kuhlman event was not like anything I had ever witnessed. George's very traditional Catholic upbringing did not include any place or space for what we were about to experience.

There were about three thousand plus waiting to go inside the conference room. George and I were standing together. The more he saw, the less he liked what he saw. I recognized his solemn sighs and restless stance. In an attempt to be agreeable, he smiled and said, "Well, whatever the woman does, she sure can draw a crowd." Suddenly, the doors opened and it was pure bedlam; people shoving and pushing and yelling. George and I got separated in the crowd and I could not find him. The frustrated ushers were trying desperately to direct everyone to quickly find their seats.

I had no way to contact George so I just took a seat and believed that we would meet later. So far, things were not what I had hoped they would be. I looked around and realized that many in the crowd had brought picnic baskets of food, drinks, and children's toys. It was at this point that I realized we were going to be here for a long time.

A young man named Dino Kartsonakis began to play the piano as a holy hush fell upon the crowd. The congregation began to raise their hands, sing, and worship the Lord. Dino was divinely anointed to draw the presence of the Lord into the room. Then, Mr. Jimmy McDonald, an African American vocalist, thrilled and filled the room with his rich baritone voice. I will never forget his passionate singing of, "His Eye Is on the Sparrow." This was becoming a very pleasant and inspiring meeting.

Then, with a very dramatic drum roll and flashing lights, I heard a deep throaty and very dramatic voice say, "Have you been waiting long?" A petite red headed woman attired in a long white silk dress with large billowing sleeves and dangling bracelets walked out upon the stage and began to teach, preach, prophesy, exhort, sing, spin around, and suddenly announce with great passion, "Someone is being healed of cancer. It's a man named Tom. Tom. Tom Johnston. It is in his liver. Where are you, Tom?" That was how it began.

She moved as though she was being controlled by some divine remote system. She would stop and start, laugh and cry. She was like a many faceted jewel absorbing and reflecting the mood and will of God. Ms. Kuhlman would speak a word of knowledge and, when you believed that the word was for you, you would go up on the stage. She would pray and you would be slain in the Spirit. The power of God was always flowing through Kathryn Kuhlman.

> Ms. Kuhlman moved as though she was being controlled by some divine remote system. The power of God was always flowing through her.

I watched in awe and wondered what George was thinking and if he was still in the room.

Hundreds and hundreds of men, women, and children were confessing that they were healed. They were getting out of wheelchairs, dropping their crutches, removing braces, and I was loving every minute of what I was seeing. Kathryn Kuhlman stopped, faced the congregation, and said, as she pointed her finger in my direction, "There is a woman located in this area." She once again pointed her long slender finger that suddenly looked ten feet long. Ms. Kuhlman continued saying, "This woman has asthma, allergies, and fights against lung diseases. The Lord has seen your suffering. Be healed in Jesus' Name."

My poor heart was beating like a drum. I knew she was talking about me but I was terrified to respond. A lady named Maggie was working with Ms. Kuhlman, walked over to me, and said, "You are being healed. Claim your healing!" I looked right at Ms.

Maggie and said, "I'm not the one. I'm not sick." Fear is a terror to good works. Ms. Kuhlman pointed in my direction again and said, "Lord, this woman can be very stubborn. She will need a sign of Your love for her."

It was as though someone unscrewed the top of my head and filled my entire being with hot oil. I began to shake uncontrollably. Maggie asked, "Are you ready to receive your healing?" I was terrified to think what would happen to me if I did not go on the stage and profess that I was healed.

As I walked toward the stage, I kept saying, "I will not fall down. I will not fall down." When I saw Kathryn Kuhlman face-to-face, I was having trouble breathing. With her red curly hair, frail body, and piercing stare, I immediately recognized her very unique personal surrender to the Holy Spirit. I just loved her right away.

She extended her hands, gently placed them on my face, prayed a most inspiring prayer, and said, "Such as God has given me, I impart to you." Well, my resolve not to be slain in the Spirit, which is to fall down, went out the window. I was not just slain in the Spirit, but my body flew across the stage and I landed under Dino's piano. When I did get up, I was charged up, changed, and totally healed! The other good news was that I found George. He was so blessed and decided that God does use women powerfully.

That happened in September, 1971, and the tuberculosis, allergies, and asthma have never returned. Over the years, I have had the most wonderful men and women of God lay hands upon me, pray, prophesy, and impart spiritual blessings and strength for my journey. My life has been enriched and empowered through believing and receiving from the lives and ministry of other great saints.

THE POWER OF GRATITUDE

After I was healed at the Kathryn Kuhlman meeting, I was like a bird that had been caged all its life, then the door to freedom was opened, and now I could fly. I am so grateful to be healed, delivered, and prosperous.

Acts of gratitude open great doors of opportunity. Every true act of gratitude will refine your soul and draw the favor of God to your life. I told everybody that would listen to me that Kathryn Kuhlman had prayed for me, the Lord had healed me, and I was grateful.

This is a story that explains the power of gratitude.

Back at home, George and I were finishing a conference we had initiated. After the meeting, someone said, "Hey everybody. George Fluitt is taking us out for a free steak dinner." George looked amazed as about 30 people began shouting, "Thank you, George. We will see you at the restaurant." George looked at me and asked, "What just happened?" I said, "I think we have been set up to buy everyone a steak." We both laughed and went to the restaurant.

It was a very festive time until George realized he did not have his check book or cash with him. The bill was going to be about $500.00. He said to me, "I'm going to run to my office and get my check book. Cover for me until I get back." I agreed and continued to visit with my friends.

I was sharing with our group about my healing with Kathryn Kuhlman and how excited I was that our local television station was airing her weekly television show. The owner of the station was a gentleman named James A. Noe. Mr. Noe had served as the Governor of our state and was an extremely wealthy and influential businessman. I was aware that his wife was very sick and had heard that was the reason he was sponsoring the Kathryn Kuhlman television show. I had never actually met Mr. Noe but knew who he was.

The doors to the restaurant opened and in walked Mr. Noe and two other gentlemen. They were seated a few tables away from our group. After a few minutes, I decided to go over, speak to him, and express my gratitude for airing the Kathryn Kuhlman television show.

I went to his table and said, "Mr. Noe, my name is Clarice Fluitt. I want to thank you and express my gratitude for hosting the Kathryn Kuhlman television show." The man looked amazed and asked, "Have you ever been to a Kathryn Kuhlman meeting?" "Oh, yes," I said, "and I was healed." He began to weep and asked me to join his friends. He asked if I knew the gentlemen with

> Acts of gratitude open great doors of opportunity. Every true act of gratitude will refine your soul and draw the favor of God to your life.

him. I assured him that I did not know either of them. He then introduced me and told me they were Kathryn Kuhlman's business managers. Mr. Noe told me that they had just told him that our city was too small for Kathryn Kuhlman to host a crusade. He continued by saying, Ms. Kuhlman's managers had just said to him, "It would take someone in this restaurant to walk up to us and say that they had been healed in a Kathryn Kuhlman meeting before we would ever commit to coming to Monroe. The city is too small." He had offered to pay all expenses and provide all the advertising for a giant Kathryn Kuhlman crusade in our city. I was their confirmation.

When George returned to pay the bill, the restaurant owner said, "Oh, Mr. Fluitt, Governor Noe paid for your party." My expression of gratitude opened amazing doors.

Mr. Noe had me give the testimony of my healing on his TV station. This caught the attention of thousands, and Ms. Kathryn Kuhlman did come to the Monroe Civic Center. Over 10,000 people attended. Thousands were saved, healed, and delivered.

Yes, I encourage you to express your gratitude and appreciation with calls, cards, e-mails, text messages, and even face-to-face encounters.

Chapter 5

Oh Lord, to Know You Is Better than Life

*P*art of my daily routine was to walk around all the churches in our neighborhood, pray, and sing praises to God. On this one special day, I was filled with deep gratitude to God and for God. I just cried out loud and said, "Oh Lord, to know You is better than life!" I heard a response that I had grown to recognize as the voice of God, "You don't know Me; you only know about Me." I immediately said, "I rebuke you satan in Jesus' Name!" The Voice continued, "You can stay where you are and heal the sick, cast out devils, and beat your tambourine on the mountain tops of life and know about Me, or you can choose to know Me." I could only say what was in my heart, "How can I know you?" The response was, "Sell all you have, give to the poor, and come and follow Me down into the valley of the shadow

I was learning that God is not who I thought He was, but He is who He says He is. I had entered a severe learning curve.

of death. "How can I do that?" I asked. "I will send two companions to guide you on this next part of your journey. Their names are sorrow and suffering. They know how to guide you to Me. You have known the things of God; now you must know the God of things. Let Me strip you of all the things that you are trusting in besides Me."

This was beyond reason, but I knew it was beyond denying. I knew what to do but not how to do it. I was learning that God is not who I thought He was, but He is who He says He is. I had entered a severe learning curve.

GOD DISMANTLED MY LIFE

I went home and told George, "The Lord said I don't know Him, I just know about Him." He said, "Oh honey, that's the devil. Look at all the things that God has used you to do." I said, "Yes, but that is not knowing Him, that's just knowing about Him." And George asked, "Well, what do you think He wants you to do?" I said, "I know what He wants me to do." George said, "What?" I replied, "God wants us to sell everything we have and give to the poor, and trust Him." George said, "Don't you be talking to God by yourself anymore." George is such a godly man that we knelt down, prayed, and said, "God, if this is what you want, we will do it." The Lord said, "This is what I want. I want you to be willing." George said, "God won't expect us to sell everything and give the money to the poor. We just need to be willing." That was not my experience.

We did sell what we had and gave the money away. We did move out of a 16 room home into a three room camp house deep in the woods with our five children who had only known the good life. Selah. We had one piece of property that we could not give away. It was 40 acres of flood land. Even the bank didn't want it.

I remember it was the day of my first born daughter's 14th birthday, October 16. Wow, happy birthday. We were all sitting on the floor in the dining room. All the furniture was gone. The silver, the china, and everything was gone. We did not know where we were going. We did not have a bed to sleep in. We had clothes on our back. We had never been this way before.

"Lord, I can see You doing it to me, but how can You do it to the children?" He said, "Do you think you love them more than I do? Everything you're holding on to, give it to Me." Now I am not telling you that you have to do it. I asked the Lord one time why it had to be so hard. He said, "It didn't have to be but this is the most expeditious way for you." Every familiar and comforting thing in my life was affected.

We left everything behind with my mother and father crying and everybody that knew us saying, "You have lost your mind."

We did experience misunderstanding, sickness, death, poverty, fire, and an endless list of life changing challenges. We did live through the amazing ministry of my two faithful companions suffering and sorrow.

THE UNFOLDING OF GOD'S PLAN

Doctor Jack and his wife Jean Davis who we used to ski with in the winter time in Aspen called and said, "We don't know what you're doing. You have this relationship with God, and then all of a sudden you've lost your mind. You've given up your real estate business. You've given up your property, and you've got five little children. You have no place to go," and he was right. We had no place to go.

Dr. Jack offered his camp house that had two little bedrooms. It was out in the backside of the earth. You had to pump sunshine to get back there. It had an indoor bathroom, sort of, and the only closet was an open back porch which George enclosed with clear plastic sheeting where we hung our clothes. Each time we needed something to wear, George had to take a fly swatter and beat the bugs and spiders off the clothes. Daily, George went on a poor man's safari. I remember Jack said, "You can stay there until you make up your mind what you're going to do."

I wanted to know God. George wanted to know God. We moved out into the camp house in the boondocks, and just when you think nothing could be worse, God's plan begins to unfold.

I started out choosing to be happy. Even though God slay me, still I'll choose to praise Him. People would drive out to look and see where we were and say, "You know, this is just what you all needed. God is going to bring the right humility to your life." Now I want you to know I would love to be able to say, "Thank you for that comment. That's helping me so much," but that was not what I was thinking.

Then George got sick. He had never been sick before. Suddenly, he had to have surgery. I was left completely alone with five children. There was a couple who lived in a nearby trailer in the woods. The wife was about 18 or 19 years old. They had three little babies. It was winter time, and their kids were all running around the yard. The wife worked at a truck stop, and her husband drank all day. I observed these children, cold and looking for a place to

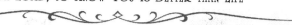

be fed, but I only had two bedrooms and a kitchen. In my state of depression I said, "They can just die out there. I'm not taking care of anything else." I had begun to lose my joy, but ultimately I took them in and cared for them like they were my own.

About this time, I had gotten extremely bitter. I decided I was mad at God, did not like His people, my husband, or my children anymore, and would have loved to have died. Now you see God wants to take you to the backside of the desert and begin to squeeze you so you will know what is really in you. You can be nice when your bank account is up, you are in charge of everything, you are looking good, and you have a job, but when you are in a fiery trial and are the despised, disgusted, mistrusted, busted, and everybody's saying, "you have lost your mind," the next thing you know, you are going to either agree with what the voices are saying or you are going to agree with God.

I remember looking into an old piece of broken mirror. I looked very old. I had not combed my hair in about two weeks and had a nasty house coat on. I would not clean up, take a bath, or brush my teeth, and I was ugly and mad. As I looked in this mirror, I said, "Devil, this is what you've done to me." The voice of God spoke to me and said, "The devil didn't have anything to do with this. I did." That's when I said, "God, if You treat your friends like this, You're not going to have many!" This is what I learned. I want you to know you can get at mad at God if you want to, but He's got more time than you do.

We are in a process, and the process is as important as the product. The only image that makes God happy is His own. He is conforming you into the image of the dear Son of God.

God is a God of glory, and He is looking for people who believe they are complete in Christ and must know they are to become launching pads for glory. They will go through the fire, but not smell like smoke. They will go through the water, and will not choke. They will have eaten the bread of misunderstanding, and come out better, stronger, and lasting longer.

> God is a God of Glory, and He is looking for people who believe they are complete in Christ and must know they are to become launching pads for glory.

After George's operation, the reality of the fact was that I had five kids who were unhappy, no car, and no money, and I kept saying, "We have nothing, nothing, nothing." As long as I kept saying, "I have nothing, nothing, nothing," that is exactly what was manifesting. Nothing, nothing, nothing!

I was at the top of my frustration level when my dad came out to our camp house. He said, "Baby, God wouldn't do this to you." My daddy never called me anything except Baby. I was always his baby. He said, "Please, let Daddy build a house for you. Daddy will do this. Daddy will do that." I heard the Lord say, "Do not lean on anything but Me."

I said, "Daddy, I don't have an answer for all of this. I don't know what God is doing, but I choose to believe God is good." He wouldn't come into my modest little camp house but said, "I can't come in because it breaks my heart."

That was the last time Daddy came to the camp house, and that was the day I allowed my faith to lay down and go to sleep while anger and discouragement took over my mind and mouth.

I cannot express the depths of despair and hopelessness that overwhelmed me. All I had ever wanted was to know and serve God. Everything in my life was filled with heart wrenching grief. My children were miserable, my husband was sick, my parents were confused, and my friends were gone. I was poor and pitiful. I could not even find the energy or ability to get up and get myself dressed. I had hit rock bottom.

I remember it was on Valentine's Day; a very cold, rainy, and dark day. George and all the children were gone for the day and I was home, sad, and alone. I was sitting in the kitchen when I felt a hand on my shoulder and heard a voice say, "Go to the door and begin to knock." I was terrified but obedient. I went to the door and began to knock. The door opened and immediately I was in heaven. I was acutely aware of my shabby appearance and shameful attitude towards the Almighty. The voice of the Holy Spirit said, "You have wanted an audience with the Father, so tell Him what you want."

Chapter 6

Run, Clarice, Run!

I fell on my face again and again and said, "Oh God, oh God, I have been so miserable and said such terrible things. Have mercy on me. Forgive me, forgive me, forgive me." The Holy Spirit said, "Stand up and tell Him what you want." I cried out, "I just want to love You. I just want to behave myself."

Again the Spirit said, "Stand up!" But I kept falling down. I had my nasty house coat on and old worn slippers. The Holy Spirit said, "Stand up and tell God what you want." I blurted out, "Lord, I just want to love You. I just want to praise You."

Again, I fell down and the Holy Ghost said, "Clarice, stand up. You have an audience with the Great I Am. Tell Him what you want." From the depths of my soul, I cried out and said, "Oh, Father, I want to marry Your Son. I want to marry Jesus Christ. I want to be Mrs. Jesus Christ!" The words came from the depths of my heart. I had never had a thought like that before. I heard the whole heaven sing out, "Let it be said, and let it be done!"

The Spirit took me back to that little room and I thought, my God, I have lost my mind. Immediately the Holy Spirit, the Giver of Life said, "Run, Clarice, run!" It was in the wintertime and I was barefooted but I began to run. I remember seeing an ugly tree I had hated and despised. Now, I fell in love with that same tree. I fell in love with the grass which was brown and scorched looking. Everything had life and was beautiful. I asked the Lord, "What is this?" I saw water and I began to quiver at its splendor and the majesty of its endless facets of beauty. I heard all of heaven singing, "Run, Clarice, run." I ran through the pasture land and began to sing again, "Ishi, Ishi, Ishi." I didn't know what it meant but it was all I could sing. God had brought me out of my deep oppression, and joy unspeakable filled with glory was in my soul. When I received the baptism of the Holy Spirit, I sang my prayers and the Scriptures but had lost my song in the wilderness until I began to run and sing, "Ishi, Ishi, Ishi."

> I heard all of heaven singing, "Run, Clarice, run." I ran through the pasture land and began to sing. God had brought me out of my deep oppression and joy unspeakable filled with glory was in my soul.

Suddenly, I was back in my camp house. I was speechless, stunned, and amazed. As I sat in that tiny kitchen, it became the most wonderful place I had ever been in. I began to cry out to the

Father, "Please keep me in this place of peace and reveal to me through Your Word just what You are doing in my life."

I picked up the Bible. It fell open to Hosea 2:14-16 and it said, "Therefore, behold, I will allure her, and bring her into the wilderness… and in that day, she shall no longer call Me Lord, but she shall call Me Ishi," [my husband]. (AMP) Could this be true; that all I could sing was, "My Husband?" I had never heard anyone teach this as a Bible truth. I said, "Oh, my God, let us call this place Bethel. Then I can stay here forever." He said, "No, now that you have overcome, we've got to go. We have another mountain to cross."

My husband George came home that night and I thought, dear God, with all that he had been through, how could I tell him, "Oh, by the way, today I went to heaven and married Jesus?" We went to bed. There were no curtains in the house. The moonlight was coming over his face and he was fast asleep. I was praying about how I was going to tell him that I had gone to heaven. I prayed to the Lord, "Everything you have ever done for us, you have always done it for both of us." Then, I took my hand, laid it on his chest and said to the Lord, "What You have done for me, please do it for him, too." Suddenly, George's eyes opened and he jumped straight up in the bed. He was jumping up and down. Tears were coming down his face. He said, "Oh my God! Oh my God! Clarice, I don't know how to tell you this. I don't want to hurt your feelings, but I am marrying Jesus. I am going to marry Jesus." The Lord met George that same day yet in a different way.

This amazing epiphany would serve to equip us for the next phase of our journey to know God.

Chapter 7

God Is a God of Restoration

All my bitterness, anger, and disappointment were gone. That little camp house became my true resting place. I had learned to truly love it. God said, "The day has come, you can leave this wilderness now. Where do you want to go?" I said, "Lord, this is the sweetest place on earth. I just want to be where You want to me to be." He said to my heart, "That's good because I'm going to put you on a dead end street with four generations of your husband's family that all think you're the anti-Christ. You're going to stay there until you love each other." They all lived on Webster Street.

George had been the golden child and I was the protestant girl that his family thought led him away from the one true church. Our work was to win their hearts and establish good relationships.

Our time living on Webster Street, in a small house close to George's family, was a continuing time of refining. George and I both decided to just be ordinary people. We lost some of that driving ambition to do great things. George reopened his real estate business and I became a stay-at-home mom. We loved the Lord and the fire to win the world was still burning but no longer raging in our hearts. We just waited on God's timing for the next several years.

Then, in the fall of 1980, I said to George that the Lord told me we were going to move. He said, "Now, Clarice, we are comfortable here and I will not go into debt to buy a home. You just need to settle down and live a normal Christian life. We are simple, ordinary people and we don't need to try to be anything else." I heard him, yet I knew what the Lord was saying. I also knew that George was speaking from a wounded spirit. I knew he was a pioneer and not a settler.

The next day, I called a realtor and made an appointment to look at homes for sale. She asked, "What is your price range?" I replied, "Price is not a factor." (Now the facts were that we had $300.00 in our bank account). The realtor asked what I was looking for and I told her. "I need six bedrooms, five baths, a living room, dining room, kitchen, study, and playroom in a first class neighborhood with about 5500 square feet of living space." She made the appointment that evening to see a beautiful home in a wonderful neighborhood. My husband asked me where I was going. I replied, "I'm going to look for a home to move into." He smiled and said, "I'm going with you so you don't embarrass yourself."

It is very important to let you know that George is a deeply spiritual man who is very sensitive to the voice of God. I thank the Lord for giving me a patient and kind hearted husband. He is also a very reasonable man. He has always honored me and trusted my gift to hear the voice of God. When we know that God has spoken to us, we must obey even when it sounds unreasonable.

We met the realtor. The home was beautiful and completely furnished inside and out. Our realtor explained that the home owner's parents had passed away and left them a large furnished mansion, and when they moved to their new home, they left everything behind.

While we were viewing the home, the owners drove up. They came into the house and the realtor introduced us. The wife asked me, "Do you like my home?" I replied, "Oh, yes, it's lovely." The lady became so attentive to me that it was as if someone sprayed 'fairy dust' in the room. She asked, "Do you like my furniture?" I said, "Yes, I do, but you need to know that we have five children and will need six bedrooms. You only have four." Then she asked, "Do you have a need for all of my household belongings?" I said, "How much will it cost?" She replied, "I'll give you everything; all the furniture, silver, crystal, lamps, etc., etc., etc." I remembered the day I gave all my belongings away, and now God was bringing our restoration! The only catch was that she needed us to move it the next day. To do that was going to cost us $300.00, and that was all we had.

> She said, "I'll give you everything: all the furniture, silver, crystal, lamps, etc." I remembered the day I gave all my belongings away and now God was bringing our restoration!

As George and I drove back home, it began to rain, and rain hard. In the south we say that a heavy downpour is a frog choking rain. George was quiet, then asked, "What are you going to do with all that stuff?" I smiled and said, "It's obvious to me we are going to furnish a big home somewhere." He was not excited.

We got home and were sitting in our living room having a cup of coffee and discussing my urgency to get ready for God to move us somewhere. George had not changed his mind but was politely listening to what I believed. At 10:00 p.m. there was a knock at our door. We did not have a porch or any covering over the front door, so whoever was out there was going to be very wet.

George opened the door, and a gentleman named John came in dripping wet and said, "I was at home and the Lord told me to come to this address and buy this house!"

George, being a real estate broker himself, said to John, "We are on a dead end street less than a mile from the university in a transitional neighborhood. The interest rates are between 16 and 18 percent for a home loan. Why do you want this house, and did my wife tell you this house was for sale?" John was smiling and replied, "No. I have not spoken to your wife, but God told me to buy this house!"

To make a very long story short, John bought the house and gave us 30 days to move. He said God had told him what he should pay, and it was twice what we had paid for it originally. We tried to talk John out of his price choice, but he emphatically said, "No!"

Now that we had some money and a lot of furniture, we could find a larger house. Our daughter Cathy had a dream and announced to us the following morning that, "I dreamed we moved back to our old home that we used to live in."

George was silent, but the next afternoon he invited me to go for a ride. He drove to our old home site and said, "Let's agree that, if we have any ungodly soul ties to this house, we break them in Jesus' name."

WHEN GOD RESTORES, HE MAKES EVERYTHING BETTER THAN IT WAS BEFORE

In the fullness of time, the north wind of chastening and the long winter passed. God sent the gentle south winds of restoration.

Through sovereign circumstances, God restored everything we gave away. He set us free of debt. The home we had left was restored to us five years later to the day. On the 16th of October God said, "Now." He took us back to the same home we had given away where we had been a prayer group that touched thousands.

On that worthless piece of land that nobody wanted, that we could not give away, gas and minerals were discovered. Once again God had sovereignly moved on our behalf.

> On that worthless piece of land that nobody wanted, gas and minerals were discovered. Once again God had sovereignly moved on our behalf.

When God restores, He makes everything better than it was originally. We were prepared and ready for the next part of the journey. Our story is one of from riches to rags and back again. I distinctly remember asking the Lord several times, "How long will this dark night of my soul continue?" His response was always the same, "Until it doesn't bother you anymore. Then you will be a victor, and not a victim."

George and I both considered ourselves as unlikely candidates to serve our Lord. We felt better about it when we found the Scripture that tells us God has chosen the weak and foolish to confound the wise and mighty.

To attain to higher levels in God, you must know that satan is truly defeated and under your feet! This revelation demands life application. To know you can go through the fires of suffering and sorrow in life and come out not smelling like smoke will promote you to the winner's circle, not the whiner's corner. Never waste your sorrow. Use it as a badge of honor that grants you access to a place of divine authority, favor, and power. Your measure of influence is increased as you choose to agree with God at every level of life.

George and I established the Eagles Nest World Prayer and Training Center in 1982 in Monroe, Louisiana. We have been very blessed to be a launching place for the revelation of the authority of the believer, the finished work of Christ, the restoration of spontaneous Biblical praise and worship, and the power of the prophetic voice of God. A new day has dawned, what was once our baby (our church) has reached the prophetic age of 33. George and I know that the ministry we have built, nurtured, and loved has matured. We are ready to move to the next spiritual phase of God's plan. Life is wonderful and full of wonder.

Now that you know a little of my history, let me relate some of the most amazing and faith building miracles that I have been honored to experience and witness.

Pictures

This is where I met Friend

God Dismantled My Life - Our home before

The camp house (many years after we left).

Cathy's new finger   When God Restores ... Our church building

Be Fruitful and Multiply -   Praying for little Goodness
Healed from barrenness

Ask Big and Receive Big – "Evidence," my R.V.

Part Two

The things of God

become yours by the

reason of use

Chapter 8

Front Row Center Seat

During the 1970s, the Oral Roberts concert choir was in great demand all over the United States. They were young, energetic, and excellent musicians. The Oral Roberts University weekly Sunday morning television show was an innovative, out-of-the-box Christian presentation. These television shows enjoyed high approval ratings nationwide. I was one of the many devoted fans and viewers.

I was really excited when I was notified that the Oral Roberts University concert choir would be performing at the Life Tabernacle Church in Shreveport, Louisiana, only a hundred miles away from my home. I immediately made plans for my husband and our five children to attend the concert.

Our dear friends, Judge Fred Fudicker, his wife, and family decided to accompany us so we planned a road trip together. We would all go to church, enjoy the concert, go to lunch, and come home.

The day before we were to go, I became very sick. I was running a high fever, sneezing, coughing, and feeling awful; but, I was determined to go. When I awoke on Sunday morning, I was feeling better, but I had completely lost my voice and developed a severe case of laryngitis. I could not talk, but still found a way to make it known that we were going to the concert. George helped get the children dressed and fed while I was gargling hot salted lemon juice, all to no avail.

We drove 100 miles in silence, which was a new experience for all of us. George bought me several packages of cough drops. When I coughed, it sounded like a big dog with a bad case of distemper, but I was going to hear the Oral Roberts University choir.

We met our friends, and George explained that I had laryngitis and could not speak a word. When we arrived, the parking lot was packed. As we went into this huge church, there were no seats available downstairs. The empty seats in the balcony were scattered and we could not sit together. I could not express my frustration because my "expresser" was not working.

When I go to church, I want to sit up close to the action. I do not want to be distracted by those who are not focused on what is happening on the platform. Well, there were no seats up close, in the middle, or on the side. George located seats in the very back, but they were not together. I began to pray, "Lord, please get me a seat up front." George was well aware of my discontent and whispered to me, "Clarice, be happy that we have a seat." I was trying, but just could not get my heart to agree to get happy. He and our three younger children ended up in one section while our two older children and I were in another area. Our friends were on their own.

Here is the scenario. The Life Tabernacle Church had a renowned choir of its own and world-class musicians. Reverend Nolan Logan was the progressive charismatic Senior Pastor and Ms. Anna Jean Price was an anointed concert pianist and chief musician. When their services would begin, their choir seemed to explode from every direction wearing beautiful robes, dancing, jumping, and singing. They would stir and release joy unspeakable that was full of glory. You just had to praise the Lord in that atmosphere.

Now, just think about all that talent and then add the incredible Oral Roberts University concert choir. My heart was crying, but my voice was silent. "Oh, Lord, I really need a seat up close!" My daughter Debra was 11 years old, Becky was 9, and both were seated with me in the back where none of us could see anything.

Pastor Logan came to the pulpit to greet everyone and explain how the event of the day would proceed. Suddenly, he paused and said, "We have a lot of visitors here with us today, and I see my good friends Clarice and George Fluitt from Monroe. Thank you for joining us." I was amazed that his eyesight was that great. I could barely see him through the large crowd. "Sister Fluitt has a beautiful and anointed voice. Church, would you like to hear her sing for us today?"

The congregation began to applaud, and I began to speak in tongues without a voice. Debra smiled and reminded me, "Mom, you promised God that you would serve Him whenever you get the opportunity. Go sing for the Lord." Becky looked at me with her big brown eyes filled with compassion and said, "Don't do it, Mom. You aren't well and you can't even whisper."

With the Life Tabernacle choir in place, and the Oral Roberts University choir waiting to perform, I boldly made my way down that long, long, long aisle, went to the pulpit, took the microphone, looked at the congregation, paused, and then in a low horse whisper asked, "Do you believe in miracles?"

I have learned to say, not pray, to the mountain in my life, "Go!" It pleases the Father to bless His children, and it pleases the children to bless the Father.

Every hand was extended in prayer toward me. I looked to Ms. Anna Jean and mouthed, "The Lord's Prayer." She immediately and dramatically attacked all 88 keys with an introduction that would have made a dead man sing. I opened my mouth and an angelic sound that was far beyond my talent came forth. I was singing with all the passion that my body, soul, and spirit could summon. People were crying and laughing as the entire church knew we were all witnessing a miracle. I concluded by hitting a perfect E above a high C note.

While the congregation was cheering, I stepped down from the stage and there it was; one seat remaining; front row, center. I said, "Thank you, Father," and took my seat.

I have learned to say, not pray, to the mountain in my life; Go! It pleases the Father to bless His children, and it pleases the children to bless the Father.

Chapter 9

Moving Your Boundaries

We received a call from a Pentecostal gentleman asking us to come to the hospital and pray for his dying wife. You have to understand. We were still in the Catholic Church and he said, "My wife has cancer and she's in a coma. The doctor says she's not going to make it through the night. We have heard that you pray for the sick. Even if you're Catholic, we're desperate!"

That was back in the day when I believed that I had to fast for three days before giving a simple answer. He said, "Woman, I don't have three days. My wife is dying. You hear me? Come on up here right now and act like you did three days of fasting."

He said, "I know somebody in the body of Christ has been fasting. We are one body so come on up and take their fast!" I thought, 'Can you do that?' I had to move my religious boundaries.

George and I along with the wife of a local doctor went to the hospital and here was this little lady. She weighed about 70 pounds. Her name was Ms. Thomas. She was laying in the bed and her husband, son, and daughter had gathered together to say goodbye. The doctor told them she wouldn't make it another hour. She had colon cancer, had also suffered a heart attack, and a stroke. She had tubes in every orifice and a deep death rattle. I hate death. It's not our friend and I believe we have the keys to hell, death, and the grave.

> We must activate God's promises with faith and let God arise. Never let anyone see you sweat and remember you are a king and a priest. Priests do not sweat.

Ms. Thomas was lying there motionless and struggling for her breath. Oh, it did not look good. The doctors had given the death sentence. She had the appearance of death, the smell of death, and the sounds of death.

My husband is reasonable. He said "Clarice, it's too late. Ms. Thomas is dying." I asked Ms. Thomas's family, "Do you believe Jesus paid the price for this woman's healing?" They answered, "YES!" I immediately felt the release to pray. Faith is simply acting on God's Word. To act is not to pretend. We must activate God's promises with faith and let God arise. Your knees may be shaking, but do not let anybody know it. Never let anyone see you sweat and remember that you are a king and a priest. Priests do not sweat.

I boldly announced, "I'm going to pray for this woman and she's going to get up and walk!" I clapped my hands and said,

"You foul spirit of death, you foul spirit of heart attack, you foul lying spirit, get off this woman." I said, "Ms. Thomas, come back here and live your life." Then she awoke from her coma, her eyes opened up, and her body supernaturally came out of that bed. George later said, "You don't know how close I came to leaving the room when you told the doubters to leave." She pulled those tubes out of her nose, came out of that bed, and lived for another 32 years.

Thanks be to God. You have been called to cast out demons, raise the dead, heal the sick, preach good news, and work miracles. Who will do the works of God? Who will agree with God's Word?

Chapter 10

The Name of Jesus Is above Everything That's Got a Name

As I was being reared Baptist, Methodist, Presbyterian, Episcopalian and Catholic, I picked up a lot of interesting doctrine which was mostly man-made.

I was totally convinced at this time in my life that a woman should not speak in a meeting where men were present. I was sincere, but I was sincerely wrong. Religion is a terrible taskmaster, but a changed heart happens when you have a relationship with Jesus.

I was convinced that I was a poor banished child of Eve, and the one that caused all the problems in the world was a lowly woman. I was guilt-ridden with traditions that held me down. Have you read that the Bible teaches us that our traditions make the Word of God to no effect? I was so confused. My heart's desire was to serve God and yet was fighting with the call because of fear of doing something wrong.

God was saying, "Come, you mighty woman of God." I was saying, "I can't. I'm like a worm. I'm just a woman." God will let you believe what you need to believe to get you where He is taking you. To break the stronghold of tradition, unworthiness, self-hate, and low self-esteem in my life, the Lord prepared circumstances to occur that I could not deny.

I was traveling with my friend, Linda. She was a wonderful musician and mighty prayer warrior. We had been on the road for about three weeks preaching, teaching, singing, and ministering the Word of God—to women only!

We were just being girls and loving Jesus. Every time I was invited to speak, I would get up and say, "My name is Clarice Fluitt and I'm the wife of George Fluitt. He's the pastor of the Church, we have five children, and I'm a homemaker. I just love Jesus and I'm just so appreciative of you giving me the opportunity to come and share the goodness of the Lord." This was before I had the understanding that religion was about to die a violent death, and I would learn to let God arise.

The Lord quickened to me one day, "You say that silly introduction one more time, and I'm going to pull your tongue out and beat you with it." He said, "What in the world does that have to do with Me?" Thank God for His loving kindness, it endures forever. I was learning that correction does not mean rejection.

We arrived at this town in Texas that I had agreed to minister at because I thought it was a lady's meeting. I found out it was a Civic Center and the marquee said, "Tonight, ordination service with Clarice Fluitt." I thought I was going to die. I went to find the man that was in charge of it to tell him that I could not minister in a meeting where men are.

Pastor Earl was a big, gregarious, outgoing guy and he said, "Well, hello there, little lady." I cautiously said, "Hello, sir, I believe we have a mistake here." He asked, "Well, what seems to be the problem?" I replied, "I don't minister where men are, it's just … well … I'm not comfortable doing that." He replied, "Well, little lady, you're all we've got, so get over it."

I was amazed and said, "I just … It's against my doctrine." He smiled and jokingly said, "Well, I tell you what, do a good job and there will be a $10 spot in it for you." "Dear Lord, he thinks I'm a hireling," I thought. This pushed all my religious buttons. All the religious spirits that had been lying dormant got challenged that day.

Linda and I went back to our hotel. I must have changed clothes 20 times trying to see how holy I could look and I thought, "Well, surely there won't be many people; this is a little bitty town."

When we arrived at the Civic Center, the place was packed. Packed, packed, men everywhere. I think one of God's names you might not know is Jehovah Trickster. Here we were. The Pastor got up, and he's a big happy fella, and said, "Well, we have the Coon Neck Choir with us tonight." I thought, "Oh, musicians. If they do a good job, I can just get up and say bless you, be ordained, and run home."

I believe that at this point, God got all the 24 elders around His throne and said, "Come watch this!" The Coon Neck Choir came in. I was expecting robes. No, they all had sweatshirts on that said, "Coon Neck." They came out happy. They were happy clappy people. The choir director was also Pastor Earl and the one running the show; the same one who told me there was a $10 spot in it for me and at this point, the only friend I had in the place. He said, "We're going to sing, 'Behold the Lamb.'"

I thought, "Oh, that's a good song, you can't mess that up." Oh, yes, they could. It sounded like a hog calling contest. I looked at Linda. She looked at me. I knew I was not supposed to speak where men were. The pastor got through, they did their yodeling, and he said, "Praise God. That was so wonderful, let's do it again for Jesus." I thought, "No, He has already been crucified."

All I can tell you is that it was twice terrible. It was awful. The whole time they were "Beholding the Lamb," the pastor was blowing kisses to them and saying, "Great, wonderful." He was determined that, if he had leadership in their lives, they would be what God said they were. He was modeling true leadership and calling the things that were not as though they were.

> When everything looks bad, a good leader will call you a champion and remind you that you are above, you are healed, and delivered. They are mentors, not tormentors.

This is the kind of leadership you need. When everything looks bad, they will call you a champion and remind you that you are above, you are the healed, and delivered. Those are the kinds of leaders we need; mentors, not tormentors. A great leader does not talk about what they do not have. They begin to build on what they have. The third time they sang, heaven filled the room and they all sang beautifully. I said, "It's a miracle. It's a miracle. God is in the house." I got so excited, I almost forgot that I was a woman and limited because of my gender.

Then the pastor got up and said, "Now, we're going to introduce you to Brother Wonderful and his Intergalactic Ministry." This man came out, talked about the 25,000 people that he ministered to, and I was over in the corner becoming the Incredible Shrinking Woman thinking, "Oh, Lord, let Brother Wonderful do this." Anyway, he got through talking and they introduced Sister Magnificent. Then finally, at the end of all of it, he said, "Come on up, Sister Clarice Fluitt." I did, but my tongue cleaved to the roof of my mouth and I could not think or speak. Fear is a terror to good works.

You know, if you believe you are cursed, you will draw unbelief to yourself. I was standing there and it seemed like every one of those men crossed their arms and implied, "Ain't nothing you got is going to get on me." I know the body language. I weakly said, "I'm really happy to be here." (Lie number one.) The Lord had already told me I could not flash my submissive wife and motherhood badges to establish my credibility.

I said, "The Name of Jesus is above everything that has a name." It was deafeningly silent. I paused. "It's above the name of cancer and is above the name of heart attack." Now remember, I've got one friend, Pastor Earl, the song leader and the one that is going to give me a $10 spot if I did well. I figured that just went down the drain. He jumped up, grabbed his chest, said, "Ahhh …," and croaked right down on the floor. My one friend and it looked like God had just killed him.

I knew women were not supposed to talk where men were. I knew it. I knew it. His children were screaming saying, "Daddy, Daddy," and his wife said, "Earl, Earl, Honey." Earl was gone. He had gone on to the great Glory Land.

Now, if you want to break a meeting up, say, "Hello," and then God kills him on the spot.

Who wants to do the works of God?

They were all screaming and crying. They called the paramedics and the paramedics came in. They got the gurney, beat on his chest, and I was just standing there. Linda looked at me and asked, "What do you want to do?" I whispered, "Disappear. What do you mean what do I want to do?" She was playing the piano while all this scene was taking place.

The Lord said, "Ah-ahm, you unlikely candidate. Do you want favor with these people?" I said, "No. I want to go home." I never wanted to cook a biscuit so bad in my life. He said, "Go and raise him from the dead." I said, "You go raise him from the dead." The Lord said, "I can't go over there. Nothing manifests in this dimension without a body. You take Me over there, you just put your hand on him and say, 'I bind the spirit of death, and I release resurrection life.'"

"Daddy, Daddy." "Honey, Earl." The piano was playing softly in the background and I said, "Let me explain to You, Lord, how this works. If I go over there, I take You over there, and if You change your mind between here and there, You might as well get two plates ready, because I'm coming to Glory Land, too. I will die right on top of him. I will hold my breath and I will never get over this. It's the end." God's response, "Go do what I tell you to do." I boldly proclaimed to the congregation, "Ladies and gentlemen, excuse me, the Lord shall raise this man from the dead." It was like the Red Sea opened.

Bob Buse, an old prophet I knew always said, "Act like you do this every day." I remember reading in the Bible that I was to do the works of God. I wanted to be an extension cord into the realm of the miraculous! I believed that I had keys to hell, death, and the grave.

There is a generation where the appointment with death has been broken. Choose what generation you want to be in. Choose what you want to believe. Will you do the works of God?

I walked over there and put my hand over Earl and started praying in tongues. The Lord asked, "What are you doing?" I said, "I'm praying." He said, "You're just racing your motors. I didn't tell you to do that. You're like a car in park that's going drrrrn, drrrrn, drrrn. You're not going anywhere. I told you to put your hand on him, bind the spirit of death and release resurrection life." I finally became obedient, followed God's instructions and said, "I bind the spirit of death and I release resurrection life." Earl's eyes opened and he got up. Death left the room and the entire congregation rejoiced. I was amazed at the end of the ordination that I had a multitude of invitations to minister. No one seemed to care that I was a woman.

> I finally obeyed God and said, "I bind the spirit of death and release resurrection life." Earl's eyes opened and the entire congregation rejoiced. No one seemed to care that I was a woman.

Faith cometh by hearing. God can take an ordinary person and fill that person with the truth of God so that you, too, will become an extension of His Love. Love not expressed is love not received. You may have the power to do all kinds of things but if you cannot be nice, if you cannot love people, cannot be kind, or cannot say hello, it just all becomes an act.

Chapter 11

The Greater Works Have Been
Given for You to Do

RAINFALL MIRACLE IN
TRANSKEI, SOUTH AFRICA

At the age of 13 during a church summer camp meeting, I had been given a vision and Word from the Lord that I would go to Africa. In this vision, I saw a place and a people that I had never seen before. I heard a Voice speak to me and say, "I am preparing you to be a deliverer for My people." I then saw an undetermined number of black faces that were crying and calling my name and saying, "Clarice, come help us! Come help us!" The faces would be clear, and then fade away, but each face and voice was sincere and compelling. I asked, "Who are these people, and where am I, and how can I help them? I'm just a young girl."

The Lord's response was, "This is a vision for another season. You are in Africa and the faces you see represent those who will be saved in one of the world's greatest reformations that will begin in Africa and sweep the world. Rest in Me, and when the time is near, I will send for you."

Forty years after this vision, His call came to pass. I received an invitation to come to the Durban Christian Center in Durban, South Africa. While I was there, I was invited by the king of the Xhosa tribe to come to his palace in the Transkei. I was told that if I came, I would be given an audience with the king.

The Xhosas are the tribe who talk with a series of clicks and are the second largest tribe in South Africa. Former President Mandela was from the Xhosa tribe. The Transkei at that particular time was a no-man's-land because of the riots preceding the democratic elections. Because we had to drive almost six hours through this region to meet the king of the Xhosas, many said to me, "You are the wrong gender, the wrong color, there is a war going on, and it is a terrible, terrible time in South Africa. You cannot do it."

Let me tell you something, if God tells you to do something, He will make a way. He can even make you invisible to your enemy. Do not worry about it. What have I got to protect? I had a Word from God and desired to do the works of God.

To make this trip it cost me R6,000 rand to rent a Combi (minibus). We were a team of five women, all unlikely candidates going to see the king of the Xhosas to share the love of God.

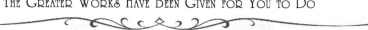

In this region, it had not rained for a long time. It was in January, which is the summer; the temperature was 116 degrees Fahrenheit, and there was not one cloud in the sky. As we traveled, we observed that the land was parched, and the crops had failed while giant termite mounds took over the landscape. People were oppressed, and starvation was everywhere. Everything screamed, "Oppression, oppression, oppression." With every inch that we went, I could hear the Lord saying, "Take the land, take the land. Don't be moved by what you see. Call the things that are not to be the things that are. Greater is He that is in you than he that is in the world."

I observed the locals transporting their hobbled sheep and goats in overcrowded trailers. They were hobbled to keep them from straying. The Lord said, "The whole country has been hobbled but I've given you a sword of the Spirit. Go cut them loose. Go cut them loose." You have to understand, all God needs is an earth suit. It does not matter what kind, what color, or what size. It just needs to be somebody that wants to do the works of God. God and you are always a majority.

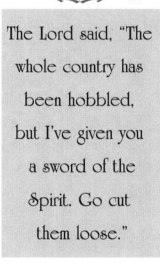

The Lord said, "The whole country has been hobbled, but I've given you a sword of the Spirit. Go cut them loose."

We traveled across the Transkei and got to the king's gate. Remember, it was 116 degrees Fahrenheit. I usually sparkle, but this time I was sweating. I put my make-up on three times, and three times it melted.

We arrived at the king's beautiful, beautiful palace. The magnificent carved doors were 24 feet tall. Much protocol was observed as they brought us into this wonderful room and said, "The king and the queen will be in." We were in a rotunda with the governor who was instructing us on acceptable protocol. They had invited us but never thought we would actually come.

Do you know that there are people that are waiting for you that never thought you would really come? You said you would come. You said you would go to the prison. You said you would go to set the captive free but you did not come because it was not convenient. Do not do that. Get yourself up and say, "Where You lead, I'll follow and what You feed, I'll swallow. I will do the works of God."

You do not come before a king without a gift befitting his office, so we were already prepared with this wonderful gift. The king's aide told us, "Whatever you do, do not turn your back to the royalty." Remember, we were in a rotunda (that is a round room) and I'm still trying to figure out who is royal. Our instructor asked, "Do you have the present?" Oh no! I realized that I had left the king's gift at our host's home. This was a serious mistake. I heard the king's aide announce, "The king and queen are ready to receive you."

They were in their big royal chairs. They had fans and we didn't. We were in this big rotunda and it was so hot. I am telling you, it was H-O-T-T-T-T-T. There was a window about 24 feet up with a little velvet curtain around it. If by accident a breeze came, it could not possibly get through all of the velvet. I was trying to maintain my dignity even after discovering that I had left my gift. What was I going to do? Punt and remember, with God all things are possible.

The king was smiling and ready to receive his gift. I said to myself, "Always act like you know what you're doing. Always."

I came before the king and said, "Your majesty, it is a great honor that you have given us to come to your wonderful country and share the Gospel of the Lord Jesus Christ, the Son of the Living God. I bring you a very great gift, an unspeakable gift."

I said to the king, "As we drove through your land, my heart was filled with great compassion when I saw your livestock languishing for lack of water, your crops withered, and your people greatly oppressed. I saw that you need water in this land. You need spiritual water and you need natural water. The Bible teaches us first the natural and then the spiritual, and I have come to bring you the gift of rain!!"

> I raised my hands, clapped, and shouted, "Rain!" Immediately, thunder struck, the wind blew the palace doors open, lightning flashed and it rained continuously for seven days and seven nights.

The king looked at me as I raised my hands, clapped, and shouted, "Rain!" Immediately, thunder struck, the wind blew the palace doors open, lightning flashed and it rained continually for seven days and nights. The king exclaimed, "Your God is God." As a wonderful result, he, his family, and his court accepted Christianity.

These are the greater works that have been given for you to do. Heal the sick. Raise the dead. Cast out demons. Multiply food. Preach good news. Stop the oppressor. Tell those storms, physical and spiritual, "You cannot come upon my land." Back them up with God's Word. You have the power in the Name of Jesus but you have to be faithful with the little things before God will give you dominion over the great things.

In 2006, I returned to South Africa to minister in several churches. I was in the country for a month and was enjoying the opportunity to reconnect with many of the friends I had met in 1993. So much had changed in South Africa for the good.

I was able to make contact with the king of the Xhosa tribe but it was a new king and queen because the ones I had been blessed to meet had passed away. The new king was very gracious and asked to have a meeting with me while I was in the area. He, his wife, and two sisters came to Johannesburg and we had a lovely time reminiscing and praying together. They were all wonderful Christians.

What a difference 21 years can make in your life. Use your years wisely.

Chapter 12

You Are a Word Sent from God

RAINFALL MIRACLE IN
QUEENSLAND, AUSTRALIA

*I*n May of 2009, I took a team of eight to Australia to reach out and minister to the residents of the Blue Mountains, which is a large rural region of communities and villages just west of Sydney. We held two conferences on consecutive Saturdays. Throughout the week, fifteen additional meetings were held in Lawson, Falconbridge, Menai, and the surrounding areas.

A miraculous highlight of the trip was a chance meeting and discussion with a Queensland couple visiting Sydney while we were waiting for the water taxi to take us to the central city. We chatted and told them why we were in Australia. They asked if I would pray for them and I asked if there was a specific need in their lives. They asked me to please pray to end the eleven year drought that had gripped the Queensland region. I assured the couple that, by a declaration of faith, the drought was now over. We were on the water taxi. I prayed in the open air with deep conviction that the rains would immediately return to Queensland and declared to the region and those present that the drought was no more. The couple smiled and said, "Well, we hope that's true." I smiled and said, "It will rain. The drought is over."

Two days later, on May 21st, The Sydney Morning Herald reported the following on page 2: "The Bureau of Meteorology reported that in the 24 hours to 7 p.m., the district received 59mm of rain, and the combined levels of the Brisbane dams had jumped by 8.22 per cent to 67.5 per cent capacity, the highest levels since 2002. Rain in the past 24 hours added 8.5 months' supply to the system. (AAP)" The resulting deluge prompted the State Government to officially declare an end to the drought. This was the highest total rainfall for May on record.[1]

Let the earth be alerted that Jesus Christ is Lord. We decree to the nations of the earth the revelation that Jesus is the Son of God, and was conceived by the power of the Holy Spirit. He was born of a virgin named Mary and for all sin, past, present, and future. He died, but on the third day, the Holy Ghost, the Lord and Giver of Life, raised Jesus from the dead!

That same Spirit that raised Jesus the Son of God, the God Man, that same Spirit, is in me. I am not an imitation. Let all the natural information bow to the supernatural revelation of the finished work. I believe that Jesus defeated hell, death, and the grave. I believe He has led captivity captive. I believe He took all the keys. I do not believe He fought for them. I believe satan immediately yielded to the power of Christ. Jesus said, "As the Father has sent Me, I send you." Selah.

As a born again believer, you are equipped with every spiritual blessing. Look within the Word of God. You are a Word sent from God. Your DNA, Divine Nature Attitude, has been released. You are not beggars and pleaders. Jesus has gone to the Father but He has sent the Holy Ghost to reveal Christ to you and conform you into the image of the dear Son of God. I release the revelation that this same Jesus will come again in glory to judge the living and the dead and there will never be an end to His Kingdom! Amen.

As a born again believer, you are equipped with every spiritual blessing. You are a word sent from God. Your DNA, Divine Nature Attitude, has been released.

---

[1] www.bom.gov.au/qld/flood/fld_reports/se_qld_may_2009.pdf; (www.smh.com.au).

Chapter 13

God Has Already Given You

the Victory

I remember that it was on a Sunday morning in February; a very beautiful but cold day. My husband George had gone on a ministry trip to Texas, and I was preparing to go to mass with our two younger children.

Debra, Becky and Trey had attended mass on Saturday, so they were to stay home. Our son, Trey, being our only boy, was an inquisitive young man and met each day with the spirit of enthusiasm and adventure. I instructed the children (Debra was 17 years old, Becky was 15, and Trey was 13) to clean their rooms, get dressed, and be ready to go to lunch by 11:30 a.m. I turned to Trey and gave him the intense "mother look" and said, "Trey, Debra is in charge while I am gone. It is too cold for you to go outside. I will be gone an hour and a half to church and when I return we will all go to lunch. Do you understand the plan?" While I was speaking, he was looking out the window and the sun was shining on his red curly hair as he nodded to me that he understood. I smiled and said, "I'm putting you in God's hands." I kissed him goodbye. The Scripture in Psalm 138:8 has always been a rhema word to my heart, "God is bringing to perfection (maturity) everything that concerns you." Wow, what a promise!

While at church, the priest, Father Bordelon, asked me to help design and redecorate the reconciliation room. (It had previously been called the confessional). I agreed and he asked if I could visit with him after the church service to discuss a plan and budget for the project. I told him that I only had 15 minutes because I had plans to meet my children for lunch. This was B.C. (before cell phones). I quickly found a phone and called home but there was no answer. I had no thought or premonition that anything bad had happened. Father Bordelon and I concluded our meeting and I was now 25 minutes late.

I called home and again no answer. I knew that Debra had her own car and my credit card and that she was quite capable of making an executive decision, especially if they were all hungry and ready to go. I was totally at peace. The weather had warmed up, it was a lovely day, and when you have five kids, it is challenging to find that desired quality time. With that thought, I said to my two little girls, "Let's go to lunch and then just the three of us will go to the movie and see Mary Poppins." They were thrilled and so was I.

We got out of the movie around 4:00 p.m. and went to get ice cream. Once again, I called home to check with the kids. Debra answered with a panic stricken voice, "Mom, where are you?" Without waiting for my response, she blurted out, "Trey has been in a terrible accident. He was burned with battery acid and has second and third degree burns on his face, chest, and arms. He's in the hospital in intensive care. I couldn't find you, Daddy is gone, and Grandmother is at the hospital. Please come home!"

Her words were filled with fear and pain. I listened intently and assured her that everything was alright. A supernatural peace filled my mind and body. I could only think of the promise of Psalm 138:8, "God is perfecting everything that concerns me." I immediately went to the hospital, but I was not prepared for what I saw or heard.

My sweet little boy was lying on his back. His face, arms, and chest were all bandaged. Only his eyes and mouth were visible. The typical hospital hook ups for meds and fluids were strategically placed on the unburned parts of his body. I had not heard from anyone how this terrible accident had occurred. As if this was not enough, I saw a pile of mud and blood spattered clothes lying in a corner. The large winter shirt was riddled with acid eaten holes that had burned through the thick fabric to Trey's flesh, the jeans were shredded, and the heavy soled tennis shoes and thick socks appeared to have melted. These facts were violently fighting with my faith.

Dr. Tom Payton was the ER physician and a close personal friend with a deep faith in God. He said, "Clarice, Trey has been burned with battery acid and has sustained second and third degree burns. We don't know how his vision will be affected. He was walking down the street and discovered a sealed container and did not know what was inside. Someone had discarded the acid in this sealed container. Trey saw it, hit it with a stick, and it exploded on to his face, chest, and arms. When battery acid comes in contact with flesh, it has the effect of thousands of needle like penetrations that burn at different degrees. His winter shirt and jeans helped to protect his body to some extent. Thank God that it was a cold day."

Dr. Payton continued to explain to me that when Trey sustained the acid explosion, he was in such agony that he jumped into a water filled ditch and splashed water and mud onto his face. "When he did that, he impacted the burn area with mud and debris. We cannot effectively clean the wounds because it will cause greater damage to his burns." The prognosis was not good. Dr. Payton told me that one of his serious concerns was that Trey could have secondary infections and possibly pneumonia. All that the doctors could do was to wait and see.

My mother-in-law was a woman of incredible faith. After hearing the doctor's report she said, "Well Doc, it seems you have done your part and now it's up to us to do our part. There is another Doctor on this case and He has another opinion." She turned to me and said with a knowing smile, "Let's take Trey home and believe God for his total restoration."

At the sound of her voice, I knew that this was a Word from God. Dr. Payton said, "As a medical doctor, I cannot endorse your decision, but as a man of God I choose to agree for a miracle for Trey."

We carefully transported our precious little "mummy" home and placed him in his bed. He could barely speak, but I understood his mumbled words, "Mom, I'm sorry."

I gathered the girls and grandmother in Trey's room to pray for him. I told Trey that satan is a defeated liar and the father of rebellion. I explained to him that, if he could not honor the instructions of his parents, he was inviting the snare of evil. But, the good news is, Jesus has defeated satan and as children of God we have the privilege to confess our sins, receive forgiveness, and become a candidate for God's grace, favor, and healing.

Immediately Trey said, "Mom, I disobeyed you and I know that it's wrong. Please forgive me and pray for me." The presence of the Lord filled our home. Gratitude, hope, love, and faith were flowing like a river. I prayed and anointed Trey with oil. I told him that faith comes to us as we hear the Word of God. I had recently listened to a lady named Betty Baxter. Betty was born hopelessly crippled and deformed. Jesus appeared to her and totally healed her. She became a world-renowned evangelist and her amazing story of God's miraculous healing power has touched and transformed millions of lives.

We all agreed to listen to the Betty Baxter story. Afterwards Trey said, "Mom, do you believe that really happened?" I replied, "Yes, I do." Trey got out of bed and began to remove his bandages. His blistered skin hung like water filled balloons. The girls were crying and telling him not to do that. He looked at me and said, "If God would do that for her, He will do it for me." He left the room and said, "I'm going to take a bath." The girls were hysterical and thought I was totally irresponsible. I said, "Girls, let's trust God with Trey."

I went into the kitchen and began to prepare the evening meal. About 15 minutes had passed and I heard Becky scream, "Mom! Mom! Come and see Trey." I ran from the kitchen into the living room and there he was. He had both of his hands on his hips standing and grinning. His wet red curls were tightly framing his beautiful scar-free face. His vision was perfect. His arms and chest did not have a sign of scars or redness. I looked at my clock. It was 7:07 p.m. Only 8 hours before he was blind, burned, and in horrible pain. What a mighty God we serve!

This amazing event is only one of the thousands of life changing stories that I have experienced involving God's divine intervention in our lives.

Later that evening when my husband George returned from his ministry trip to Texas, he came in exploding with amazing testimonies of how God had moved so sovereignly during his meetings. All the family was waiting to tell Dad our "Trey Story." I said, "Let me show you something." I held up Trey's shirt, jeans, and shoes that had been destroyed by the battery acid. George gasped, caught his breath, and said, "How in the world did that happen?"

My faith challenged girls could not stop telling their dad how amazing God is. Trey was enjoying the favor of God.

> His face was scar-free. His vision was perfect. His arms and chest did not have a sign of scars or redness. Only 8 hours before he was blind, burned, and in horrible pain. What a mighty God we serve!

Trey is now grown, married, and has two fine sons of his own. He is a quick-witted overcomer with amazing faith building testimonies. When Trey relates this amazing story, he tells us that when he was in the ditch screaming with pain, a man appeared, picked him up out of the water filled ditch, ran three blocks with this large 13 year old terrified child, brought him home, and told Debra to take him to the hospital. We have no idea just who this strong, kind man was or where he came from on that cold wintery day. We have never seen or heard from him again.

Thanks be to God who always causes us to win.

Who will do the works of God? Who desires to say, "Here I am in the army of God?" Regardless of what you have to overcome, God has already given you the victory. You will experience times and seasons that look bleak but the Word of God says, "Don't pray to that mountain." Say to it, "Be thou removed and cast into the sea."

I command the blessings of God upon those that have ears to hear, those that have the favor to fear God, not to fear what people think, not to fear what man would say, or fear that what they do may be wrong. I release you with an apostolic prophetic voice to do exploits, and to say, "As for me and my house, we will serve the Lord." You do not need to pray, "Do something to me." "You need to pray, "Do something through me."

The Word of God has the power to perform itself.

The Word of God teaches us that God has defeated every enemy. The war's been won while the battles of life rage. You're walking through this valley of the shadow of death (it is only a shadow) but you can have whatever you say, whether it is good or bad. Faith is like a muscle. If you do not use it, you will lose it. Make a choice. Prophesy to your circumstances and tell them to bow before your covenant promises from God.

Chapter 14

God Will Let You Believe What You Need To Believe to Get You Where He's Taking You

I was invited to minister at the international worship symposium in Singapore. My assignment was to teach for five days during the 10:00 a.m. to 12:00 p.m. sessions. The keynote speaker for the evening was the brilliant and anointed Steve Fry. Steve had just released his great "Thy Kingdom Come" album.

The team for this massive event was vast and varied. There were the A, B, and C teams and it became quite obvious who was who. The A team were guests in a beautiful five star hotel and spa. The B team were guests in a local two star motel. The C team was being domiciled at the local Y.M.C.A. that consisted of one very small room without air conditioning or a fan furnished with two small beds and a plastic no stain mattress. We were situated over the very popular 24 hour McDonald's restaurant. The aroma of fried meat was always permeating the atmosphere. Singapore in the summer is hot! Yes, you guessed it. I was on the C team. I was reminded of the famous comedian Don Rickles who was always saying, "I just can't get any respect."

One of the names of God that I have encountered could be, "Jehovah Trickster," (no dishonor intended) but, I have learned that God will let you believe what you need to believe to get you where He's taking you. I was beginning to feel a bit underappreciated, insignificant, inconvenienced, and real hot in the 112 degrees Fahrenheit humid jungle heat.

I chose to put on my happy face and make the best out of my situation. I went to my classroom and, to my amazement, hundreds of people were lined up to get into a room prepared for about 60 attendees. The event coordinator was moving the morning keynote speaker from the large auditorium into what was to be my room, and moving me and my class to the main auditorium. (Note: This is not the way to build new friends among the A group). I spoke on the Songs of Solomon and the call to be a worshipper from beyond the veil. The Lord favored me, and the class was successful.

A beautiful young married couple, Frankie and Julie, asked to speak to me after the meeting. They were the leaders of a large visual arts department at the famous His Sanctuary Church. Their bishop was Bishop Rodrick Tay. They had phoned him and told him about my class. Bishop Tay asked them to arrange a meeting for him to meet with me.

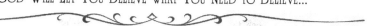

I expressed my gratitude but, since I had no transportation available, I could not arrange a time to meet. Frankie quickly told me that Bishop Tay had taken the liberty to send a limousine to transport me to the meeting. Out of curiosity, I said yes.

As I arrived at the His Sanctuary Church, the chauffer graciously escorted me to the grand and elegant reception area. Bishop Tay was a tall slender Chinese gentleman in his 40s. He was handsomely dressed from head to toe. One could not help but notice his thick black hair and that it was perfectly groomed. He stood erect and did not speak until he stood directly in front of me and bowed. With tears in his eyes he said, "Dear prophetess of God, have mercy on our blindness and forgive our peoples' insensitivity for not recognizing and acknowledging you as a gift that God has sent to us. Please be welcome as a royal dignitary to our nation and allow me the privilege of accommodating you and your team to the finest hotel in Singapore. Let me serve your every need." I was stunned. Never had I been more honored. Needless to say, Bishop Tay and his lovely wife Salley became my dear friends.

When I returned to my Y.M.C.A. dwellings, I found my other C team members. We sacked, packed, and moved to the prestigious and beautiful Mandolin Bay Hotel.

Bishop Tay had completed building a large new church and had invited Dr. Daisy Osborn to dedicate the opening of the building. He also invited me to minister at this great celebration. All the dignitaries of the area had accepted their invitation to this great event. The local church had worked tirelessly around the clock preparing for the big day.

If you have not heard of Dr. Daisy and her husband Dr. T. L. Osborn, let me explain what spiritual giants they were and are. They were missionaries to Africa and measured their congregations by the acres. Some of the most amazing miracles of healing have been reported and certified. Millions have come to know God through their life changing explosions of almightiness.

Dr. Daisy was a petite, spunky, and very fashionable red haired dynamo. She walked and talked with amazing authority and I was thrilled to have the opportunity to meet and minister with her. I had read all of the Osborn's books. They had changed my life and helped prepare me for a life of miracles.

I vividly remember the day she arrived in Singapore. I was with Bishop Tay and we were waiting in the hotel lobby for her grand entrance. When I saw her, I was immediately aware of the presence of the Lord that surrounded her. She was exquisitely dressed and looked like the royalty that she was.

Bishop graciously greeted her and introduced me to her. I quickly blurted out, "Oh, Ms. Daisy, I am so blessed to meet you and I look forward to learning great wisdom from you." I was like a six year old kid who had just found their first ice cream cone. Dr. Daisy smiled politely and released her wisdom on me immediately. Her piercing blue eyes fixed on me as she said, "Know this, my dear young woman, you must learn to either lead in life, follow in life, or get out of the way of life; and for God's sake, get a new hairdo!" I was not offended, but her

> Dr. Daisy's piercing blue eyes fixed on me as she said, "Know this, my dear young woman, you must learn to either lead in life, follow in life, or get out of the way of life; and for God's sake, get a new hairdo!"

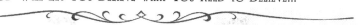

words empowered me. She cut me with her prophetic laser sword and those religious spirits that had kept me in bondage to the traditions that taught me to look peculiar, never be stylish, always walk 10 steps behind any man and call it submission rather than unworthiness was completely severed.

I knew immediately that my choice was to lead, so I heard her heart and got a real spunky hair cut that day. I have never looked back.

Dr. Daisy imparted her understanding that, in Christ, there is neither male nor female. She has since gone on to her reward, but I know she would be proud of me today. I did not know that this would be one of her last ministry trips. At this time, she was battling stage four cancer but you would not have known by looking at or listening to her.

The Osborn's had an amazing reputation in all of Asia. Their ministry of healing and deliverance had impacted the Middle East. Thousands came to the meeting. The sick, lame, and halt were everywhere. I was so blessed to be in this great meeting.

NEVER LET ANYBODY SEE YOU SWEAT

Dr. Daisy came on stage. She exhorted the crowd, released the miracle anointing, and told the crowd to prepare for an unprecedented outpouring of healing miracles. The musicians and singers were praising, the crowds were clapping and shouting, and I was sobbing and absorbing all that was happening. Dr. Daisy extended her hands to the crowd and said, "Everyone who wants a miracle come forth." The place erupted and the entire audience was pushing to get to the altar.

She quieted the people and announced that God had sent a great healing prophet from the U.S.A. to pray for each person. This prophet was there to lay hands on and pray for all the sick. I could not imagine who she was talking about, but I was ready to get in line.

"Ladies and gentlemen, I want to introduce Prophetess Clarice Fluitt from the U.S.A., God's agent for miracles!" I was the most unprepared and shocked person in the place and I was getting ready to run to the altar to be prayed for. "Come up here and take the service, prophetess Clarice." The crowds clapped as I came on to the stage and I remembered what I had learned from an old prophet named Bob Buse, "Never let anybody see you sweat and act like you know what you're doing. That's what faith is all about."

With great authority, I took the microphone and Dr. Daisy left and went to the hotel. Then I began to activate other ministers in the leadership to start praying with me for the people until we had an extraordinary corporate ministry. For the next five hours great healings and miracles were reported. I continue to hear Dr. Daisy say, "Lead, follow, or move!"

Great opportunity always travels with fear, doubt, and risk. Learn to push through, because victory is sweet.

As we left the building after the meeting, people were already lining up for the next service. The grand celebration for dedicating the new sanctuary was to begin at 10:00 a.m. I was exhausted after the meeting and got back to my room around 2:00 a.m.

At 6:30 a.m. my phone rang and Bishop Tay was barely whispering, "Prophetess, I have laryngitis, Dr. Daisy is sick, my worship leader has lost his voice, and my master of ceremonies has a virus. Help!" "Bishop," I said, "What do you want me to do?"

He responded, "I want you to M.C. the entire event, introduce all the dignitaries, lead the worship, preach the dedication message, receive the offering, make the altar call, and pray for salvation and healing of the people. This will be the largest crowd that has ever been to the sanctuary. You have to help me!"

I have never been more challenged. I fell on my face and began to declare the Word of God over myself, "Thanks be to God who causes me to triumph in everything." I knew that I could not do this in my human strength. I arrived at the church at 8:30 a.m. Bishop whispered his very specific instructions, and gave me a list of oriental names that only God could pronounce. I met the musicians, and PRAYED. I met with the arts department, and PRAYED.

The church was filled inside and out with standing room only by 9:08 a.m. Everyone was expecting to see Ms. Daisy, and the atmosphere was charged with faith.

Promptly at 10:00 a.m. the mighty musicians began to play, and dancers in magnificent costumes and brilliant banners were being unfurled. Bishop Tay, his wife Salley, and yours truly came on stage to the sound of a roaring crowd that was ready to praise God. There was not a need to speak, so we all yielded to the spirit of limitless praise and worship. The Spirit orchestrated the entire service. Outstanding healing

Outstanding miracles occurred, goiters disappeared, people came out of wheelchairs, arthritic hands were open, demons had to flee. The atmosphere was charged with the realm of the miraculous.

113

miracles occurred, goiters disappeared, people came out of wheelchairs, arthritic hands were opened, demons had to flee, and people were saved and baptized in the Holy Spirit by the hundreds. The atmosphere was charged with the realm of the miraculous.

It was a most successful dedication. I really learned that with God all things are possible. We are expected to make plans, but God always has His purpose.

Chapter 15

Champions Live Differently than Ordinary People

JOHOR BAHRU

While I was in Singapore, I began to get homesick. I had been ministering for over two months. When you get away from home for a long time and nothing's familiar, you begin to wonder if anything is really being accomplished. Have you ever felt like you've just done and done and done and wondered if you have accomplished anything? Is my life accounting for anything, or am I just running around? Am I seeing anything take place? I was really in need of some encouragement.

I traveled to a city called Johor Bahru, which is not far from Singapore, into Malaysia where we conducted a meeting. There were Malaysian, Chinese, and Tamil-speaking people in attendance. I had three interpreters. I would say, "Good evening," and after each interpreter spoke and it was time for me to speak again, I had forgotten what comes after good evening. The whole process was just a study in frustration. Then I said to the interpreters, "Just call the people to the altar and let's pray."

I prayed even though they did not know what I was saying. I just kept praying for them, and they would be healed or fall over. Many Hindus were there. There was a young girl who was obviously a Buddhist. I prayed for her and she looked at me with a big smile. She spoke a little English, but it was very broken English. I prayed and she said something but the only thing I could understand was something like, "My name Mae Bu."

The meeting was in a place where there were open sewers. Awful fumes coming into this hot and overcrowded room with only one small fan to combat the inside temperature of 112 degrees Fahrenheit was not what I would call pleasant, but I was obedient to do the best I could.

I went back to my room that night very exhausted and homesick and said, "Lord, is anything really happening in these meetings?"

From Johor Bahru I went to Kuala Lumpur to meet Ms. Daisy Osborn. We were doing another meeting together. She was lovely, sweet, beautiful, and anointed. I knew she was going through a battle with cancer, but she never broke her stride. She was a champion.

Champions live differently than other people. You may be down in the valley, but you do not need to take other people down there with you.

I was getting dressed to go to the meeting and I was thinking about being away from my family and people who love me. I was feeling alone and sorry for myself.

The phone rang. This sweet young girl said to me, "You Clarice Fluitt?" I said, "Yes." She said, "My name Mae Bu. You pray for me last night. You pray for me. Spirit of living God come on me. I Buddhist. Jesus appeared to me. I receive Jesus as my Lord and Savior." I said, "Praise God, Mae Bu." She said, "You must know. I crazy woman. I have nervous breakdown. I was great piano player, but after last night, Jesus Christ come and He heal. My mind come back." I said, "That's wonderful, Mae Bu." She said, "I go back to my school. The students come and say, "Oh Ms. Mae Bu, what happened to you?" I tell them, "I go to meeting. Prophet woman lay hand. Jesus appeared. I received Jesus in my heart. He healed me. All my children say, we want Jesus."

Suddenly, I was feeling better about being in a foreign land. Mae Bu said, "My uncle Buddhist priest. He is very sick man. I go to see him. He look at me. He say, "Mae Bu, what happened to you?" "I go prophet woman. Lay hand on me. Jesus come into my heart, save me, heal my mind. He say, "I want Jesus now." My uncle Buddhist priest."" I said, "Oh, Mae Bu, thank you, thank you for encouraging me." She said, "No call to encourage. Woman, Mae Ling, in hospital. She die. She have brain cancer. I tell her your story. She said, "Oh you think she pray for me?" She said I give you phone number. Call hospital.""

About this time, I felt like Clark Kent looking for a telephone booth. I called the hospital and said, "I want to speak to Mae Ling." They said, "Oh no, she very sick. She dying." I said, "My name is Clarice Fluitt. I am from the United States of America, and sent by the most high, sovereign God into this country to

> I called the hospital and said, "I have been sent by the most high, sovereign God into this country to talk to Mae Ling." At the end of that day, Mae Ling was healed, her children were saved, and the Buddhist priest professed Jesus as Lord and Savior.

talk to Mae Ling." The person on the other end of the line said, "We put her on phone right now." "This Mae Ling, hello." I said, "In the authority of the name of Jesus Christ, I call you the healed." Mae Ling said, "I believe." Her response got me very excited. I was ready for the evening meeting.

That night we went to the meeting and thousands of people were there. As I was telling the story, there were three Buddhist priests in saffron robes that came to the meeting bringing Mae Ling's three little children to be saved. At the end of that day, Mae Ling was healed, her children were saved, and the Buddhist priests professed Jesus as their Lord and savior.

Never doubt the power of prayer to our awesome and loving Father God. Choose to be a champion and go the distance even when your flesh is complaining.

Chapter 16

God Has a Plan

I was in Manila to help lead a worship service for a Benny Hinn Crusade. We were having a wonderful time. Two of the leaders of our meetings had traveled to Hong Kong to speak to a beautiful woman that had a business called Club Bravo. Their intention was to invite her to come to the Benny Hinn miracle meetings in Manila. She was from the Philippines, and owned and operated a business in Hong Kong (a gentleman's social club).

Many thousands of beautiful young Filipino women had moved to Hong Kong to become "hostesses" because they had to help take care of their family members. This ancient occupation provided food and shelter for their families. People were starving.

About five or six of these ladies attended the meetings along with their head mistress by the name of Cora. They were lovely young women dressed like little dolls. The meeting began and the minister invited the ladies from Hong Kong to come up on stage. He did not give them an explanation, just an invitation. When they did, he threw his jacket on them and said, "Receive Jesus. I absolve you of your sins." I thought, "Can he do that?"

I was sitting on stage in the front thinking to myself, "He is really messing with my theology." The ladies were squirming around trying to get up when he came back, threw his jacket again, and said, "Receive the baptism of the Holy Ghost." I thought, "You did not even talk to them about sin. You cannot get people saved unless you talk about sin. This is just emotion." The next thing I heard was the sound of a new prayer language bubbling up from the Hong Kong ladies.

After the meeting, the staff went to the green room back stage. It was like who is who in the zoo; all the wonderful name brand people. Bishops, pastors, ministers, governors and all the people were being so kind. We were all talking about what God was doing and how wonderful and amazing the healing meetings were going.

Suddenly, this beautiful woman Cora walked in where we were, and with tears mingled with mascara running down her face, said, "Hey! Somebody in here tell me, now that I got Jesus in my heart, how am I supposed to make a living?" The bishop from Singapore looked at me and said, "Ah, Pastor Clarice, you go to Hong Kong. Start church." I replied, "I don't think so." He said, "Oh yes, this job for woman. You get a church started and I will send a pastor later."

To make the long story short, the next day I was on a plane going to Hong Kong thinking if that little gang of mine back home could see me now. I had never been in a bar. The only thing

I had going bad in my life were things like pride, arrogance and self-righteousness; those good sins. How was I ever going to relate with these women?

The ladies greeted me at the airport with a big stretch limousine, flowers, candy, expressed their appreciation, and said, "We so happy you come, Pastor Clarice. You come to Club Bravo." I asked, "What time will the service be this evening?" They smiled and said, "We don't have service evening time. We work night time." I had no response. I went to the hotel, and the next day about 2:00 p.m., they came and took me to Club Bravo.

I entered a dark room that was filled with young women. It seemed that they all had little brown cigarettes. There were enough whiskey bottles on the wall that you could float a battle ship, and mirrors on the ceiling. It is an unusual place. My heart was pounding. I said, "Oh my God, oh my God, oh my God." The Lord said, "Shut up!" I asked, "Lord, Lord, what do you want to me to tell them?" He said, "Tell them I love them." I said, "Then can I tell them about sin?" He said, "Never speak of it. You just tell them I love them, and you mean it." I said, "Yes, Sir."

> The dark room was filled with young women. There were whiskey bottles on the wall and mirrors on the ceiling. My heart was pounding. I asked, "Lord, what do you want me to tell them?" He said, "Tell them I love them."

Cora got up to introduce me and said, "I go to Benny Hinn meeting. Same Spirit of God on Benny Hinn is on Cora. I have power to heal! Spirit of Holy Ghost on me. I now speak in tongue.

Pastor Clarice Fluitt from the United States of America come to tell you about Jesus the Son of God."

I got up and simply said, "I want to tell you all about Jesus. He has paid the price for all sin, sickness, and poverty. Jesus is the Son of God. How many of you want Jesus to be your Savior and want to spend eternity with Him?" Every hand went up. I said, "Alright, I am going to pray for you. Just put your hand on your heart and say with me, I believe in Jesus. He is the Son of God. I am a sinner."

The Lord asked, "What are you doing?" I said, "I am praying the sinner's prayer." He said, "Involve yourself in their life." You have a nice, safe position up here. Now go down and touch every one of them." I said, "Touch everyone." He said, "Trust Me." I said, "God, there are too many of them." He said, "Trust Me." I said, "Lord, I do trust You, but have You counted? I am going to be here forever. This harvest is too big for one woman to take care of it. Something has got to happen." He said, "Trust Me. I have a plan. You do what's possible. I'll do what's impossible." I said, "Okay."

I walked to this first girl and said, "Do you want Jesus to be your Savior?" She said, "I want Jesus to be my Savior." I said, "Then just say, 'Come in, Jesus, take me just as I am.'" She said, "Jesus, take me as I am." She started praying and said, "Praise God." They were like ripe apples falling in a basket. I thought, "I may move to Hong Kong. I may even take up nightclubbing." Everything was going so good and easy.

We all need to remember that God is bound to His Word but not necessarily to our interpretation of it. We may have a plan, but God has a purpose.

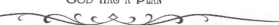

I got to the tenth girl and was feeling good when the Lord asked me, "What are you doing?" I said, "I am getting these people saved." He said, "You must pray for them to be empowered." I said, "What do you mean?" He said, "Pray for them to get the baptism of the Holy Ghost." I said, "Lord, they don't understand." He said "Neither do you. Pray in faith with these girls." I went back to the first girl and asked her, "Do you want the power of God in your life?" She responded, "I want power in my life to serve Jesus." I said, "Ask Jesus to baptize you in the Holy Spirit and just receive the power of God." She began speaking in tongues. I began to wonder if it was Chinese or Tamil but the Lord reminded me again, "Just trust Me. You do your part and I will do Mine." Every one of those ladies that I had already prayed for were now praying in tongues.

Into about the fifteenth person, I was feeling really good about what I was doing. There was this one particular girl with her head down. I asked her, "Do you want Jesus to be your Savior?" She looked up at me, but all I could see were the whites of her eyes. There were no pupils and this deep horrible voice came out of her and said, "We will kill you!"

I thought, "Oh, rats!" That girl started manifesting demons and bedlam broke out all over the place. Bottles were breaking, people were screaming, and I thought, "Well, God, I guess You brought me here to kill me." I ran through the people as fast as I could saying, "I bind you devil. I take authority. Loose this woman." Suddenly I heard the people that I had previously prayed for saying, "You loose my sister in Jesus' name!" They were following my lead, and the power of God was releasing every prisoner.

When all the drama was over they all got born again, were baptized in the Holy Ghost and set free from demonic activity.

> Nobody told them about sin. Nobody told them they could not be the hand of God extended. There were no laws that day, just mercy and love. I learned that you have to catch a fish before you can clean it.

We were shouting and singing. We were all screaming, Jesus! Nobody told them about sin. Nobody told them they could not be the hand of God extended. There were no laws that day, just mercy and love. They just believed God in a place called Club Bravo in Hong Kong. I learned that you have to catch a fish before you can clean it.

I said, "Well, God, You do have a purpose. You know how to get the harvest done. You are bringing people in, teaching them Your Word, and turning them loose."

It was so wonderful. Joyfully, I announced to all of them, "You have all had a divine encounter and experience with God. Tonight when we meet together, I will teach you God's wonderful Word and explain the doctrine of what has happened to you." They said, "Oh, Pastor, we work nighttime." I thought, "Oh my God, I have turned them into twice the children of hell." The Lord said, "You sure have a lot of confidence in yourself." I went back to the hotel, wept and cried, and acted like a fool.

The next day at 2:00 p.m., Cora came to get me, and was all smiles. I said, "Well, Cora, what kind of evening did you have, dear?" "Very good!" She said, "My paramour, very rich diamond merchant. He Buddhist. He called last night. He very sick. He have bleeding ulcer. He said, "Oh Cora, I very sick."" She said, "I told him same spirit of living God on Benny Hinn on Cora and I have power to heal you. I lay hands on him and cast the demon out. He gave me more money last night than ever before."

I felt like I was in Cornelius' house. I can tell you so many stories about the sovereignty of God. Club Bravo became a Church and I was part of it. I went back to Club Bravo three years later. Cora moved back to Manila, and she and her husband established a church work in Manila.

God has a plan. Is anything impossible for God?

Chapter 17

Change Your Perception

PROPHETIC DECLARATIONS

Every judgment that has been made of your life; every doctrine that you have embraced as truth that was not truth; everything that has tried to smother you, and to put out your fire; everything that has come to wound, cut, bruise, confuse, or to discourage you, I reach into the ever-present now with an apostolic voice, and carefully remove those things God had nothing to do with. In the authority of the name of Jesus, I speak to the heavens and declare that we have sent up the vapor, and God is sending down the rain. Lord, let our deserts bloom again. (Job 36:27 AMP)

Beloved, preach glad and not mad; for God has redeemed our lives from destruction; crowned us with loving kindness and tender mercy; as you satisfy your mouths with good things, your youth will be renewed like the eagles. (Psalm 103:4-5)

Who will be a fire pot for God? Thank you Lord that we are each a signed, sealed, unique individual that both reflect and absorb an element of God's glory that no one else has ever had. Thank you Lord that we are not oppressed, depressed, suppressed, repressed, or possessed. Father, we agree with what You say, and we are standing in the stead of Christ. (2 Corinthians 5:20)

Teach us to be sensitive to the needs and desires of others. Teach us to cover and not smother. Let our eyes behold the goodness of the Lord in the land of the living. Teach us how to love ourselves so we can love others. Lord, thank you for setting us free from everything that has to do with unworthiness, self-hate, and low self-esteem. You have set us free from every ill-perceived conception and perception that was once our reality and from everything that had been programmed into us from negative words, thoughts and ideas. (Psalm 27:13) Amen

> "[What, what would have become of me] had I not believed that I would see the Lord's goodness in the land of the living!" (Psalm 27:13 AMP)

Chapter 18

I Know God Has Given You
Your Miracle

It began as an ordinary day in the middle of an event that I had been hosting. I came home after having had a wonderful dinner with friends anticipating a quiet evening of rest and relaxation.

Out of nowhere, I began to experience severe stomach pain and was rushed to the hospital. At the recommendation of Dr. Owen Meyers, my primary care physician who met me at the hospital, I underwent a series of tests. When the results were read by Dr. Meyers, he was perplexed and amazed. He showed me the ultra sound of where my stomach was supposed to have been. The results indicated that my esophagus was trying to become my stomach, and my stomach had become strangulated and was reduced to nothing more than a withered looking string. He immediately recommended the additional expertise of a gastrointestinal specialist. After collaboration and consultation with Dr. Meyers, the G.I. specialist recommended surgery the following morning. I had nothing to say except, "I trust You, Jesus."

Dr. Tandie, my Executive Assistant, had been observing all of these happenings and is well informed on medical procedures. She was smiling, but I knew her extremely logical mind was being challenged by this experience.

My dear friend, Dr. Marian Stewart, is a spirit-filled medical doctor and was in town attending the event I was hosting. She is motivated by the love and compassion of the Lord to help the sick and suffering whenever she can. She is also a seer with prophetic insight. Dr. Stewart loves the realm of the supernatural and the working of miracles.

She had come to be with me in the hospital and said, "Let's pray," and pray we did. As she stood over me she said, "By faith and through spiritual enactment, I am going to operate on you right now." I must admit, I did not fully understand what she was talking about.

With her eyes closed she said, "I see inside your stomach." Dr. Stewart, using her medical knowledge and prophetic giftings, began calling each body part to come into alignment with the Word of God in the order that God originally intended it to be, and how

> Dr. Stewart, using her medical knowledge and prophetic giftings, began calling each body part to come into alignment with the Word of God.

He originally intended each part to function. The prayer lasted less than ten minutes. She said, "Dr. Clarice, they won't have to operate now. Be sure you get a new ultra sound in the morning." Dr. Stewart left and, as she went to the door, she said, "I know God has given you your miracle."

The morning came, and so did three doctors, all of whom were ready to go surgically exploring. I asked for another test, and they complied. When the results came back, all three of them were amazed. There, in full view, was my stomach. They didn't ask, and I didn't tell!

I was dismissed from the hospital and went home to eat a lovely meal. May this miracle bring great faith to you as you face your own trials and testings knowing that God has spare parts, and is pleased to demonstrate the outcome when we act in faith. Believe Him for ridiculous miracles!

With God, all things are possible.

Chapter 19

Don't Limit God

THE GOD MAKER

was on a missionary outreach with my ministry team, and we had one day off. We were in Kuala Lumpur, Malaysia. The oldest city in Malaysia is the city of Malacca, and I wanted to visit that ancient place. I did not realize that the very day I went to Malacca was one of their great feast days, sort of like Mardi Gras in New Orleans. This old city had cobblestoned streets that were about nine feet wide. It was just a little teeny, tiny place. When we got into the city, there was no way to get out. The traffic had become so congested that there was no way to get down the street. We were trapped in Malacca. I want you to know that if you are trapped in Malacca, you are really trapped. There was nowhere to go and the only thing available to eat was fungus soup, fish heads, and some other delicacies that I was trying to acquire a taste for. It is amazing how different our taste is, but I was trying and believing that with God all things are possible.

> When you are walking with God, you are alive for His purposes. He says, "I need a body to manifest My will. I need a set of hands, I need eyes, and I need ears. If you'll just take Me where I want to go, I'll do what I've got to do."

Do you believe the steps of the righteous have been ordered by God? Here I was in Malacca on my one day off. Let me explain something I have experienced. When you are walking with God, you do not get a day off. Every day is a work day. You do not belong to you anymore. You are alive for God's purposes. He says, "I need a body to manifest My will. I need a set of hands, I need eyes, and I need ears. If you'll just take Me where I want to go, I'll do what I've got to do." Wonderful things happen when God mixes with man.

Nothing on this earth manifests without a body. The demons have to have one. Jesus has to have one. Which one are you going to yield to? It's an either/or; we are either going to manifest the old nature, or we are going to manifest Christ. So, we are learning to walk as the sons of God. We have been called and equipped to create with God. When things look terrible, do not be moved by what you see. Remember the Word of God. If you cannot remember anything else, just say, "Jesus is Lord." Do not open your mouth and let negative words come out.

Here we were in Malacca. All over the Far East, every home and every business has a little god box attached to their buildings. They all have a god of some kind, and in these god boxes they have fresh fruit. The fresh fruit is used to appease the multitude of gods. They also have a special kind of incense paper which is made to burn for 12 hours. Every 12 hours you replace these burning papers so that the smell of incense is everywhere that these little god houses are. Whoever has the market on the incense papers and the god houses is one rich dude!

It happened to be that the head god maker in all of Asia lived in Malacca and his shop was on the street where I got stuck. I was with my Christian host and said "I want to go in there." He said "Oh, no, no, no. That's the god maker's place." I felt like a Tom Sawyer spirit got me. "Just wait a minute," I said. "We're going to go in there and look around." I could not leave, so I might as well fit into the plans of God. You have to understand that when the enemy says, "Aha, I've got you now. You can't do anything," that is when you are going to do the most good if your faith is in God.

The god maker's occupation was to design and construct the structures referred to as god houses. These god houses provide a proper place for the incense to burn and the offerings of fruit and cakes to be displayed in order to appease their polytheistic beliefs (belief in a multitude on gods).

This could be compared to our construction of bird houses to accommodate a multitude of different birds. Some are simple and others are very elaborate. The god maker of Malacca was the ultimate entrepreneur, or god house designer.

So I went in the god maker's market and as far as I could see there were these papers. Papers, papers, papers; all of these papers, and all of these different god houses. I was walking through and my thought was, "Well, Jesus turned water into wine." I'm going to say, "Father, every time these papers are lit, they are going to become a praise to You. I reverse the curse of false religion and release the truth of God wherever I go. Father, I just thank You that everywhere these papers go I release the revelation of Your love and power."

This little old Malaysian man came out from the back of the store with his long beard, long thin nails, his cigarette, and yellow nicotine stained fingers from years of smoking. It was the god maker himself. He had no teeth and was bent over. He was very old; very, very old, and very honorable.

My friend that spoke the language said to the god maker, "This is a woman of God from the United States." He said, "Aw!" My friend told me the god maker wanted to have tea with me. I said, "Of course. I'll be happy to meet with him." My friends were all challenged because they wanted to protect me. I believe I was created to stir things. I am a stirring instrument. I am a spoon for God. Wherever it is, just stir it up and bring it to the surface. We went into his resting place in the back of the store for tea. Everybody venerated this old god maker.

His servants prepared some sweets. I thought they were sweet, but you have to understand the Eastern taste buds are quite different than Western taste buds. Where we put sugar in things, they use salt. They brought these little salt cakes to go with this very strong tea. I have learned to endure all kinds of things for the sake of the gospel; we can eat that which is set before us, and act as though it is good. We sat there with our interpreter. I learned that on this high, holy day all of the demon entities were going to be parading in the streets and it was also the god maker's birthday.

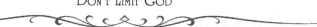

He was 88 years old and the most venerated and wealthiest man in all of Asia. He invited me and my team to be his special guest at his birthday banquet. Don't you just love it? It is a set up. You have to let your faith arise. Faith cometh by hearing, and hearing by this testimony. This is not about testing and moaning. This is about the power of God; of God taking things that are impossible, putting His breath on it, and watching God touch the world with His love. Not the world system; but God loves god makers; little idol makers. He loves big people, little people, small people, great people, all people. We are, after all, in the people business.

So, choose not to be clannish. God is after anybody that has a body. If you are prejudiced or fearful, people will know it. Be real. If you are fake, people can see right through a facade.

Here we go. My team asked, "Do you really want to go to the god maker's birthday banquet?" I said, "By the hair of my chinny chin chin, you are going to let me in. Where else do you think I am going tonight? Am I going to walk the streets of Malacca? This is an open door. We are going to this big, fine hotel and be in the midst of the most prominent people in Malaysia. I am going to sit right up in the high places with the king of the Rama-Jamas, they are going to parade by me, and I am going to loose God's love and conviction on every float. The demons and dragons don't have a prayer."

There I was, the unlikely candidate at the god maker's birthday banquet. It was a 15 course meal in the most incredible palatial hotel. The food was culturally enriching, absolutely beautiful, but food that I had not acquired taste for. The little old god maker and his wife were sitting at the head of the table.

All of his children, grandchildren, great-grandchildren, and great great-grandchildren filled the room. He had such honor because he was the patriarch and the source of wealth.

Did you know that when you are filled with the Holy Spirit, the word platho, to be filled, means that you have received the source of all wealth resident within you? So, you need to let God out, let Him rule, reign, lead, and guide.

The god maker sent a messenger to me and said, "You are a woman of God. We have many gods, but my wife has diabetes and is blind. Can your God heal my wife?"

The little old god maker, his wife, and all of their heirs were in the room with us. While we were eating rotten egg soup and duck that had to be rotted for its head to fall off, I was saying, "Mmm, yummy, yummy, yummy; got duck in my tummy." That is honor. People know whether or not your honor is genuine. I really liked the little god maker. I did not agree with what he did, but he was a kind, sweet man who had not yet had the revelation of Jesus Christ as Lord and Savior. Why would you beat a blind man up for not knowing what the color blue is? If you do not have the power to give him sight, do not find fault with him. May God's power be revealed to us and through us so that the things we do will be so obviously of God that no flesh could glory.

The time came when the old gentleman sent a messenger to me and said, "You are a woman of God. We have many gods but my wife has diabetes and is blind. Can your God heal my wife?" Oh yeah. Oh yeah. I know why I am here now. Let us manifest something besides an opinion. All the people that are with me are getting really nervous. This is one of those times when it is either do it, or don't do it. So, I went up to the front table. All the heirs were waiting for Granny to get healed with this God that I told them about, this Jesus, the Son of the living God, the Key, the Deliverer, the Mighty God, the One True God.

I said to the god maker through my interpreter, "Sir, all of your gods are false gods. They have no power or authority. When my God heals your wife, will you renounce all your gods?" The old god maker took his wife's hands and with tears coming down his face looked at her and they both said, "Yes." He put his hands on her face and touched her with such gentleness, such reverence, and such love. He said to me, "If your God heals my wife, then your God is God."

The Kingdom of God has come and continues to come to me and you. What the world wants to see is a healing, delivering, all-powerful God that when you walk in, all of hell backs up. Ha! Oh, this is a joyous time.

Here we have this little old god maker, his little old blind wife, and my squeamish but hopeful team. I have the god maker that had just said in front of all of his heirs who were seeing their money fly out the door, "If your God heals my wife and opens her eyes, I will relinquish everything I have to do as being the god maker."

I took her sweet face and placed it in my hands. I knew they were no longer my hands. I became aware that the substance of faith had moved into the shadow and that the Lord was saying, "Thank you, Clarice. Thank you for letting Me touch her." I said, "Now, blindness, you foul spirit from the pit of hell, release this woman.'" Some would say, Oh, but she is not a believer. Shh! God starts from the end and goes to the beginning. He always starts at the finish and backs up. Tears began coming down her face. It was not a long prayer. It was just, "Receive your sight." She blinked her eyes. It was very quiet. Suddenly she said, "Oh!"

The god maker began to weep and kissed her. All of her children and grandchildren began to cry when she said, "I see you! I see you!" The little children came and gathered around her, children she had never seen. The god maker of Malacca became a born-again believer! About a year later, I received a thank you letter from the god maker's grandson thanking me for presenting the Gospel to his family and appreciating the fact that his grandmother had received her sight.

Let God arise and the enemy be scattered. He is a mighty God. He is a God to be adored and glorified. Hallelujah to the King. He is the One that reaches to the nations of the world. Nothing is impossible for Him. Nothing is impossible.

Chapter 20

Be Fruitful and Multiply

A lovely young couple moved into the house next door to our home. Larry was a handsome aspiring attorney and Mary a perky homemaker and community advocate. One evening they came over to our house for a visit. After a few minutes of polite conversation Mary said, "Dr. Fluitt, we know that you pray for people. We want you to pray for us to have a baby." She explained that they had been through a fertility clinic but to no avail. They had been married for six years and both really wanted a baby. My husband George and I prayed and anointed them with oil. We rebuked the devil and called this couple to become fruitful and multiply. One month later Mary came over giggling with the good news that she was pregnant. We all rejoiced and when their precious little girl arrived they were ecstatic.

When their firstborn baby was six months old, Larry came by our home and asked, "Dr. Fluitt, are you still praying for us to be fruitful and multiply?" I smiled and said, "I have been thanking the Lord for your family." Larry laughed and said, "You can stop praying now. We just learned that Mary is pregnant again, this time with triplets." She delivered three little boys. Imagine four babies under the age of two.

Mary had a twin sister that was having the same problem and she desperately wanted a child. Mary and Larry brought the husband and wife to our home and asked us to pray for them. We did, and God blessed and sent them a baby ten months later.

JUST BELIEVE

There is a wonderful church located in Indiana, Pennsylvania, named Divine Destiny. The Pastors are Drs. Scot and Tammie. I was preaching at their church and when the time came to pray, the altar was filled with faithful folks desiring a touch from the Lord. There was one particular lady who approached me and asked me to pray for her. She told me that, for seventeen years she had not been able to have children because of complications. She had even taken fertility treatment at her doctor's recommendation. She had carried this burden of barrenness for 17 years knowing that children were a blessing from God yet she was unable to conceive. I prayed for her, prophesied over her, and told her that by this time next year she would have a baby. She just looked at me and smiled.

The following year when I returned to Divine Destiny, the same smiling lady came up to me and said, "I have someone to introduce to you." Cuddled in her father's arms was a beautiful little girl.

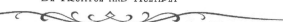
The lady told me that she remembered my teaching during that time. At that meeting the year before I had told her she must line up her words with the Word of God and speak to the things that are not as though they were. She related that, although this was a real step for her to take, every day on her way to work she would talk to the Lord and thank Him for her children. She just kept praising God and thanking Him for what He was going to do. Three months later she discovered she was pregnant. She had taken the first test at home but followed it up by making an appointment with her doctor for a second test because she just did not believe the first one. Both she and the doctor were amazed when the test confirmed her pregnancy. She carried the baby for the entire term without one single complication.

She told me that, although there were many lessons she learned through this process, the one that stood out is that God loves us and, just like us with our own children, would do anything for us if we just believe.

LITTLE BABY, HEAR MY VOICE!

I was a guest speaker in Rock Hill, South Carolina, at this big prophetic meeting at the Shield of Faith Church pastored by Drs. Larry and Kathy. Suddenly the weather changed. A weather bulletin had reported that there was going to be a blizzard and not to get on the roads.

Snow was everywhere. Obviously, the services got cancelled and we were provided with a stay at home day. Pastor Larry was just frustrated. He had made all these wonderful plans for the meetings. How many of you know God will let you make plans, but He has a purpose? So here we were. It was cold and snowy and the Pastor was not a happy camper. He had spent a lot of time and money advertising the meeting. What was the purpose? I had traveled a long way just to take a seat, watch the snow, and enjoy the fireplace with a hot cup of coffee with some great friends?

A group of about 20 young people between the ages of 18 and 24 from the Master's Commission had traveled approximately 100 miles to attend the prophetic meetings. Their representative called Pastor Larry and said, "There's no one at the church!" He said, "Well, there's a weather bulletin that said there was going to be a blizzard and not to get on the roads." The caller said, "Well, we didn't get the memo. Could we just come to the house and meet Dr. Fluitt?" Pastor Larry said, "Sure, come on over."

God will let you believe what you need to believe to get you where He's taking you. He's so extravagant but never wasteful with His love and grace.

So they came and we all had lunch and sat around the table. I said, "Let's talk about the Lord. Is there anything you've ever wondered about? Let's talk about it." This pretty young woman sitting on the end said, "Dr. Clarice, I have something I've just got to tell you. I'm 18 years old, and I was reared Baptist. When I was a little girl two and three years old, I used to take all my dolls, line them up, and I knew that I was called to be a missionary to all nations. I would say, 'You African dolls, and you doll from Egypt,' and I would preach to them, when I was two, three, and four years old. My mother and father would tell me not to get my mind on religion. But I've always known that God called me to do something as far as missions were concerned."

"When I was seventeen I applied to join the Master's Commission of the Assemblies of God church to become a missionary and it's just been wonderful. I'm learning so much. I was with one of the ladies in the church and she was listening to a CD. I asked, "Who is that?" She said, "Oh, that's Dr. Clarice Fluitt from Louisiana." I asked if I could please borrow her CDs. She agreed so I took the CDs home and listened over and over and over again. I didn't have a clue what you were talking about, but there was a certain frequency to your voice that I seemed to recognize and I continued to listen over and over and over again. My father came into my room and said, "Who in the world are you listening to?" I said, "This lady from Louisiana, and she's a prophet. Her name is Dr. Clarice Fluitt." He said, "I know her." I said, "Daddy, you're Baptist. You live in South Carolina. You couldn't know her." And he said, "Oh, I know her. When your mother and I found out that we were expecting a baby, some friends of ours told us there was a meeting going on and a prophet in town. That was 18 years ago. We were Southern Baptist and attended this meeting where this woman was prophesying and singing opera. Your mom and I were standing in the corner thinking, what is this? We had NEVER seen anything like that. That woman smiled at us, came over, and took your mother's hand. She then put her hand on your mother's stomach and said, "Little baby, hear my voice. God has chosen you as a missionary. You will NEVER escape God's voice."" (The prophetic voice of God) She said, "When I heard your voice on a CD, I knew I had to find you because you had imparted a word in me while I was in my mother's womb!" (Luke 1:41)

Never underestimate the power of the prophetic word.

GOODNESS LIVES

The House of Mercy is a mission church located in Newark, New Jersey. Pastors Sam and Tilly Giresi and their daughter Tilly Ann have established a safe haven and church home for many who are severely burdened with poverty, homelessness, sickness, hunger, and a multitude of life challenges on a daily basis. I have an oversight of their work.

The Giresi's and their staff demonstrate the love of God as they graciously respond to their calling to love, reach, teach, and equip the whosoevers. To observe this team in action is a study in how to live a sacrificial yet extremely joyful life. As I write this story, I can hear the deep contagious laughter of the tiny Pastor Tilly. It has been well said that dynamite comes in small packages.

Here is an amazing story that I experienced on one of my visits to minister at their church.

Pastor Tilly had befriended a lovely young Christian woman who had recently moved to America from Nigeria. The woman's name is Toby. Toby had two little boys with her; a two year old named Mercy, and a three week old named Goodness Ore Oluwa Ajibade.

Little Goodness was very sick with a life threatening heart defect. He had recently been released from a three week stay at the neo-natal intensive care unit at the Beth Israel Medical Center in Newark.

Pastor Tilly called Toby and invited her to bring Goodness to church so I could pray for him. She was a stranger in a foreign land where nothing was familiar and had to organize everything that was needed to tend to two babies. It was an incredible act of faith on her part to secure transportation and overcome the fear of exposing fragile little Goodness to a public environment.

I arrived. Toby and her children were already there. I recognized the necessity to pray. Little Goodness was a beautiful baby that was experiencing erratic breathing. I visited with Toby and then anointed Goodness with oil. I laid my hand on his chest and prayed for a new heart. I also secured a red prayer cloth to his clothing and prophesied that he would live and serve the cause of Christ. His breathing became calm and he went to sleep; but, much more drama was to follow.

We gathered after the meeting to share a fellowship luncheon. Goodness woke and Toby began to nurse him. The baby lost his breath and was struggling for his life. It was a very tense moment. Pastor Tilly took the limp baby in her arms and everyone rallied and began to quote the promises of God over the baby. Once again Goodness took a breath, became calm, and settled in his mother's arms.

Toby's story continues. The next day she took Goodness to the doctor. The doctor immediately sent the baby to the emergency room with the diagnosis of the strong possibility of heart failure. Goodness was transferred to the NIC unit where they scheduled him for immediate heart surgery at New York University Langone; but, before he could be transferred from New Jersey to New York, he experienced heart failure. His body turned blue and he stopped breathing. A nurse took him into another room. Goodness' lungs had collapsed and he had died.

No one told Toby that her baby had died. She asked where he was and someone gave her the room number. When Toby went unknowingly into the room and saw her baby completely lifeless and covered with a sheet, she tore off the sheet, grabbed him, and began calling on the Name of Jesus. She remembered the prophetic word that Goodness would live and serve the Lord. She called her son's name and commanded him to come back.

Goodness revived and a gifted Muslim surgeon performed a critical surgery on him. Later, the doctor told Toby that Goodness was deathly sick and so fragile that something miraculous had kept him alive. Toby smiled and said, "Yes, it was Jesus!" The doctor also smiled and said, "I need to know this Jesus."

All of this happened in 2011. I am happy to report that today Goodness is now a happy, healthy, and very active little boy. Thank You, Jesus.

ASK BIG AND RECEIVE BIG

While ministering in Florida, I had the opportunity to visit with a family that had just purchased a brand new 60 foot recreational vehicle (R.V.). It was an amazing piece of art and science that appeared to have merged into something like a traveling Taj Mahal. The interior was akin to any 5 star hotel that I have ever seen. The exterior was an explosion of colorful metal and glass that reeked of money. It was a viable expression of what first class really means.

I was impressed! A tantalizing thought slipped through my mind. Wow, I wonder what it would be like to have something like this to take on the road? I caught myself really thinking about the possibilities of owning my own R.V.

I had been traveling on the road since 1971, and flying had become quite challenging. I continued to think, and then I said, out loud, "The Lord is going to give me my own R.V. It will be a new first class trouble free vehicle that will give glory to God and comfort for me!"

That evening during the service I said out loud to the congregation, "Next month will be my birthday and I am going to get a beautiful debt free R.V." The congregation applauded and agreed with what I said.

When I arrived home, I told George, "God is going to give me a beautiful new R.V. for my ministry!" George smiled and said, "Ok."

About a week later, I received a phone call from a lady who lived in Virginia. Now, this lady was not in the meeting where I made my declaration concerning the R.V, but she had been blessed by some of my teaching CDs and called to express her gratitude. We chatted and, out of the blue she said, "I really know that the Lord has put it on my heart to buy you an R.V. for your ministry." I immediately began to question her as if she had asked me to rob a bank.

Although I had this inspired thought that led to me speaking the word, and both the thought and the word had been launched into the atmosphere, now, when the action to produce the manifestation that I desired appeared, I met it with doubt and unbelief. This not only caused me to react in fear, but also to examine her generosity by fear rather than by faith.

This is an amazing process that we do to ourselves. We will have an inspired thought (which can be seen as a seed), then we speak a word (which is like planting the seed); then when the time comes to harvest our dream crop and put our faith into action to believe so we can receive our crop, unbelief, doubt, and unworthiness close us down.

Well, this precious lady answered my interrogation. I asked what kind of R.V.? I must have a new one. You can't travel with me (she didn't want to travel with me). Can you afford such a gift? Are you going to pay the taxes? On and on and on I went, and then I said, "Let me pray about this and call you later." It became obvious to me that I had the faith to ask big, but not the grace to receive big.

The next day another call came from a church in Virginia. The pastor lovingly said, "Dr. Clarice, our church wants to buy you a new R.V. so you can travel in comfort and style."

My first thought was, I must have over prayed. It was beginning to look like I might end up with a fleet of R.Vs.

The church group went to a nearby town where executive RVs were designed and made for celebrities. They were drawn to a very beautiful and sleek R.V. The interior was top class and all luxury. The business manager approached them and asked if they were interested in purchasing an R.V. The leader said yes. "Oh," said the manager, "Is this coach for you?" "No," said the leader. "We are buying this for a lady prophet that lives in Louisiana. Before we decide, we will pray over the R.V. and anoint it with oil." The manager was a bit shocked but agreeable. They prayed and said they would be back.

The following day, the first lady who had called me happened to be driving through the same town and passed the R.V. business. She stopped, went into the parking lot, and immediately went to the same R.V. that the church group had prayed over. She said, "This is it. I'll buy this one." The manager smiled and said, "You must be with the church group that was here yesterday." The lady said, "No. I'm not with anyone but myself." The manager responded with, "Are you purchasing the coach for yourself?" "No.

I'm buying it for a lady prophet that lives in Louisiana." He was very confused. "The church group said they were buying it for a lady prophet from Louisiana, but they wanted to anoint it with oil and bless the R.V. before buying it."

Well, to make a long story short, the generous lady bought the same R.V. before the church group did, paid all the taxes, filled it with gas, sent me the pink owner's slip, and a nice card that said, "Enjoy, and rest assured I can easily afford to bless you with the R.V."

What a blessing she was to my life. I named the R.V. "Evidence" because it was the evidence of what I asked God for. The beautiful R.V. served me well and I had the opportunity to use it as a traveling office and prayer room. I have lost count of how many people were saved and baptized in the Holy Spirit in this anointed chariot.

There is an additional story as to how this gift became the gift that kept on giving.

My precious mother suffered a double stroke. Mom was a great Christian overcomer. Her physical condition began to wane and it became necessary to provide her with full time nurses and caretakers. I am an only child and I was honored to care for her needs during her sickness.

It does not take long to empty your reserve when you are confronted with a lengthy illness.

I was in our home church on a Saturday morning preparing for the Sunday service. A gentleman walked in and asked who owned that R.V. with the name "Evidence" written on the front. I answered, "I own the R.V." He said, "I would like to buy it today and I'll pay cash for it now." Well, the price was right! I sold my evidence, paid my bills, and was able to spend quality time with the Mom without financial concerns.

I had a thought: I want an R.V.

I spoke a word: I want an R.V.

I acted on my want: I got my R.V. I got my "Evidence."

Don't give up your dream!

Spontaneous Unrehearsed Prophetic Poem

by Dr. Clarice Fluitt

I Am a Candidate for Miracles

Miracles, miracles, miracles we cry

Miracles, miracles we prophesy.

Miracles in our mind

Miracles so divine.

Supernatural power of the Holy Ghost

Come on God, You're the One in whom we boast.

Miracles today.

Miracles, miracles, miracles today.

Miracles, miracles, let us see Your great display.

Your holy Word is spoken ... Tells us every curse is broken

We have not because we ask not now

O my God, I am understanding how.

Miracles ... Flow where we walk

When we learn how to talk.

Stretch Your mighty, mighty hand

Release, Lord, Your awesome plan.

Miracles … let's see them now

O my God, Only You know how

Miracles…

Miracles in our family … let the oppressed go free

Change their hearts and mind, O God … and give them liberty.

Miracles in our families … Miracles in our land

Miracles in our government … Reveal Your awesome plan.

Miracles…

Miracles … we implore

Miracles that You've got in store.

You say we have not because we don't ask

O my God, that season has past.

I ask for Miracles…

Miracles in the government … miracles in this earth

Miracles for those that are alone

Miracles for those without a home.

Miracles for those who are oppressed

Miracles for healing in our flesh

Miracles…

Miracles we do implore

O my God, You know the score.

You say "Now we will be released"

When we speak as kings and priest

Miracles...

Going to cry for the miracles God has said

Going to cry for the miracles to raise the dead.

Going to speak to the miracles to be released

Are you believing you're the kings and priest?

Miracles...

Miracles of healing, deliverance too

Make me believe God's Word is true.

You've got to choose to decide today

Open up your mouth let me hear you say

Miracles...

Who wants to see the lame man leap?

Who wants to hear the mute man speak?

Who wants to know that the deaf can hear?

Anybody wants to say "I know it's near."

Miracles...

Miracles in relationships
Miracles helping us to be equipped.
Miracles in the things we say
Miracles, miracles night and day.
Miracles…

Somebody prophesy to the dry earth
Somebody prophesy amazing new birth
Where there's a drought and things are dry
Come on, saints, let's prophesy
Miracles…

Miracles of healing in your flesh
Miracles you've prayed for and make request.
Miracles for your home and life
Miracles that put an end to strife.
Miracles that open blind eyes
Miracles that don't think of lies
Miracles that let God arise
Miracles…

Who's waiting on who?

Who's waiting upon who?

You say "Lord, I've been waiting…

waiting upon the Lord."

And the Lord says

"Did I not send a prophet into your house?

to speak of My mercy and amazing grace?

Did I not send My Son to say

"I am the author, the Finisher

I am the starter without delay

What have you started…that I could breathe upon?

You speak and I'll breathe."

Miracles…

"Can these bones live again" asked the Lord long ago.

And the prophet said,

"Lord, why would You ask me. How could I know?

You are God in charge of all things"

Now that religious answer will never do a thing.

Miracles happen … when you do not doubt.

Miracles happen … when you choose to shout.

Miracles…

These bones can live again.

Don't be moved by death or doom

Miracles are happening in your house

You're releasing them with your mouth

You'll never leave where you are now

Until you understand and know how

You decide where you'd rather be

Are you a captive or are you free?

You've got to choose, you've got to say

"O my Lord, no more delay.

I am a candidate for miracles."

Miracles...

I'm not moved by things that I see

Your rewards in life are determined by the things that

you do to set others free

Miracles...

Got to understand in the depth of your mind

You're not natural, you're holy and divine.

When you're looking at your finances

You've got to know that I really do live

You say "Lord, it doesn't really add up"

I am the portion but you are the cup.

Pour Me out…

Pour Me out with your mouth

Summon those winds from the north and south.

Speak My words of liberty

Come My Beloved and decree

All men fail, the great ones rise up

When you go down let Me hear the sound

Miracles…

There are those who have really been bound

And they've heard that wonderful sound

"Come to Jesus, come to Jesus, Come today"

"Come to Jesus, Come to Jesus, no more delay."

"Come to Jesus, Come to Jesus, that's the call"

"Come to Jesus, Come to Jesus, one and all."

Miracles…

There's a miracle awaiting for you to see

Miracles that set other men free

No more talking about you and me

Come on now have you seen the King?

Miracles…

Set the stage in your house

Open up your heart, open up your mouth

Say Miracles today…

Miracles of healing and deliverance, it's true

Miracles flowing out of me and you

Lend a hand for others to see

Bring them over the wall … liberty.

Miracles…

Going to sell that property this very day

Do everything that the Lord does say

You begin and the Lord will bless

Open up your heart and simply confess

Miracles…

Miracles of attitude that you win

Miracles that say "I'm forgiven of sin."

Miracles that say "I always win."

Miracles of changing your mind today

We'll be justified by what we say

Miracles...

You've been waiting for God to fall down

To wear a wonderful, marvelous crown

To lift you up in the day and stand

But let me say "You don't understand the plan."

Miracles they must be released

From the mouth of the kings and priests

Stir yourself up like the spoon from the Lord

Get your conversation in accord

Miracles...

Miracles in this day

Listen to the word and understand what I say

Never complain about what you allow

Understand you've got to be God's plow

Praise, praise, praise and raise

Miracles...

Don't you complain about what you allow

Understand God says "we're equipped ...

For miracles..."

Miracles are here today

Miracles are in what you say

Open up your eyes that you really can see

The miracle of Christ in you and me

Miracles...

Declarations on the Power and Purpose in the Realm of the Miraculous

Thanks be to God who always, every time causes me to triumph. Before there is release, pull back the bow before you let your arrows flow. You'll never possess what you're not willing to pursue. There needs to be a whole lot of tension in you. Tension and release the story of life.

Now learn and be aware that you house destiny. When fatigue walks in, faith walks out. Do not allow yourself to grow weary in doing good, for when fatigue walks in, faith walks out and unbelief nests in your upper most branches. Anybody who wants to say, "O my Father God, there is no more delay. Whatever You say I simply say yes. I'm going to press in and conquer this flesh with Your miracles...."

Lay your hands on yourself right now and say: "Father, in Jesus' Name, I decree, I proclaim. I am who You say that I am. I command fatigue, weariness, frustration, laziness, impropriety,

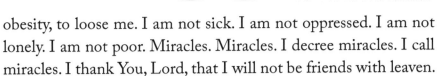

obesity, to loose me. I am not sick. I am not oppressed. I am not lonely. I am not poor. Miracles. Miracles. I decree miracles. I call miracles. I thank You, Lord, that I will not be friends with leaven. I will not just exist from day to day. I will open my heart and believe what You say.

Everything God has not told me to do I command it to set me free. I refuse to empower the religious traditions of the mind of man. I have focus, vision, perception, and discernment. I walk as a savior upon this earth. I carry the antidote to every negative situation. The things that I have failed in, I call it fertilizer. I put it under my feet. I refuse to look back thinking about defeat.

This is the day that the Lord has made. This is the day I plow under everything that God did not originate. Every seed that God did not plant, I'm taking it out. I'm plucking it out. I'm commanding depression to leave me. I refuse to spend my money, energy, or time on anything that God has not originated.

I will not seek the living among the dead. I hear God. I fear God. I am a candidate for the realm of the miraculous. Hear me, O God, as I prophesy "These bones shall live again."

I am a head and not a tail. I am above and not beneath. I am healed. I am delivered. I am prosperous. I am who God says that I am.

It's time to fly like an eagle.

Choose to Agree with God

God is calling us and wooing us and He says, "I have created you to walk in the realm of the miraculous. I have created you not to be a thermometer, but a thermostat. I've created you to change things; to have a life-giving spirit, and to speak words that have the power to perform themselves."

When you see the sick, the lonely, the oppressed, the hurting, you are the antidote to their situation. You are not just a natural human being. You may look like a natural human being *but as a man thinketh in his heart so is he.* God's Word has the power to perform itself. The Scripture says in Isaiah 55:11 that the Word will not return void or empty, but it will accomplish what God sent it forth to do.

God has destiny, your DNA, your divine nature attitude. You are to accomplish something in this life that is supernatural. The natural things that you do are just the shuck on the corn. It's not the corn. And God says "the thing that will remain forever is His Word." Sow the Word!

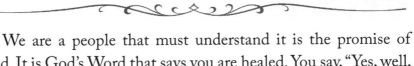

We are a people that must understand it is the promise of God. It is God's Word that says you are healed. You say, "Yes, well, we've prayed for the sick and we haven't seen everybody healed." It yet remains to be seen. You see, temporal things are passing away. Choose to agree with God.

Things that you see are passing away. Things that you do not see are eternal and here to stay. We must have spiritual eyes to see from God's perspective. The Word of God has the power not to just inform us and speak to our soul, but to transform us from the inside out. This transformation will cause something divine to germinate inside of you. The divine Word of God goes in your spirit, changes your mind, and changes your opinion about things.

Today I am speaking the Word of God to you. I am giving you a gos-pill and I am telling you it is imperative for you to believe that you are healed. Whatever growth is growing in your body, whatever bad report is going on, whatever you lack or have too much of, whatever is going on in your body, it is a day of the manifestation of miracles to come forth in your life. It is a day that you must choose to believe that heaven and earth will pass away, but the Word of God has the power to perform itself and remain forever.

Lay hands on your body right now. If you have something growing in your body that you know about or you don't know about, you need to speak to it today because the Word of God says that God has given abundant life. He says, *"I have come to give life and that you may have it more abundantly."*

Through the Word of God that flows out of your mouth you can say, "No deadly thing can stay in my body. I command it out in the Name of Jesus. I refuse to be oppressed. I refuse to be poor. I refuse to be bound. I refuse to be a victim. I am a victor through God. Heavenly Father, I attend to Your Word and I incline mine ears to all Your sayings. I will not let them depart from my eyes and I keep them in the midst of my heart for they are life and healing to all of my flesh. They are life and healing to all of my flesh."

In Revelation 12:11, the Scripture says, "And they overcame him by the Blood of the Lamb and the word of their testimony."

Speak against the spirit that tries to take your eyesight and your hearing, in the authority of the Name of Jesus. I command a refreshing to your eyes and your ears.

Declare, "God is with me. God is for me. God has paid the price. In the authority of the Name of Jesus let my proclamation be that no evil shall befall me, nor shall any plague come near my dwelling for God has given His angels charge over me. They keep me in all my ways; in my pathway of life, in healing, and in health. I refuse to be sick. I make a decision to talk to my body and say, "Body, you will respond to healing and wholeness." I will do my part. I will do what I can. I will eat right, sleep right, and live right. I will take care of my body the best that I can, and I will trust God."" Angelic beings are waiting to respond to the Word of God.

Take these gos-pills and begin to say, "Lord, I present my body for it is the temple of the Living God. You dwell in my life and permeate my spirit, soul and body. I am filled with the fullness of God."

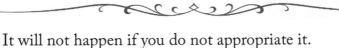

It will not happen if you do not appropriate it.

How many of us bought a bunch of vitamins but never took them? We spent the money and thought it was a good idea at the time. If we do not take them, they will not help us. It does not matter what God has said if we do not apply it to our life. If we desire the benefit then there is a procedure.

Jesus bore the curse for me; therefore, I forbid growths, tumors and cysts to inhabit my body. The life of God within me dissolves growths and tumors and my life and my strength are totally restored.

When you begin to call the things that are not to become the things that are, and when you command ...

Come here, healing, and hear Jesus' holy Name.

I summon the realm of the miraculous

Come, come, come unto me

For the Word of God says "I'm already free."

Who would choose to believe? Who would say "Lord, by faith I receive." My heartbeat is normal. My heart beats with the rhythm of life.

The Kingdom of God is a Kingdom of words. Are you going to believe every cell that does not promote life and health in your body? Cut it off from its life source. Command deterioration out of your bones, out of your teeth. Command sickness, disease, and viruses to go in Jesus' Name.

Say, "I am redeemed from the curse of the law. The Spirit of life of God's Word flows in me. It cleanses me. I am washed by the water of the Word of God."

In Jesus' Name I forbid my body to be deceived anymore. "Body, you will not be deceived by viruses or disease, germs or negative reports. Neither will you work against life or health in any way. Every cell in my body supports life and health. This same Spirit that raised Jesus from the dead has quickened my mortal body. He dwells in me, permeating His life through my veins, sending healing throughout my body."

The Scripture says, "The law of the Spirit of life in Christ Jesus has already made me free from the law of sin and death." Therefore, I will not allow sin, sickness, or death to come in here. It is against the law to die.

Father, I resist the enemy in every form that he comes against me. I command my body to be strong, healthy, wealthy, and wise. I enforce it, infuse it, and impart it with Your Word. I reject the curse. I am blessed. I enforce the law of life in this body in the authority of Jesus Christ the Son of the Living God.

You are a candidate for a miracle today. Every report that God has not made over you, I call it null and void and I set a new report over you; your mind, emotion, and every cell in your body.

Father, we thank You that we are candidates for the realm of the miraculous. You are the Healer, You're the Deliverer, You're the Mighty God. You have given us Your Word. You have encouraged, exhorted, edified, and built us up.

We thank You, Lord, that You always do exceedingly abundantly above that which we could ask or desire.

About Dr. Clarice Fluitt

Dr. Clarice Fluitt is an internationally recognized Christian leader, accomplished businesswoman and entrepreneur with a history in real estate development. She is also a much sought-after Life Strategist, Personal Advisor, Author, and Motivational Speaker.

Dr. Fluitt is a time proven prophetess with laser like accuracy. Reports of amazing miracles and healings with positive life changing evidence continually follow her ministry. Dr. Clarice's life is a remarkable chronicle of hilarious real-life stories, tragic trials, tests, and moving visitations of the Lord. Unpretentious and friendly, she is a highly esteemed minister and conference speaker.

Her high impact speaking engagements at Lead and Succeed Business Seminars have joined forces with other speakers that include Bill Cosby, Larry King, Rudy Giuliani, Steve Forbes, Suze Orman, Michael J. Fox, Les Brown, Rick Belluzzo, Daymond John, Shaquille O'Neal, Joe Montana and other legendary speakers. These innovative and supercharged events provide individuals with proven methods, formulas, strategies and keys that skyrocket individuals to higher levels of success.

MORE RESOURCES BY DR. CLARICE FLUITT

The Law of Honor (Book)

CD SETS

- Seeing the Invisible Clearly
- Healing Everywhere
- Don't Give Up Your Dominion
- The Believer's Job Description
- The Mentality of an Overcomer
- Moving On
- Invading the Marketplace
- They Didn't Meet on Facebook
- The Sovereignty of God
- Awaken to God's Love

MINISTRY CONTACT INFORMATION

Clarice Fluitt Ministries

P O Box 7888

Monroe, LA 71211

Phone: 318.410.9788

E-mail: claricefluitt@claricefluitt.com

Websites:

www.claricefluitt.org

www.claricefluitt.com

Made in the USA
Middletown, DE
10 July 2016

Bright Lights,
Big City

JAY McINERNEY

BRIGHT LIGHTS, BIG CITY

BLOOMSBURY

LONDON · BERLIN · NEW YORK

FOR MY MOTHER AND FATHER, AND FOR MERRY

First published in Great Britain by Penguin Books
First published in the USA by Vintage, a division of Random House, Inc.
1984
This Bloomsbury paperback edition published 2007

Portions of this work were previously published in *Paris Review* and
Ploughshares

Grateful acknowledgement is made to Index Music Inc. for permission
to reprint an excerpt from the lyrics to 'Cross-Eyed and Painless' by
David Byrne and Brian Eno.
Copyright © Bleu Disque Music Co. Inc. and E. G. Music Ltd
by permission of David Byrne and Brian Eno, 1980

Bloomsbury Publishing Plc, 36 Soho Square, London W1D 3QY

A CIP catalogue record for this book is available from the British Library

ISBN 978 0 7475 8920 4

10 9 8 7 6 5

Typeset by RefineCatch Limited, Bungay, Suffolk
Printed in Great Britain by Clays Ltd, St Ives plc

www.bloomsbury.com/jaymcinerney

'How did you go bankrupt?' Bill asked.
'Two ways,' Mike said. 'Gradually and then suddenly.'

—THE SUN ALSO RISES

CONTENTS

BRIGHT LIGHTS, BIG CITY

IT'S SIX A.M.
DO YOU KNOW
WHERE YOU ARE?

You are not the kind of guy who would be at a place like this at this time of the morning. But here you are, and you cannot say that the terrain is entirely unfamiliar, although the details are fuzzy. You are at a nightclub talking to a girl with a shaved head. The club is either Heartbreak or the Lizard Lounge. All might come clear if you could just slip into the bathroom and do a little more Bolivian Marching Powder. Then again, it might not. A small voice inside you insists that this epidemic lack of clarity is a result of too much of that already. The night has already turned on that imperceptible pivot where two A.M. changes to six A.M. You know this moment has come and gone, but you are not yet willing to concede that you have crossed the line beyond which all is gratuitous damage and the palsy of unraveled nerve endings. Somewhere back there you could have cut your losses, but you rode past that moment on a comet trail of white powder and now you are trying to hang on to the rush. Your brain at this moment is

I

composed of brigades of tiny Bolivian soldiers. They are tired and muddy from their long march through the night. There are holes in their boots and they are hungry. They need to be fed. They need the Bolivian Marching Powder.

A vaguely tribal flavor to this scene—pendulous jewelry, face paint, ceremonial headgear and hair styles. You feel that there is also a certain Latin theme—something more than the piranhas cruising your bloodstream and the fading buzz of marimbas in your brain.

You are leaning back against a post that may or may not be structural with regard to the building, but which feels essential to your own maintenance of an upright position. The bald girl is saying this used to be a good place to come before the assholes discovered it. You don't want to be talking to this bald girl, or even listening to her, which is all you are doing, but just now you do not want to test the powers of speech or locomotion.

How did you get here? It was your friend, Tad Allagash, who powered you in here, and he has disappeared. Tad is the kind of guy who would be at a place like this at this time of the morning. He is either your best self or your worst self, you're not sure which. Earlier in the evening it seemed clear that he was your best self. You started on the Upper East Side with champagne and unlimited prospects, strictly observing the Allagash rule of perpetual motion: one drink per stop. Tad's mission in life is to have more fun than anyone else in New York City, and this involves a lot of moving around, since there is always the likelihood that where you aren't is more fun than where you are. You are awed by his strict refusal to acknowledge any goal higher than the pursuit of pleasure. You want to be like that. You also think he is shallow and dangerous. His friends are all rich and spoiled, like the cousin from Memphis you met earlier in the evening who would not accompany you below Fourteenth Street because, he said, he didn't have a lowlife visa. This cousin had a girlfriend with cheekbones to break your heart, and you knew she was the real thing when she steadfastly refused to acknowledge your presence. She possessed secrets— about islands, about horses, about French pronunciation—that you would never know.

You have traveled in the course of the night from the meticulous to the slime. The girl with the shaved head has a scar tattooed on her scalp. It looks like a long, sutured gash. You tell her it is very realistic. She takes this as a compliment and thanks you. You meant as opposed to romantic.

'I could use one of those right over my heart,' you say.

'You want I can give you the name of the guy that did it. You'd be surprised how cheap.'

You don't tell her that nothing would surprise you now. Her voice, for instance, which is like the New Jersey State Anthem played through an electric shaver.

The bald girl is emblematic of the problem. The problem is, for some reason you think you are going to meet the kind of girl who is not the kind of girl who would be at a place like this at this time of the morning. When you meet her you are going to tell her that what you really want is a house in the country with a garden. New York, the club scene, bald women—you're tired of all that. Your presence here is only a matter of conducting an experiment in limits, reminding yourself of what you aren't. You see yourself as the kind of guy who wakes up early on Sunday morning and steps out to cop the *Times*

3

and croissants. Who might take a cue from the Arts and Leisure section and decide to check out an exhibition—costumes of the Hapsburg Court at the Met, say, or Japanese lacquerware of the Muromachi period at the Asia Society. The kind of guy who calls up the woman he met at a publishing party Friday night, the party he did not get sloppy drunk at. See if she wants to check out the exhibition and maybe do an early dinner. A guy who would wait until eleven A.M. to call her, because she might not be an early riser, like he is. She may have been out late, perhaps at a nightclub. And maybe a couple of sets of tennis before the museum. He wonders if she plays, but of course she would.

When you meet the girl who wouldn't et cetera you will tell her that you are slumming, visiting your own six A.M. Lower East Side of the soul on a lark, stepping nimbly between the piles of garbage to the gay marimba rhythms in your head. Well, no, not *gay*. But she will know exactly what you mean.

On the other hand, almost any girl, specifically one with a full head of hair, would help you stave off this creeping sense of mortality. You remember the Bolivian Marching Powder and realize you're not down yet. No way, José. First you have to get rid of this bald girl.

In the bathroom there are no doors on the stalls, which makes it tough to be discreet. But clearly you are not the only person in here to take on fuel. Lots of sniffling going on in the stalls. The windows are blacked over, and for this you are profoundly grateful.

Hup, two, three, four. The soldiers are back on their feet. They are off and running in formation. Some of them are dancing, and you must follow their example.

Just outside the door you spot her: tall, dark and alone, half hidden behind a pillar at the edge of the dance floor. You approach laterally, moving your stuff like a Bad Spade through the slalom of a synthesized conga rhythm. She jumps when you touch her shoulder.

'Dance?'

She looks at you as if you had just suggested instrumental rape. 'I do not speak English,' she says, when you ask again.

'*Français?*'

She shakes her head. Why is she looking at you that way, as if tarantulas were nesting in your eye sockets?

'You are by any chance from Bolivia? Or Peru?'

She is looking around for help now. Remembering a recent encounter with a young heiress's bodyguard at Danceteria—or was it the Red Parrot?—you back off, hands raised over your head.

The Bolivian Soldiers are still on their feet, but they have stopped singing their marching song. You realize that you are at a crucial juncture vis-à-vis morale. What you need is a good pep talk from Tad Allagash, but he is not to be found. You try to imagine what he would say. *Back on the horse. Now we're really going to have some fun.* Something like that. You suddenly realize that he has already slipped out with some rich Hose Queen. He is back at her place on Fifth Ave., and they are doing some of her off-the-boat-quality drugs. They are scooping it out of tall Ming vases and snorting it off of each other's naked bodies. You hate Tad Allagash.

Go home. Cut your losses.

Stay. Go for it.

You are a republic of voices tonight. Unfortunately, that republic is Italy. All these voices waving their arms

5

and screaming at one another. There's an *ex cathedra* riff coming down from the Vatican: *Repent. Your body is the temple of the Lord and you have defiled it.* It is, after all, Sunday morning, and as long as you have any brain cells left there will be a resonant patriarchal basso echoing down the marble vaults of your churchgoing childhood to remind you that this is the Lord's Day. What you need is another overpriced drink to drown it out. But a search of pockets yields only a dollar bill and change. You paid twenty to get in here. Panic gains.

You spot a girl at the edge of the dance floor who looks like your last chance for earthly salvation. You know for a fact that if you go out into the morning alone, without even your sunglasses—which you have neglected to bring, because who, after all, plans on these travesties?—the harsh, angling light will turn you to flesh and bone. Mortality will pierce you through the retina. But there she is in her pegged pants, a kind of doo-wop Retro ponytail pulled off to the side, as eligible a candidate as you are likely to find this late in the game. The sexual equivalent of fast food.

She shrugs and nods when you ask her to dance. You like the way she moves, the oiled ellipses of her hips and shoulders. After the second song, she says she's tired. She's at the point of bolting when you ask her if she needs a little pick-me-up.

'You've got some blow?' she says.

'Is Stevie Wonder blind?' you say.

She takes your arm and leads you into the Ladies'. A couple of spoons and she seems to like you just fine, and you are feeling very likable yourself. A couple more. This woman is all nose.

'I love drugs,' she says, as you march toward the bar.

6

'It's something we have in common,' you say.

'Have you ever noticed how all the good words start with D? D and L.'

You try to think about this. You're not quite sure what she's driving at. The Bolivians are singing their marching song, but you can't make out the words.

'You know. Drugs. Delight. Decadence.'

'Debauchery,' you say, catching the tune now.

'Dexedrine.'

'Delectable. Deranged. Debilitated.'

'Delinquent.'

'Delirium.'

'And L,' she says. 'Lush and luscious.'

'Languorous.'

'Librium.'

'Libidinous.'

'What's that?' she says.

'Horny.'

'Oh,' she says, casting a long, arching look over your shoulder. Her eyes glaze in a way that reminds you precisely of the closing of a sandblasted glass shower door. You can see that the game is over, although you're not sure which rule you broke. Possibly she finds H words offensive. A purist. She is scanning the dance floor for a man with a compatible vocabulary. You have more: *detumescence*, for instance. *Drowning* and *depressed*; *lost* and *lonesome*. It's not that you're really going to miss this girl who thinks that *decadence* and *Dexedrine* are the high points of the language of Kings James and Lear. But the touch of flesh, the sound of another human voice . . . You know there is a special purgatory waiting for you out there in the dawn's surly light, a desperate half sleep which is like a grease fire in the brainpan.

7

The girl waves as she disappears into the crowd. There is no sign of the other girl, the girl who would not be here. There is no sign of Tad Allagash. The Bolivians are mutinous. You can't stop their treacherous voices.

It is worse even than you expected, stepping out into the morning. The glare is like a mother's reproach. The sidewalk sparkles cruelly. Visibility unlimited. The downtown warehouses look serene and restful in this beveled light. An uptown cab passes and you start to wave, then realize you have no money. The cab stops.

You jog over and lean in the window. 'I guess I'll walk after all.'

'Asshole.' He leaves rubber.

You start north, holding a hand over your eyes. Trucks rumble up Hudson Street, bearing provisions into the sleeping city. You turn east. On Seventh Avenue an old woman with a hive of rollers on her head walks a German shepherd. The dog is rooting in the cracks of the sidewalk, but as you approach he stiffens into a pose of terrible alertness. The woman looks at you as if you were something that had just crawled out of the ocean trailing ooze and slime. An eager, tentative growl ripples the shepherd's throat. 'Good Pooky,' she says. The dog makes a move but she chokes it back. You give them a wide berth.

On Bleecker Street you catch the scent of the Italian bakery. You stand at the corner of Bleecker and Cornelia and gaze at the windows on the fourth floor of a tenement. Behind those windows is the apartment you shared with Amanda when you first came to New York. It was small and dark, but you liked the imperfectly patched pressed-tin ceiling, the claw-footed bath in the

8

kitchen, the windows that didn't quite fit the frames. You were just starting out. You had the rent covered, you had your favorite restaurant on MacDougal where the waitresses knew your names and you could bring your own bottle of wine. Every morning you woke to the smell of bread from the bakery downstairs. You would go out to buy the paper and maybe pick up a couple of croissants while Amanda made the coffee. This was two years ago, before you got married.

Down on the West Side Highway, a lone hooker totters on heels and tugs at her skirt as if no one had told her that the commuters won't be coming through the tunnels from Jersey today. Coming closer, you see that she is a man in drag.

You cross under the rusting stanchions of the old elevated highway and walk out to the pier. The easterly light skims across the broad expanse of the Hudson. You step carefully as you approach the end of the rotting pier. You are none too steady and there are holes through which you can see the black, fetid water underneath.

You sit down on a piling and look out over the river. Downriver, the Statue of Liberty shimmers in the haze. Across the water, a huge Colgate sign welcomes you to New Jersey, the Garden State.

You watch the solemn progress of a garbage barge, wreathed in a cloud of screaming gulls, heading out to sea.

Here you are again. All messed up and no place to go.

THE DEPARTMENT OF
FACTUAL VERIFICATION

Monday arrives on schedule. You sleep through the
first ten hours. God only knows what happened to
Sunday.

At the subway station you wait fifteen minutes on the
platform for a train. Finally a local, enervated by graffiti,
shuffles into the station. You get a seat and hoist a copy
of the New York *Post*. The *Post* is the most shameful of
your several addictions. You hate to support this kind
of trash with your thirty cents, but you are a secret fan
of Killer Bees, Hero Cops, Sex Fiends, Lottery Winners,
Teenage Terrorists, Liz Taylor, Tough Tots, Sicko Creeps,
Living Nightmares, Life on Other Planets, Spontaneous
Human Combustion, Miracle Diets and Coma Babies.
The Coma Baby is on page two: COMA BABY SIS PLEADS:
SAVE MY LITTLE BROTHER. There is a picture of a four- or
five-year-old girl with a dazed expression. She is the
living daughter of a pregnant woman who, after an
automobile accident, has been lying in a coma for a
week. The question that has confronted *Post* readers

for days is whether or not the Coma Baby will ever see the light of the delivery room.

The train shudders and pitches toward Fourteenth Street, stopping twice for breathers in the tunnel. You are reading about Liz Taylor's new boyfriend when a sooty hand taps your shoulder. You do not have to look up to know you are facing a casualty, one of the city's MIAs. You are more than willing to lay some silver on the physically handicapped, but folks with the long-distance eyes give you the heebie-jeebies.

The second time he taps your shoulder you look up. His clothes and hair are fairly neat, as if he had only recently let go of social convention, but his eyes are out-to-lunch and his mouth is working furiously.

'My birthday,' he says, 'is January thirteenth. I will be twenty-nine years old.' Somehow he makes this sound like a threat to kill you with a blunt object.

'Great,' you say, going back to the paper.

When you next look up the man is halfway down the car, staring intently at an ad for a business training institute. As you watch, he sits down in the lap of an old lady. She tries to get out from under him but he has her pinned.

'Excuse me, sir, but you're sitting on me,' she says. 'Sir, sir. Excuse me.' Almost everyone in the car is watching and pretending they're not. The man folds his arms across his chest and leans farther back.

'Sir, please get off of me.'

You can't even believe it. Half a dozen healthy men are within spitting distance. You would have jumped up yourself but you assumed someone closer to the action would act. The woman is quietly sobbing. As each moment passes it becomes harder and harder to do anything without calling attention to the fact that you hadn't done anything earlier. You keep hoping the man will stand up and leave her alone. You imagine the headline in the *Post:* GRANNY CRUSHED BY NUT WHILE WIMPS WATCH.

'Please, sir.'

You stand up. At the same time, the man stands up. He brushes his coat with his hands and then walks down to the far end of the car. You feel silly standing there. The old lady is dabbing at her eyes with a Kleenex. You would like to see if she's all right, but at this point it wouldn't do much good. You sit down.

It's ten-fifty when you get to Times Square. You come up on Seventh Avenue blinking. The sunlight is excessive. You grope for your shades. Down Forty-second Street, through the meat district. Every day the same spiel from the same old man: 'Girls, girls, girls—check 'em out, check 'em out. Take a free look, gentlemen. Check it out, check it out.' The words and rhythm never vary. Kinky Karla, Naughty Lola, Sexsational Live Revue—girls, girls, girls.

Waiting for a light at Forty-second, you scope among the announcements of ancient upcoming events, strangling the lamppost like kudzu, a fresh poster with the headline MISSING PERSON. The photograph shows a smiling, toothy girl, circa Junior Prom. You read: *Mary O'Brien McCann; NYU student; blue eyes, brown hair, last seen vicinity Washington Square Park, wearing blue jumper, white blouse.* Your heart sinks. You think of those left behind, the dazed loved ones who have handlettered this sign and taped it here, who will probably never know what happened. The light has changed.

You stop at the corner for a doughnut and coffee to go. It's 10:58. You've worn out the line about the subway breaking down. Maybe tell Clara you stopped to take a free look at Kinky Karla and got bitten by her snake.

Into the lobby, your chest constricting in anticipation, your throat getting dry. You used to feel this way walking into school Monday mornings. The dread of not having finished your homework—and where were you going to sit at lunch? It didn't help being the new kid every year. The stale disinfectant smell of the corridors and the hard faces of teachers. Your boss, Clara Tillinghast, somewhat resembles a fourth-grade tyrant, one of those ageless disciplinarians who believes that little boys are evil and little girls frivolous, that an idle mind is the devil's playground and that learning is the pounding of facts, like so many nails, into the knotty oak of recalcitrant heads. Ms. Clara Tillinghast, aka Clingfast, aka the Clinger, runs the Department of Factual Verification like a spelling class, and lately you have not accumulated many gold stars. You are hanging on by the skin of your chipped teeth. If the Clinger had her way you would have been expelled long ago, but the magazine has a tradition of never acknowledging its mistakes. The folk history of the place has it that no one has ever been fired: not the narcoleptic theater critic who confused two different off-Broadway premieres and ran a review that combined elements of a southern family saga and a farce about Vietnam; not the award-winning plagiarist who cribbed a five-thousand-word piece direct from a twenty-year-old issue of *Punch* and signed her name to it. It's a lot like the Ivy League, from which its staff is mostly drawn, or like a cold, impenetrable New England family which keeps even the black sheep suffocating within the fold. You, however, are a minor cousin at best; if there were a branch of the family business in a distant, malarial colony, you would have been shipped off long ago, *sans* quinine. Your transgressions are numerous. You can't call them specifically to mind, but Clingfast has the list in one of her file cabinets. She takes it out from time to time and reads you excerpts. Clara has a mind like a steel mousetrap and a heart like a twelve-minute egg.

Lucio, the elevator operator, says good morning. He was born in Sicily and has been doing this for seventeen years. With a week's training he could probably take over your job and then you could ride the elevator up and down all day long. You're at the twenty-ninth floor in no time. Say so long to Lucio, hello to Sally, the receptionist, perhaps the only staffer with a low-rent accent. She's from one of the outer boroughs, comes in via bridge or tunnel. Generally people here speak as if they were weaned on Twinings English Breakfast Tea. Tillinghast picked up her broad vowels and karate-chop consonants at Vassar. She's very sensitive about coming from Nevada. The writers, of course, are another story—foreigners and other unclubbables among them—but they come and go from their thirtieth-floor cubbyholes at strange hours. They pass manuscripts under the doors at night, and duck into empty offices if they spot you coming at them down the hallway. One mystery man up there—the Ghost—has been working on an article for seven years.

The editorial offices cover two floors. Sales and advertising are several floors below, the division emphasizing the strict independence of art and commerce in the institution. They wear suits on twenty-five, speak a different language and have carpeting on the floors, lithographs on the walls. You are not supposed to talk to them. Up here, the air is too rarefied to support broadloom, the style a down-at-the-heels hauteur. A shoeshine or an overly insistent trouser press is suspect, quite possibly Italian. The layout suggests a condo for high-rise gophers: the private offices are rodent-sized, the halls just wide enough for two-way pedestrianism.

You navigate the linoleum to the Department of Factual Verification. Directly across the hall is Clara's office, the door of which is almost always open so that all who come and go from the kingdom of facts must pass her scrutiny. She is torn between her desire for privacy, with all the honors, privileges, et cetera, appertaining to her post, and her desire to keep a sharp eye on her domain.

The door is wide open this morning and you can do nothing but make the sign of the cross and walk past. You sneak a glance over your shoulder as you enter the department and see that she's not at her desk. Your colleagues are all in place, except for Phoebe Hubbard, who is in Woods Hole researching a three-part piece on lobster-ranching.

'Good morning, fellow proles,' you say, slipping into your seat. The Department of Factual Verification is the largest room in the magazine. If chess teams had locker rooms they might look like this. There are six desks— one reserved for visiting writers—and thousands of reference books on the walls. Gray linoleum desktops, brown linoleum floors. An absolute hierarchy is reflected in the desk assignments, with the desk farthest from Clara's office and closest to the windows reserved for the senior verificationist, and so on down to your own desk against the bookshelves next to the door—but in general the department is a clubhouse of democratic fellowship. The fanatic loyalty to the magazine which rules elsewhere is compromised here by a sense of departmental loyalty: us against them. If an error slips into the magazine, it is one of you, and not the writer, who will be crucified. Not fired, but scolded, perhaps even demoted to the messenger room or the typing pool.

Rittenhouse, who has served notice to falsehoods and commended facts for over fourteen years, nods and says good morning. He looks worried. You assume that Clingfast has been looking for you, that the notion of last straws has been aired.

'Has the Clinger been around yet?' you ask. He nods and blushes down to his bow tie. Rittenhouse enjoys a touch of irreverence but can't help feeling guilty about it.

'She's rather perturbed,' he says. 'At least it seemed so to me,' he adds, demonstrating the scruples of his profession. For half of his life this man has been reading some of the better literature and journalism of his time with the sole aim of sorting out matters of fact from matters of opinion, disregarding the latter, and tracking the alleged facts through dusty volumes, along skeins of microfilm, across transcontinental telephone cables, till they prove good or are exposed as error. He is a world-class detective, but his dedication makes him wary of speech, as if a fiery Clara Tillinghast stood guard on his larynx, ready to pounce on the unqualified assertion.

Your nearest neighbor, Yasu Wade, is checking a science piece. This is a mark of favor—Clingfast usually reserving the science articles, the factual verification of which is so urgent and satisfying, for herself. Wade is on the phone. 'Okay now,' he says, 'where does the neu-

16

trino fit into all of this?' Wade grew up on Air Force bases until he escaped to Bennington and New York. His speech is Sunbelt Swish—a lisp on a twang, occasionally supplemented by feigned R and L confusion, particularly when he has a chance to use the phrase 'President-elect.' His mother is Japanese, his father an Air Force Captain out of Houston. They married in Tokyo during the Occupation, and Yasu Wade is the unlikely result. He calls himself the *Yellow Nonpareil*. Wade is irreverent in every direction, yet somehow manages to amuse where you offend. He is Clara's favorite, not counting Rittenhouse, who is so naturally adapted to his environment as to be invisible.

'Tardy, very tardy,' Wade says to you when he hangs up the phone. 'This won't do. Facts wait for no man. Tardiness is a species of error with regard to Greenwich Mean Time. Greenwich Mean Time is now fifteen-fifteen hours, which means that Eastern Daylight Saving Time, which many of us observe hereabouts, is eleven-fifteen. Starting time here at the office is ten A.M.—hence an error in your disfavor of one hour and fifteen minutes.'

In fact, things are more casual than Wade would have it: Clingfast likes to assert her prerogatives by coming in somewhere between ten-fifteen and ten-thirty. As long as one is at one's desk by ten-thirty, one is relatively safe. Somehow you manage to miss this banker's deadline at least once a week.

'Is she pissed?' you ask.

'I wouldn't put it that way,' Wade says. 'I like that word better the way the British use it—colloquial for intoxicated: e.g., Malcolm Lowry's consul getting pissed on mescal in Quauhnahuac, if I remember the name of the town correctly.'

'Can you spell it?' you ask.

'Of course. But to return to your original question—yes, Clara is a tad peeved. She is not pleased with you. Or perhaps she is pleased to see you confirming her worst expectations. I think she's got the scent of blood. If I were you . . .' Wade looks toward the door and raises his eyebrows. 'If I were you, I'd turn around.'

Clingfast is in the door, looking like a good candidate for a Walker Evans Depression-era photo; flinty-faced and suspicious. The guardian of the apertures, the priestess of Webster's Second Edition *Unabridged Dictionary*, eagle eyes and beagle nose. She gives you a look that could break glass, and then steps out. She's going to let you suffer for a while.

You dig into your desk and pull out a Vicks inhaler. Try to plow a path through some of the crusted snow in your head.

'Still got that nasty sinus problem, I see.' Wade gives you a knowing look. Though he prides himself on being hip, he is too fastidious to do anything dangerous or dirty. You suspect that his sexual orientation is largely theoretical. He'd take a hot piece of gossip over a warm piece of ass any day of the week. He's always telling you who's sleeping with whom. Not that you mind. Last week it was David Bowie and Prince Rainier.

You try to settle down to an article about the French elections. It is your job to make sure that there are no errors of fact or spelling. In this case the facts are so confused as to suck you deep into vast regions of interpretation. The writer, a former restaurant critic, lavishes all his care on adjectives and disdains nouns. He describes an aging cabinet minister as 'nubbly' and a rising socialist as 'lightly browned.' You believe that

Clingfast gave you this piece in order to see you hang yourself. She knew the piece was a mess. She probably also knew that the claim of fluency in French on your résumé was something of a whopper, and that you are too proud to admit it now. Running down the facts requires numerous phone calls to France, and you made a fool of yourself last week doing your *je ne comprends pas* with various sub-ministers and their assistants. Plus you have your own personal reasons for not wanting to call Paris or speak French or be reminded of the goddamned place. Reasons that have to do with your wife.

There is no way you will be able to get everything in this article verified, and there is also no graceful way to admit failure. You are going to have to hope that the writer got some of it straight the first time, and that Clingfast doesn't go through the proofs with her usual razor-tooth comb.

Why does she hate you? She hired you, after all. When did things start to go wrong? It's not your fault that she never married. Since your own marital Pearl Harbor, you have understood that sleeping alone goes a long way toward explaining nastiness and erratic behavior. Sometimes you have wanted to tell her: *Hey, I know what it's like.* You have seen her at that little piano bar off Columbus, clutching her drink and waiting for somebody to come up and say hello. When she's bitching you out, you have wanted to say: *Why don't you just admit you hurt?* But by the time you understood this it was too late. She wanted your hide.

Maybe it all began with the John Donlevy deal. You had been at the magazine only a few weeks and Clara took a week off. Donlevy was doing a book review for the magazine, flexing his synapses after his second

Pulitzer prize. Book reviews were considered walk-throughs in the department, and Clara left the piece in your hands. In your innocence you not only fixed up the occasional citation error; you went on to suggest some improvements in the prose and to register questions regarding interpretation of the book. You handed in the proofs and went home well pleased. Something happened in Collating; your proofs were sent to Donlevy in place of the editor's proofs. The editor, a youngish woman fresh from the Yale alumni magazine, was in awe of her sudden proximity to Donlevy, and was horrified when she learned what had happened and looked over your proofs. You were summoned to her office and upbraided for your unprecedented presumption. To tamper with the prose of John Donlevy! Horrible. Un*think*able. You, a mere stripling of a verificationist. If you had gone to Yale, you might have learned some manners. She was trying to decide how best to explain the outrage to Donlevy when he called to say that he appreciated the suggestions and that he was taking several of the changes. You got that part of the story from the switchboard operator, who listened in on the conversation. The editor never spoke to you again. After Clara returned, there was another lecture, much the same, with the addition of the idea that you had embarrassed her and the entire department. When the issue came out, you noted with some satisfaction that your best stuff was incorporated in the review. But it was the end of Clara's warm maternal act.

To give Clara her due, lately you have not been impeccable in the performance of your duties. It's a matter of temperaments. You try and you try, but you can't see this as God's work, or even Man's work. Aren't computers supposed to free us from this kind of drudgery?

In fact, you don't want to be in Fact. You'd much rather be in Fiction. You have cautiously expressed this preference several times, but there hasn't been an opening in Fiction in years. The people in the Verification Department tend to look down on fiction, in which words masquerade as flesh without the backbone of fact. There is a general sense that if fiction isn't dead, it is at least beside the point. But you'll take a new story by Bellow over a six-part article on the Republican convention at the drop of a hat. All the magazine fiction passes through the department, and since no one else wants it you take it upon yourself to do the routine checking— make sure that if a story set in San Francisco contains a psycho named Phil Doaks, there is no Phil Doaks in the San Francisco phone book who might turn around and sue. It's the opposite of verifying a factual piece. To confirm that the story doesn't unintentionally coincide at any point with real people and events. A cursory process, it does give you a shot at some decent reading. At first Clingfast seemed pleased that you were taking on a job no one else wanted, but now she accuses you of spending too much time on the fiction. You are an idler in the kingdom of facts. Meanwhile, the Fiction people are none too thrilled when you inform them that a story which contains a fly-fishing scene incorrectly has a hatch of Sulfur Duns occurring on a stream in Oregon where, in fact, no Sulfur Duns have ever hatched. You are an unwilling emissary from the land of pedantry. 'So what the hell does hatch in goddamned Oregon?' the editor asks. 'Salmon-flies, for one,' you say. You want to say: It's my job—I don't like it either.

Megan Avery comes over to your desk. She picks up the framed needlepoint sampler Wade embroidered for your last birthday, which reads:

Facts all come with points of view
Facts don't do what I want them to.
—TALKING HEADS

When Wade gave it to you you weren't sure whether to be grateful for his time and effort or insulted by the implied comment on your professional incapacities. Megan asks, 'How's everything going with you?' You say you can't complain. 'Are you sure?' Megan makes honesty seem like a viable alternative. She is a person who could give lessons in sanity. Why have you never confided in her before? She's older and wiser. You're not sure how old; she doesn't seem to have a particular age. You would describe her as striking, or attractive, but she has such an earnest, practical nature that it is hard for you to envision her as a sexual being. Although married once, she seems the West Village type meant to run her own life and help her friends through their many disasters. You admire her. You don't know many sensible people. Maybe you could have lunch sometime.

'I'm okay, really,' you say.

'Need any help with the French piece? I'm not real busy just now.'

'I think I can manage. Thanks.'

The Clinger appears in the doorway. She nods at you. 'We've decided to move the French thing up an issue. That means I need it on my desk before you leave today. We're closing tomorrow afternoon.' She pauses. 'Can you handle it?'

There is not a snowball's chance in hell and you suspect she knows it. 'I could just give it directly to Collating tonight and save you the trouble.'

'My desk,' she says. 'Tell me now if you're going to need help.'

You shake your head. If she sees the shape the page proofs are in at the moment, you're screwed. You have not followed procedure. You have used pen where you should have used pencil, red pencil where you should have used blue. Phone numbers written in the margins, coffee rings in the columns. You have done all the things that the 'Manual of Factual Verification' tells you not to do. You've got to try and find a clean copy of the proofs to work from. The Clinger is large on procedure.

The prospect of the work in front of you resurrects the unspeakable headache with which you woke. You're already exhausted. You're so tired. Eight days of sleep would put you right. A boatload of Marching Powder might get you through this ordeal. But simply to face it seems like more than you can do. You should protest the change in scheduling. Why the hell didn't someone ask you if it was almost ready to go? Even if you could speak French, it would take several more days. If you were not afraid of having Clara or the Druid examine your proofs as they stand, you would protest.

If you were Japanese, this would be the time to commit *seppuku*. Pen a farewell poem about the transience of cherry blossoms and the fleet transit of youth, wrap the sword blade in white silk, plunge it home and pull upward, rightward through your intestines. And no whimpering or sour expressions, please. You learned all about the ritual while checking an article on Japan. But you lack that samurai resolution. You are the kind of guy who always hopes for a miracle at the last minute. Manhattan does not lie in an earthquake zone, but there is always the possibility of nuclear war. Short of that, nothing you can imagine would alter the publishing schedule.

At a little after noon the Druid tiptoes past the office on his way to lunch. Because you happen to be staring out the door at nothing in particular you catch his eyes, famously nearsighted. He bows formally. The Druid is elusive; one has to look very closely, and know what to look for, to see him at all. While you have never actually seen a Victorian clerk, you believe this is what one would look like. At the magazine, his temperamental reticence has been elevated to a principle. Fourth in a dynastic succession, he has run the show for twenty years. Trying to discover what he is thinking is the preoccupation of the entire staff. Nothing passes into the magazine without his enthusiastic approval and his own final edit. There is no arbitration and no explanation. It pains him that he requires a staff to assist him, but he is invariably polite. There is officially no second-in-command, because that would imply an eventual changing of the guard, and the Druid cannot imagine the magazine without himself. The Kremlin must be a lot like this. Perhaps because he suspects he is mortal, fiction that deals too directly with death is unwelcome here; most references to myopia are edited out. No detail is too minute for his attention.

The only direct contact you have had with the Druid was when he called you up one day to worry about the English usage of the President of the United States. You were checking a piece in which the President warned

24

against *precipitous* action. The Druid felt that *precipitate* was the word the President was looking for. He asked you to call the White House and get approval for the change. You dutifully called the White House and tried to explain the importance of this distinction. You spent several hours on hold. Those who actually believed you were serious would not commit themselves. Others just cussed you out. Meanwhile, the magazine was going to press. The Druid called three times and encouraged you to keep trying. Finally, with the composing room screaming for the final pages, an accommodation of sorts was reached, unknown to the President and his staff. While Webster's Second distinguished the meanings of the two words, the racier Third Edition listed them as synonyms. The Druid gave you a final call to explain this and to approve—not without trepidation—the original quote. The magazine went to press. Government continued apace.

At one o'clock you go out for a sandwich. Megan asks you to bring her a Tab. Downstairs, you semi-revolve through the doors and think about how nice it would be not to have to return at all, ever. You also think about how nice it would be to hole up in the nearest bar. The glare from the sidewalk stuns you; you fumble in your jacket pocket for your shades. Sensitive eyes, you tell people.

You shuffle off to the deli and pick up a pastrami-on-rye and an egg cream. The bald man behind the counter whistles cheerfully as he slices the meat. 'Nice and lean today,' he says. 'And now for a little mustard—just how your mom used to make it.'

'What do you know about it?' you ask.

'Just passing the time, pal,' he says, wrapping it all up. All of this, the dead meat on ice behind glass, everything, puts you off your meal.

Outside, waiting for a light, you are accosted by a man leaning up against a bank.

'My man, check it out here. Genuine Cartier watches. Forty dollars. Wear the watch that'll make 'em watch you. The genuine article. Only forty bucks.'

The man stands beside the torso of a mannequin, the arms of which are covered with watches. He holds one out to you. 'Check it out.' If you take it, you'll feel committed. But you don't want to be rude. You take the watch and examine it.

'How do I know it's real?'

'How do you know anything's real? Says *Cartier* right there on the face, right? Looks real. Feels real. So what's to know? Forty bucks. How can you lose?'

It appears authentic. Slim, rectangular face, regal roman numerals, sapphire-tipped winding knob. The band feels like good leather. But if it's real, it's probably hot. And if it isn't hot it can't be real.

'Thirty-five bucks to you. My cost.'

'How come so cheap?'

'Low overhead.'

You haven't owned a watch in years. Knowing the time at any given moment might be a good first step toward organizing the slippery flux of your life. You've never been able to see yourself as the digital kind of guy. But you could use a little Cartier in your act. It looks real, even if it isn't, and it tells time. What the hell.

'Thirty dollars,' the man says.

'I'll buy it.'

'At that price you ain't buying it. You're stealing it.'

26

You wind your new watch and admire it on your wrist. 1:25.

Once you reach the office you realize you have forgotten Megan's Tab. You apologize and tell her you'll go back for it. She says not to bother. While you were gone she took two messages, one from Monsieur Somebody at the Department of Something, and one from your brother Michael. You don't really want to talk to either of them.

By two o'clock it's eight in Paris and everyone has gone home for the day. For the rest of the afternoon you will try to fill in the holes with reference books and calls to the consulate in New York. Your eyelids feel as if they are being held open by taxidermy needles. You push on blindly.

Your new watch dies at three-fifteen. You shake it, then wind it. The winding knob falls off in your hand.

The editor of the piece calls to ask how it's going. You say it's going. He apologizes for the scheduling change; he wanted to save it till next month at the earliest. For no clear reason, the Druid moved it up. 'I just wanted to warn you,' he says. 'Take nothing for granted.'

'That's my job,' you say.

'I mean especially in this case. He hasn't left Paris in twelve years, and spends most of his time in restaurants. He never double-checks anything.'

Jesus wept.

Twice during the afternoon you call the writer to ask him where he picked up his facts. The first time you call you go through a list of errors and he concedes each point cheerfully.

27

'Where did you get this about the French government owning a controlling interest in Paramount Pictures?' you say.

'Don't they? Well, shit. Run a line through that.'

'Your next three paragraphs depend on it.'

'Damn. Who told me that?'

By the end of the second call he is annoyed, as if the errors were of your devising. This is the way it goes with the writers: they resent you to the degree that they depend on you.

Late in the afternoon a memo arrives addressed to 'staff.' It is signed by the Druid's assistant, which makes it gospel.

It has come to our attention that a Mr. Richard Fox is writing an article about the magazine. Some of you may already have been approached by Mr. Fox. We have reason to believe that the intentions of this reporter are not coincident with the best interests of the magazine. We would like to remind all staff members of the magazine's policy with regard to the press. All queries and requests for interviews should be referred to this office. Under no circumstances should any employee presume to speak for the magazine without prior clearance. We remind you that all magazine business is strictly confidential.

The memo occasions amusement in the Department of Factual Verification. The magazine has been involved in many freedom of press trials, but in this gag order there is not a glimmer of irony.

Wade says, 'I wish Richard Fox would call me.'

Megan says, 'Forget it, Yasu. I know for a fact that Richard Fox is straight.'

'For a *fact*? I'd be very interested to hear about your verification procedure.'

'I know you would,' Megan says.

'At any rate,' Wade says, 'I only meant that I would be fantastically curious to know how many pieces of silver some of the institutional dirty laundry is worth. But don't get me wrong—it's not that I don't find Fox attractive.'

Rittenhouse is tugging at his glasses, indicating that he wishes to speak. 'I, for one, do not feel that Richard Fox is an objective reporter. He has a penchant for sensationalism.'

'Of course,' Wade says. 'That's why we love him.'

The possession of dangerous information excites a brief feeling of power here in the Department of Factual Verification. You wish Richard Fox or anyone else cared enough about Clara Tillinghast to perform a character assassination.

By seven everyone is gone. They all offered to help, and you waved them away. There is a shabby nobility in failing all by yourself.

Clara sticks her head in the door as she's leaving. 'My desk,' she says.

My ass, you think.

You nod and, in token of your earnestness, hunker down over the page proofs. From this point on it's a matter of covering your tracks, running pencil lines through anything that you have not been able to verify and hoping that nothing important slips through.

At seven-thirty Allagash calls. 'What are you doing at the office?' he says. 'We have plans for the evening. Monstrous events are scheduled.'

Two of the things you like about Allagash are that he never asks you how you are and he never waits for you to answer his questions. You used to dislike this, but when the news is all bad it's a relief that someone doesn't want to hear it. Just now you want to stay at the surface of things, and Tad is a figure skater who never considers the sharks under the ice. You have friends who actually care about you and speak the language of the inner self. You have avoided them of late. Your soul is as disheveled as your apartment, and until you can clean it up a little you don't want to invite anyone inside.

Allagash tells you that Natalie and Inge are dying to meet you. Natalie's father runs an oil company and Inge is soon to be in a major television commercial. Moreover, the Deconstructionists are playing the Ritz, one of the modeling agencies is sponsoring a bash for Muscular Dystrophy at Magique and Natalie has cornered a chunk of the Gross National Product of Bolivia.

'I'm going to be working most of the night,' you say. Actually, you are about to give up, but a night of Allagash is not the remedy for your blues. You're thinking of bed. You are so tired you could stretch out right here on the linoleum and slip into a long coma.

'Give me a time. I'll pick you up,' Tad says.

The phrase 'last-ditch effort' jumps out from the column of print in front of you. It makes you ashamed of yourself. You think of the Greeks at Thermopylae, the Texans at the Alamo, John Paul Jones in his leaky tub. You want to rally and whip hell out of falsehood and error.

You tell Tad you will call him back in half an hour. Later, when the phone rings, you ignore it.

At a little after ten you put the proofs on Clara's desk. It would at least be a relief if you could tell yourself that this was your best shot. You feel like a student who is handing in a term paper that is part plagiarism, part nonsense and half finished. You have scoped out and fixed a number of colossal blunders, which serves only to make you more aware of the suspect nature of everything you haven't verified. The writer was counting on the Verification Department to give authority to his sly observations and insidious generalizations. This is not cricket on his part, but it is your job to help him out and it is your job that is on the line. There has only been one printed retraction in the magazine's history and the verificationist responsible for the error was immediately farmed out to Advertising. Your only hope is that the Clinger won't read it. A fire of mysterious origin might sweep through the offices. Or Clara might get sloshed tonight, fall off a barstool and crack her head open. She might get picked up by a Sex Killer. Any *Post* reader will tell you it's possible. Happens every day.

There was a cartoon you used to watch, at least you think there was, with a time-traveling turtle and a benevolent wizard. The turtle would journey back to, say, the French Revolution, inevitably getting in way over his head. At the last minute, when he was stretched out under the guillotine, he would cry out, 'Help, Mr. Wizard!' And the wizard, on the other end of the time warp, would wave his wand and rescue the hapless turtle.

* * *

31

Already you feel a sense of nostalgia as you walk down the narrow halls past all the closed doors. You remember how you felt when you passed this way for your first interview, how the bland seediness of the hallway only increased your apprehension of grandeur. You thought of all the names that had been made here. You thought of yourself in the third person: *He arrived for his first interview in a navy-blue blazer. He was interviewed for a position in the Department of Factual Verification, a job which must have seemed even then to be singularly unsuited to his flamboyant temperament. But he was not to languish long among the facts.*

Those first months seem now to have been filled with promise. You were convinced of the importance of your job and of the inevitability of rising above it. You met people you had admired half your life. You got married. The Druid himself sent a note of congratulations. It was only a matter of time before they realized your talents were being wasted in Fact.

Something changed. Somewhere along the line you stopped accelerating.

Mrs. Bender, the senior grammarian, is working late. You say good night. She asks you about the French piece and you tell her it's finished.

'What a mess,' she says. 'It reads as if it was translated literally from the Chinese. These damn writers want us to do all their work for them.'

You nod and smile. Her complaint is refreshing, like rain at the end of a muggy day. You linger in the doorway while she shakes her head and clicks her tongue.

'Going home soon?' you say.

'Not soon enough.'

'Can I get you something from downstairs?'

She shakes her head. 'I don't want to feel as if I'm settled in here.'

'See you tomorrow.'

She nods and returns to her proofs.

You walk to the elevator and press the Down button.

THE UTILITY OF FICTION

You see yourself as the kind of guy who appreciates a quiet night at home with a good book. A little Mozart on the speakers, a cup of cocoa on the arm of the chair, slippers on the feet. Monday night. It feels like Thursday, at least. Walking from subway to apartment, you tell yourself that you are going to suppress this rising dread that comes upon you when you return home at night. A man's home, after all, is his castle. Approaching your building on West Twelfth Street, you observe the architect's dim concept of European fortresses: a crenelated tower atop the building conceals the water tank and the entrance is fitted with a mock portcullis. You let yourself in the front door and gingerly unlock the mailbox. No telling what might be inside. One of these days there could be a letter from Amanda explaining her desertion, begging forgiveness or asking you to send the rest of her stuff to a new address.

Tonight there is an overdue notice from VISA; a solicitation from Recording for the Blind; a letter from Jim

Winthrop in Chicago, college roommate, best man at your wedding; and something corporate for Amanda White. You open Jim's letter first. It starts 'Hey stranger,' and ends with 'regards to Amanda.' The letter to Amanda is a printout on an insurance company letterhead, her name typed into the salutation:

Let's face it—in your business, your face is your greatest asset. Modeling is an exciting and rewarding career. In all likelihood, you have many years of earning ahead of you. But where would you be in the event of a disfiguring accident? Even a minor injury could spell the end of a lucrative career and the loss of hundreds of thousands of dollars in potential income.

You ball up the letter and arc it into the wastebasket beside the elevator. You press the button. *Where would you be, for instance, if a spurned husband threw acid in your face?* No. Stop this. This is not your better self speaking. This is not how you feel.

The sound of the tumblers in the locks of your apartment door puts you in mind of dungeons. The place is haunted. Just this morning you found a makeup brush beside the toilet. Memories lurk like dustballs at the backs of drawers. The stereo is a special model that plays only music fraught with poignant associations.

This was the second apartment you shared with Amanda, the place into which you moved in order to accommodate the wedding gifts. Amanda wanted to live on the Upper East Side, where the other models lived. She brought home prospecti for co-ops and then, when you asked her where the money was going to come

35

from, suggested you could get a loan from your father. You asked her what made her think that even if your father had that kind of money on hand, he would want to fork it over. She shrugged. 'Anyway, I'm doing really well right now,' she said. For the first time you realized that she thought your family was rich, and by the standards of her childhood they were. 'Come look at this kitchen plan,' she said.

This place was your compromise—an uptown sort of building downtown: high ceilings, daytime doorman, working fireplaces. You both liked the wood paneling and the wainscoting. Amanda said it was a place in which you would not feel ridiculous eating off the new china with the sterling flatware. Flatware, china and crystal occupied much of her concern as the wedding approached. She insisted that you buy a starter set of Tiffany sterling: the price of silver was going through the ceiling and she was convinced that it would double or triple by the time of the wedding. A famous designer told her so. With the earnings of three weeks' showroom work she bought six settings. A few days later silver collapsed, and the six settings were worth about what she paid for one.

When she heard you had a family crest she wanted to put it on the sterling, but you drew the line at your monograms and feared the sense of urgency in her new acquisitiveness. She seemed eager to provision you all at once for a lifetime. Then, within a year of this prenuptial buying spree, she was gone. Now you eat out of paper cartons and the wainscoting doesn't cheer you. What's more, you can't really afford the rent. You keep meaning to look for a new place, and to do the dishes and the laundry.

You close the door and stand in the foyer, listening. For some time after Amanda left, you would pause here in the hope that you would hear her inside, that she had returned, that you would discover her, penitent and tender, when you stepped into the living room. That hope is mostly gone, but still you observe this brief vigil inside the door, gauging the quality of the silence to see if it is only the melancholy silence of absence, or whether it is full of high-register shrieks and moans. Tonight you are uncertain. You step into the living room and throw your jacket on the love seat. You hunt up your slippers and read the spines of the books in the shelves, determined to make a go of this quiet-night-at-home idea. A random sampling of titles induces vertigo: *As I Lay Dying, Under the Volcano, Anna Karenina, Being and Time, The Brothers Karamazov*. You must have had an ambitious youth. Of course, many of these spines have never been cracked. You have been saving them up.

Nothing seems to be what you want to do until you consider writing. Suffering is supposed to be the raw stuff of art. You could write a book. You feel that if only you could make yourself sit down at a typewriter you could give shape to what seems merely a chain reaction of pointless disasters. Or you could get revenge, tell your side of the story, cast some version of yourself in the role of wronged hero. Hamlet on the battlements. Maybe get outside autobiography altogether, lose yourself in the purely formal imperatives of words in the correct and surprising sequence, or create a fantasy world of small furry and large scaly creatures.

You have always wanted to be a writer. Getting the job at the magazine was only your first step toward literary celebrity. You used to write what you believed to be urbane sketches infinitely superior to those appearing in the magazine every week. You sent them up to Fiction; they came back with polite notes. 'Not quite right for us now, but thanks for letting us see this.' You would try to interpret the notes: what about the word *now*—do they mean that you should submit this again, later? It wasn't the notes so much as the effort of writing that discouraged you. You never stopped thinking of yourself as a writer biding his time in the Department of Factual Verification. But between the job and the life there wasn't much time left over for emotion recollected in tranquillity. For a few weeks you got up at six to compose short stories at the kitchen table while Amanda slept in the other room. Then your night life started getting more interesting and complicated, and climbing out of bed became harder and harder. You were gathering experience for a novel. You went to parties with writers, cultivated a writerly persona. You wanted to be Dylan Thomas without the paunch, F. Scott Fitzgerald without the crack-up. You wanted to skip over the dull grind of actual creation. After a hard day of work on other people's manuscripts—knowing in your heart that you could do better—the last thing you wanted to do was to go home and write. You wanted to go out. Amanda was the fashion model and you worked for the famous magazine. People were happy to meet you and to invite you to their parties. So much was going on. Of course, mentally, you were always taking notes. Saving it all up. Waiting for the day when you would sit down and write your masterpiece.

You dig your typewriter out of the closet and set it up on the dining-room table. You have some good twenty-pound bond from the supply cabinet in the office. You roll a sheet, with backing, onto the platen. The white-ness of the sheet is intimidating, so you type the date in the right-hand corner. You decide to jump immediately into the story you have in mind. Waste no time with preliminaries. You type:

He was expecting her on the afternoon flight from Paris when she called to say she would not be coming home.

'You're taking a later flight?' he asked.

'No,' she said. 'I'm starting a new life.'

You read it over. Then you tear the sheet out of the type-writer and insert a new one.

Go farther back, maybe. Try to find the source of this chaos. Give her a name and a place.

Karen liked to look at her mother's fashion maga-zines. The women were elegant and beautiful and they were always climbing in and out of taxis and limousines on their way to big stores and res-taurants. Karen didn't think there were any stores or restaurants like that in Oklahoma. She wished she looked like the ladies in the pictures. Then maybe her father would come back.

This is dreadful. You tear the sheet into eighths and slide them into the wastebasket. You insert another piece of paper; again you type the date. At the left margin you type, 'Dear Amanda,' but when you look at the paper it reads 'Dead Amanda.'

Screw this. You are not going to commit any great literature tonight. You need to relax. After all, you've been busting ass all day. You check the fridge; no beer. A finger of vodka in the bottle on the sink. Maybe you will step out and get a six-pack. Or wander over to the Lion's Head, as long as you're going out, to see if there's anybody you know. It's not impossible there to meet a woman *avec* hair, *sans* tattoo, at the bar.

The intercom buzzes while you're changing your shirt. You push the Talk button: 'Who is it?'

'Narcotics squad. We're soliciting donations for children all over the world who have no drugs.'

You buzz him up. You're not sure how you feel about the advent of Tad Allagash. While you could use company, Tad can be too much of a good thing. His brand of R & R is nothing if not strenuous. Nonetheless, by the time he gets to the door, you're glad to see him. He's looking *très sportif* in J. Press torso and punked-out red SoHo trousers. He presents his hand and you shake.

'Ready to roll?'

'Where are we rolling?'

'Into the heart of the night. Wherever there are dances to be danced, drugs to be hoovered, women to be Allagashed. It's a dirty job but someone's got to do it. Speaking of drugs, are you in possession?'

You shake your head.

'Not a single line for young Tad?'

'Sorry.'

'Not even a mirror I can lick?'

'Suit yourself.'

Tad goes over to the mahogany-and-gilt-framed mirror that you inherited from your grandmother, the one Amanda was so afraid your cousin was going to nab. He runs his tongue over the glass.

40

'There's something on here.'

'Dust.'

Tad smacks his lips. 'In this apartment the dust has better coke content than some of the shit we buy by the gram. All us coke fiends sneezing—it adds up.'

Tad runs his finger across the length of the coffee table. 'It looks like you could teach a course in dust here. Did you know that ninety percent of your average household dust is composed of human epidermal matter? That's skin, to you.'

Perhaps this explains your sense of Amanda's omnipresence. She has left her skin behind.

He walks over to the table and leans over the typewriter. 'Doing a little writing, are we? *Dead Amanda*. That's the idea. I told you you'd get more nookie than you can shake a stick at if you tell the girls that your wife died. It's the sympathy vote. More effective than saying she fit you with horns and kited off to Paris. Avoid the awful taint of rejection.'

Tad's first reaction, when you told him about Amanda's departure, contained a grain of genuine sympathy and regret. His second reaction was to tell you that you could make a fine erotic career for yourself by repeating the story just as you had told it to him, adding touches of pathos and cruel irony. Finally, he advised you to say that Amanda had died in a plane crash on her way home from Paris on the day of your first anniversary.

'You're sure there aren't any drugs around here?'

'Some Robitussin in the bathroom.'

'I'm disappointed in you, Coach. I've always thought of you as the kind of guy who saves something for a rainy day. The temperate sort.'

'I've fallen in with bad companions.'

41

'Let's get on the phone,' Tad says. 'We must locate party fuel. *Cherchez les grammes*.'

All the people who might have drugs aren't home. The people who are home don't have drugs. There is a pattern here. 'Damn Warner,' Tad says. 'He never answers his phone. I just know he's sitting there in his loft on top of a pile of toot, ignoring the phone.' Tad hangs up and checks his watch, which tells him the time in selected major cities of the world, including New York and Dubai, Persian Gulf, Oman. 'Eleven-forty. A little too early for Odeon, but once we're downtown, it's happy hunting ground for sneeze and squeeze. Ready?'

'Have you ever experienced this nearly overwhelming urge for a quiet night at home?'

Tad reflects for a moment. 'No.'

The glittering, curvilinear surfaces inside Odeon are reassuring. The place makes you feel reasonable at any hour, often against bad odds, with its good light and clean luncheonette-via-Cartier deco decor. Along the bar are faces familiar under artificial light, belonging to people whose daytime existence is only a tag—designer, writer, artist. A model from Amanda's agency is sitting at the bar. You do not want to see her. Tad cruises right over and kisses her. At the other end of the bar you order a vodka. You finish it and order a second before Tad beckons. The model is with another woman. Tad introduces them as Elaine and Theresa. Elaine, the model, has a punk high-fashion look: short, razor-cut dark hair, high cheekbones, eyebrows plucked straight. Metallic and masculine are the adjectives that come to mind. Both M words. Theresa is blonde, too short and busty to

42

model. Elaine looks you over as if you were an impulse purchase that she might return to the department store.

'Aren't you Amanda White's boyfriend?'

'Husband. I mean, I was.'

'She was in Paris showing the fall collections,' Tad says, 'and she got caught in a crossfire between Palestinian terrorists and the French police. Totally fluke thing. Innocent bystander. Senseless death. He doesn't like to talk about it.' Tad's delivery is entirely convincing. You almost believe him yourself. His air of being privy to dark secrets and inside stories gives credence to outrageous statements.

'That's terrible,' Theresa says.

'Tragic is what it is,' Tad says. 'Excuse me, but I've got to do some business. Back in a minute.' He bows and then heads out the door.

'Is that true?'

'Not really.'

'What is Amanda doing these days?' Elaine asks.

'I don't know. I think she's in Paris.'

'Wait a minute,' Theresa says. 'Is she alive?'

'We just sort of split up.'

'Too bad for you,' Elaine says. 'She was yummy.' She turns to Theresa. 'Sort of this slinky girl-next-door look. Farm fresh. Very ingenuous.'

'I don't understand this,' Theresa says.

'Me neither,' you say. You'd just as soon change the subject. You don't like this role of bird with broken wing, especially since that's exactly how you feel. The lame-duck husband. You'd rather be an eagle or a falcon, pitiless and predatory among the solitary crags.

'Aren't you some kind of writer?' Elaine says.

'I do some writing. I'm sort of an editor actually.'

43

'Oh, God,' Theresa says, when you mention the name of the magazine. 'I've been reading it all my life. I mean, my parents get it. I always read it at the gynecologist. What's your name? Should I know you?' She asks you about writers and artists on the staff. You dish up a standard portion of slander and libel that would never pass the Clinger's requirements of verification.

Without getting too specific you imply that your job is extremely demanding and important. In the past you could often convince yourself as well as others of this, but your heart is no longer in it. You hate this posturing, even as you persist, as if it were important for these two strangers to admire you for all the wrong reasons. It's not much, this menial job in a venerable institution, but it's all you've got left.

Once upon a time, you assumed you were very likable. That you had an attractive wife and a fairly interesting job seemed only your due. You were a good guy. You deserved some of the world's booty. After you met Amanda and came to New York, you began to feel that you were no longer on the outside looking in. When you were growing up you suspected that everyone else had been let in on some fundamental secret which was kept from you. Others seemed to know what they were doing. This conviction grew with each new school you attended. Your father's annual job transfers made you the perennial new kid. Every year there was a new body of lore to be mastered. The color of your bike, your socks, was always wrong. If you ever go into psychoanalysis, you will insist that the primal scene is not the encounter of parents in coitus: it takes the shape of a ring of schoolchildren, like Indians surrounding a wagon train, laughing with malice, pointing their

44

vicious little fingers to insist upon your otherness. The scene repeated itself in schoolyards across the country. Not until you reached college, where everyone started fresh, did you begin to pick up the tricks of winning friends and influencing people. Although you became adept, you also felt that you were exercising an acquired skill, something that came naturally to others. You succeeded in faking everyone out, and never quite lost the fear that you would eventually be discovered a fraud, an impostor in the social circle. Which is just about how you feel these days. Even now, as you puff yourself up with tales of high adventure in magazine publishing, you can see Elaine's eyes wandering out over the room, leaving you behind. She's drinking champagne. As you watch, she dips her tongue into the tulip bowl and slides it around inside the glass.

A woman who looks vaguely famous glances up from her table and waves. Elaine waves back. Her smile goes sour when the woman turns away.

'Check that out,' Elaine says. 'Silicone implants.'

'I don't know. She looks pretty damn flat to me.'

'Not the tits—the cheeks. She's got fucking silicone implants to make it look like she has cheekbones.'

Tad comes back, pleased with himself. 'Bingo,' he says.

It's somewhere past midnight. Anything that starts now is not going to end at a reasonable hour. You think about slipping out and heading home. All sorts of beneficial effects are rumored to accrue from a good night's sleep. On the other hand, you wouldn't mind a taste of that toot. Just enough to boost your morale.

In a moment you are all en route to the bathroom downstairs. Tad lays out some fat lines on the toilet

45

seat. Elaine and Theresa take their turns. Finally, Tad hands you the bill. The sweet nasal burn hits like a swallow of cold beer on a hot August day. Tad fixes another round and by the time you all troop out of the bathroom you are feeling omnipotent. You are upwardly mobile. Certainly something excellent is bound to happen.

'Let us locomote out of here,' Tad says.

'Where to?' Theresa says. 'Where the boys are?'

'Where the girls are,' Elaine says. You're not sure if this is just having fun with movie allusions or something more pointed.

Your merry band decides that Heartbreak is the destination. A cab is procured for the short hop uptown.

Outside the door there is a crowd of would-be Heartbreakers with a uniform outer-borough look. Tad pushes through the supplicants, confers with the bouncer and then waves the three of you in. Elaine and Theresa are chatting away when it comes time to pay, so you cover one and Tad covers the other. Inside, there is still room to move.

'It's early,' Tad says. He is disappointed. He hates to arrive before everyone else is in place. He takes pride in his timing, being on time by being the latest.

Elaine and Theresa disappear and you don't see them for fifteen minutes. Tad discovers some friends, advertising people, at a table. Everyone is discussing the new *Vanity Fair*. Some are for and some against. 'Utter confusion,' says Steve, a copywriter. 'It's the Abstract Expressionist approach to publishing. Throw ink at paper. Hope for pattern to emerge.'

You go off to buy a drink, keeping both eyes peeled for lonely women. There don't seem to be any at the moment. Everyone knows everyone else. You are on the anti-cline of your first rush. You are also experiencing the inevitable disappointment of clubs. You enter with an anticipation that on the basis of past experience is entirely unjustified. You always seem to forget that you don't really like to dance. Since you are already here, though, you owe it to yourself to make a sustained assault on the citadel of good times. The music pumps you up, makes you want to do something, not necessarily dance. The drugs make you feel the music and the music makes you want to do more drugs.

At the bar someone thumps your shoulder. You turn around. It takes you a minute to place the face, but in the time it takes to shake hands you come up with a name: Rich Vanier. He was in your dining club at college. You ask what he's been doing. He's in banking, just back from South America tonight, after saving a banana republic from bankruptcy.

'What the hell, I restructured, gave the generals a few more months of high living. So what are you doing to keep body and soul together. Still the poet?'

'I do a little South American business myself.'

'I heard a rumor you married an actress.'

'*Activist*. I married a beautiful activist. She was the illegitimate daughter of Che Guevara. A few months ago she went home to visit her mother and got herself arrested and tortured by a series of rich South American generals. She died in prison.'

'You're kidding, right?'

'Do I look like I'm kidding?'

Rich Vanier can't get away from you fast enough. He says you'll have to have lunch sometime.

Walking back to the table you see Theresa and Elaine heading off with Tad. You catch up with them just

47

outside the Men's Room. The four of you occupy a stall. Elaine sits on the tank and Theresa sits on the seat.

'Seems like I spend about half my life in bathrooms,' Theresa says as she blocks off a nostril.

Later you run into a woman you met at a party. You can't remember her name. She acts embarrassed when you greet her, as if something shameful had once passed between you, though all you can remember is a discussion about the political ramifications of The Clash. You ask her if she wants to dance and she says sure.

Out on the floor, you invent your own dance step. You call it the New York Torque. 'Some Girls' segues to 'Shattered.' You keep outstripping the prevailing tempo. Your partner sways back and forth metronomically. When you look at her, she seems to be studying you sympathetically. After you have soaked through your shirt you ask her if she wants to take a break. She nods her head vigorously.

'Is there something the matter?' You have to shout in her ear to be heard.

'Not really.'

'You seem nervous.'

'I heard about your wife,' she says. 'I'm so sorry.'

'What did you hear?'

'About what happened. About the, you know, leukemia.'

You are riding the Bolivian Local up through the small mountain villages into the lean oxygen of the Andean peaks.

'We've got Terrain and Elisa eating out of our hands,' Tad says. 'I think it's time we suggested that we all slip out to someplace more comfortable.'

You are in the bathroom again. Elaine and Theresa are in the Ladies' on legitimate business.

'I do not appreciate this leukemia bit,' you say. 'Not funny.'

'Just trying to boost sales. Consider me your agent.'

'I'm not amused. Bad taste.'

'Taste,' says Tad, 'is a matter of taste.'

You are dancing with Elaine. Tad is dancing with Theresa. Elaine moves with an angular syncopation that puts you in mind of the figures on Egyptian tombs. It may be a major new dance step. Whatever it is, she is making you feel self-conscious. She's a tough act to accompany. You feel like a recent transplant from the Junior Prom. You are not particularly attracted to Elaine, who's too hard-edged in your view. You do not even think she is a particularly nice person. Yet you have this desire to prove that you can have as good a time as anyone, that you can be one of the crowd. Objectively, you know that Elaine is desirable, and you feel obligated to desire her. It seems to be your duty to go through the motions. You keep thinking that with practice you will eventually get the knack of enjoying superficial encounters, that you will stop looking for the universal solvent, stop grieving. You will learn to compound happiness out of small increments of mindless pleasure.

'I really enjoyed Amanda,' Elaine says between songs. 'I do hope I see her again.' There is something confidential in her manner, as if you shared a secret with regard to Amanda. You would be happier if she had said she didn't like Amanda. Being still unable to think the worst of her, you need other people to think it and speak it for you.

49

Tad and Theresa have disappeared. Elaine excuses herself and says she will be right back. You feel abandoned. You consider the possibility of conspiracy. They have planned to meet at the door and ditch you. You are doing bad things to their mood. Or, worse yet, you are missing out on drugs. You get yourself a drink. You wait five minutes and then decide to reconnoiter. You check the Men's Room first and then the Ladies'. A woman in a leather jump suit is teasing her hair at the mirror. 'Plenty of room,' she says. You hear sounds coming from one of the stalls. Giggling. Looking down, you see Elaine's pumps and Theresa's sandals under the door.

'Save a little for me,' you say, pushing on the door of the stall, which yields just enough to allow you to stick your head in and discover Elaine and Theresa engaged in an unnatural act. You look on in wonder and confusion.

'Want to join the party?' Elaine asks.

'*Bon appétit*,' you blurt, and you lurch out of the Ladies' Room. You emerge into a din of bodies and music.

It is very late.

A WOMB WITH A VIEW

You dream about the Coma Baby. You sneak into the hospital, past the nurses and reporters. Nobody can see you. A door with a plaque reading *L'Enfant Coma* opens into the Department of Factual Verification. Elaine and Amanda are doing lines on Yasu Wade's desk and swearing in French. The Coma Mom is stretched out on your desk in a white gown. IV bottles are hanging from the bookshelves, tubes plugged into her arms. The gown is open around her midsection. You approach and discover that her belly is a transparent bubble. Inside you can see the Coma Baby. He opens his eyes and looks at you.

'What do you want?' he says.

'Are you going to come out,' you ask.

'No way, José. I like it in here. Everything I need is pumped in.'

'But Mom's on her way out.'

'If the old lady goes, I'm going with her.' The Coma Baby sticks his purple thumb in his mouth. You try to reason with him, but he does a deaf-and-dumb routine. 'Come out,' you say. Then there is a knock on the door, and you hear Clara Tillinghast's voice: 'Open up. It's the doctor.'

'They'll never take me alive,' the Baby says.

The phone is ringing. The receiver squirts out of your hand like a trout. You keep expecting things to be solid and they're not. You recover the receiver from the floor and apply it to your face. One end goes next to your ear and the other next to your mouth.

'Allô?' You expect the speaker to be French. It's Megan Avery. She wanted to make sure you were awake. Oh yes, you were just making some breakfast. Sausage and eggs.

'I hope you don't mind,' she says. 'But I didn't want you getting in Dutch with Clara again. I thought I'd just make sure you were awake.' *In Dutch?* You make a note to look up this expression in Partridge's dictionary of slang when you get to work. The clock says nine-fifteen. You slept through the eight-thirty alarm. You thank Meg and tell her you will see her at work.

'You're sure you're awake?' she says.

It certainly feels like it: headache, sour stomach—all the vital signs.

The generalized dread attendant upon regaining consciousness becomes localized around the image of Clara Tillinghast. You can face the fact that you will probably lose your job, but you do not think you can face Clara. Not on four hours of teeth-grinding sleep. Nor can you stand the sight of those page proofs—the evidence of your failure. In your dreams you have been on the phone to Paris, waiting for the piece of information that would save your life. You were barricaded inside the Department of Factual Verification. Someone was pounding the door. You were holding the line. The operator broke in intermittently, speaking in a language you could not even partly understand. The palms of your hands have been flayed by your fingernails. All night you lay with your arms held rigidly at your sides, your fists clenched.

You consider calling in sick. She would call up sometime during the day to say you were fired and you could hang up before she got abusive. But the magazine goes to press tomorrow and your absence would put pressure on your colleagues. And hiding would rob your failure of dignity. You think of Socrates, the kind of guy who accepted his cup and drank it down. More than this, you cling to the hope that you will somehow escape your fate.

You're dressed and out of the house before ten. The train pulls in just as you make the platform. You consider letting it go by. You're not quite ready yet. You need to hone the steel of your resolution, consider your strategy. The doors close with a pneumatic hiss. But someone in the back is holding one open for a man who is running up the platform. The doors open again. You step onto the train. The car is full of Hasidim from Brooklyn—gnomes in black with briefcases full of diamonds. You take a seat beside one of them. He is reading from his Talmud, running his finger across the page. The strange script is similar to the graffiti signatures all over the surfaces of the subway car, but the man does not look up at the graffiti, nor does he try to steal a peek at the headlines of your *Post*. This man has a God and a History, a Community. He has a perfect economy of belief in which pain and loss are explained in terms of a transcendental balance sheet, in which everything works out in the end and death is not really death. Wearing black wool all summer must seem like a small price to pay. He believes he is one of God's chosen, whereas you feel like an integer in a random series of numbers. Still, what a fucking haircut.

At Fourteenth Street three Rastafarians get on, and soon the car reeks of sweat and reefer. Sometimes you feel like the only man in the city without group affiliation. An old lady with a Macy's bag sitting across from you looks around as if to ask what the world is coming to between these Dracula Jews and zonked-out Africans, but when you smile at her she quickly looks away. You could start your own group—the Brotherhood of Unfulfilled Early Promise.

The *Post* confirms your sense of impending disaster. There's a Fiery Nightmare on page three—an apartment blaze in Queens; and on page four a Killer Tornado that ravaged Nebraska. In the heartland of the country, carnage is usually the result of acts of God. In the city it's man-made—arson, rape, murder. Anything that goes wrong in other parts of the world can usually be attributed to the brutishness of foreigners. It's a nice, simple world view. The Coma Baby is buried on page five. No developments: 'COMA BABY LIVES.' The doctors are considering a premature Caesarean delivery.

It's ten–ten when you come up on Times Square, ten-sixteen when you enter the building. The first elevator down is operated by a kid who looks like his last job was purse snatching. You say good morning and step into the back. After a minute he turns around.

'You gonna tell me what floor or do I gotta be psychic?'

You tell him twenty-nine. Accustomed to Lucio and his gracious peers, this kid strikes you as a rude interloper. He swings the gate closed and latches the door. Halfway up he takes out a Vicks inhaler and snorts on it. This makes your nose twitch sympathetically.

'Twenty-nine,' he says when you get to the floor. 'Ladies' undies and accessories.'

No armed guards waiting for you. You ask Sally, the receptionist, if Clara is in yet.

'Not yet,' she says. You're not sure if this is good news or bad. It could be a case of prolonging the agony. Your colleagues are all huddled around a copy of the New York *Times*, the newspaper of record and of choice here in Fact. Clara told you when you were hired that all members of the department were expected to read the paper thoroughly, excluding the new features sections, but you haven't looked at it in weeks.

'Is it war?' you ask.

Rittenhouse tells you that one of the magazine's writers, a favorite among members of the Department for her scrupulous research and general lack of snottiness toward underlings, has just won a big award for her series on cancer research. *Cancer*. Rittenhouse is particularly pleased because he helped research the articles. 'How about that?' he says. He holds up the paper so you can see the article. You are about to nod your head and impersonate enthusiasm when you see the ad on the facing page. You take the paper from Rittenhouse. There are three women modeling cocktail dresses and one of them is Amanda. You feel dizzy. You sit back on the desk and look at the picture. It's Amanda, all right. You didn't even know she was in New York. The last you heard she was in Paris and planning to stay. She might have had the decency to call as long as she's here. But, then, what is there to say?

Why does she have to haunt you like this? If she would just work in an office like everyone else. Right before she left she mentioned a billboard contract, and you have dreamt of seeing her face, monstrously enlarged, on the wall across from your apartment.

'I think we can all be proud of her,' Rittenhouse says.

'What?'

'Is anything wrong?' Meg asks.

You shake your head and fold up the paper. *Leukemia, Tad said.* Meg tells you that Clara hasn't come in yet. You thank her for the wake-up call. Wade asks if you finished the French piece and you say, 'More or less.'

On the first Tuesday of the month, everyone gets one of the short pieces from the front section of the magazine. The articles have already been divvied up: yours is a report on the annual meeting and reception of The Polar Explorers Society, held this year at the Sherry Netherland. The Polar Explorers are predictably eccentric. They wear divers' watches and obscure military decorations. The hors d'oeuvres at the reception include blubber and smoked Emperor Penguin on Triscuits. You underline *Emperor Penguin* and make a note to check the spelling and whether or not it is edible. Also check spelling on *Triscuits.* As Clara says, one can't be too careful. If you botch a brand name the manufacturer will never let you hear the end of it. If there were no such thing as an Emperor Penguin, or if it were an Empress, three hundred letters would land in the mailroom by the middle of next week. The magazine's most fanatic readers are exactly the sort who would know about

Penguins; ornithology seems to be a particular field of scrutiny, and the slightest error or even vagueness of fact brings a flurry of vigilant correspondence. Just last month an innocuous sketch on birdfeeder activity raised a storm. Readers protested that a certain type of finch couldn't possibly have been at a feeder in Stonington, Connecticut, when the writer claimed to have seen a pair. The letters are still coming in. The Druid called Meg, who worked on the piece, and asked for the opinion of the Audubon Society. The matter is still under advisement. You once wrote a spoof on this genre called 'Birds of Manhattan,' which amused your colleagues but disappeared without a trace when you sent it upstairs to Fiction.

First stop on the present assignment is volume E for Emperor of the *Encyclopaedia Britannica*. No sign of penguins, but there's a fascinating article about embryology with sequential pix of the human egg changing from a salamander at ten days into a homunculus at ten weeks. Eventually you replace E on the shelf and reach for P, one of your favorites. *Paralysis; Paranoid Reactions; Parasitology*, for fun and profit, sub-chapters on rhizopods, ciliates, flagellates and sporozoans. *Pardubice*, a town in the East Bohemian section of Czechoslovakia, an important junction on the Brno–Prague line. *Paris*, with color pix; *Particles, Elementary; Pascal; Pavlov; Peccary*, the New World counterpart of the swine (w. pic.); *Pedro*, the name of five kings of Portugal. Finally, *Penguins*. Flightless and clumsy on land. You know the feeling. The Emperor reaches a height of four feet. No mention of edibility. In the picture they look like eccentric Polar Explorers dressed for a reception at the Sherry Netherland.

Your colleagues are abuzz with details from their own pieces. Wade has one about an inventor who has just received his hundredth patent, for a rotary nose-hair clipping device. Wade gets the inventor on the phone and learns that he was also responsible for the automatic toilet-bowl cleaning revolution, although the big companies stole the idea out from under him and made millions. He gives Wade a long account of this injustice and then says he can't discuss the matter because it's under litigation. All this should be wonderfully diverting, yet there is a forced quality to your laughter. You find it hard to listen to what other people are saying, or to understand the words of the article on which you are ostensibly working. You read the same paragraph over and over, trying to remember the difference between a matter of fact and a matter of opinion. Should you call up the president of the Polar Explorers and ask if it's true that someone was wearing a headdress made out of walrus skin? Does it matter? And why does the spelling of *Triscuit* look so strange? You keep watching the door for Clara. Odd phrases of French run through your brain.

The first thing to do is call the writer and get from him the number of someone who can confirm that such a society exists, that it had a reception at the hotel mentioned, on the date mentioned, that this is a matter of fact and not fiction. Names are named. You must find out if these names belong to real people and, if so, how they are spelled.

Rittenhouse announces that he's just had a call from Clara, who is sick and won't be in: the reprieve you have been waiting for. The boa constrictor wrapped around your heart eases its grip. Who knows? The illness might prove serious.

58

'Actually,' Rittenhouse continues, 'what she said is that she would not be in *this morning*. She's not certain if she will be feeling well enough to come in this afternoon. She can't say at this point.' He pauses and tugs on his glasses, considering whether further qualification is necessary, and then concludes, 'Anyone wishing to consult her may call her at home.'

You ask Rittenhouse if there are any messages.

'Nothing specific,' he answers.

Here is your chance to redeem yourself. A day's work might pull you into the clear with the French piece. You could get the guys in Typesetting to cut you a few hours' slack on the deadline. You could get the Penguin thing out of the way in half an hour and then buckle down to it.

Alors! Vite, vite! Allons-y!

An hour later, the Polar Explorers are put to bed. It's a little after noon, and your energy is flagging. What you need is some lunch to set you right. Return to the French elections with renewed vigor. Maybe pick up *une baguette* with ham and Brie to get you into the proper frame of mind. You ask if anybody wants anything from the outer world. Megan gives you money for a bagel.

On the way out you see Alex Hardy standing in front of the water cooler staring into the aquamarine glass. He looks up, startled, and then, seeing it's only you, he says hello. He turns back to the water cooler and says, 'I was just thinking it could use some fish.'

Alex is a Fiction Editor Emeritus, a relic from the early days, a man who speaks of the venerable founders by their nicknames. He started out as an office boy, made his rep as a writer of satiric sketches of Manhattan high life that abruptly stopped appearing for reasons which are still the subject of speculation, and became an editor. He discovered and encouraged some of the writers you grew up on, but he has not discovered anybody in years and his main function seems to be as the totem figure of Continuity and Tradition. Only one story has emerged from his office in the time you have been on the staff. No one can say whether his drinking is a function of his decline or whether it is the other way around. You expect cause and effect are inextricable in these cases. Mornings he is thoughtful and witty, if somewhat ravaged. In the afternoons he sometimes wanders down to the Department of Factual Verification and waxes nostalgic. You believe he likes you, insofar as he likes anyone. He attached detailed memos to several of your short-story submissions, critiques both blunt and encouraging. He took your work seriously, although the fact that it ended up on his desk was perhaps an indication that it was not taken seriously in the Department of Fiction. You are fond of this man. While others view him as a sunken ship, you have a fantasy: Under his tutelage, you begin to write and publish. His exertion on your behalf renews his sense of purpose. You become a team, Fitzgerald and Perkins all over again. Soon he's promoting a new generation of talent—your disciples—and you're evolving from your Early to your Later Period.

'The old crew would have thought of that,' he says. 'Siamese fighting fish in the water cooler.'

You try to think of a retort along the lines of 'a scale off the fish that bit you,' but it doesn't quite come.

'Where are you headed?'

'Lunch,' you say, before you can think better of it.

The last time you told Alex you were on your way to lunch you needed a stretcher to get you back to the office.

He consults his watch. 'Not a bad idea. Mind if I join you?'

By the time you compose an excuse it seems too late, indeed rude, to say that you're meeting a friend. You don't have to match him drink for drink. You don't have to drink anything, although one wouldn't kill you. One pop would cut neatly through this headache. You'll just tell him you've got a big piece going to press. He'll understand. You could use a friendly presence. You might even confide in him. Tell him some of your problems. Alex is a man familiar with trouble.

'Have you ever considered getting an MBA?' he asks. He has taken you to a steakhouse off Seventh Avenue, a smoky place favored by *Times* reporters and other heavy drinkers. He is dropping ashes on his steak, which lies cold and untouched. Already he has informed you that it is impossible to get a good steak anymore. Beef isn't what it used to be; they force-feed the cattle and inject them with hormones. He is on his third vodka martini. You are trying to stretch your second.

'I'm not saying necessarily go into business. But write about it. That's the subject now. The guys who understand business are going to write the new literature. Wally Stevens said money is a kind of poetry, but he didn't follow his own advice.' He tells you there was the golden age of Papa and Fitzgerald and Faulkner, then a silver age in which he played a modest role. He thinks we're now in a bronze age, and that fiction has nowhere to go. It can run but it can't hide. The new writing will be about technology, the global economy, the electronic ebb and flow of wealth. 'You're a smart boy,' he says. 'Don't be seduced by all that crap about garrets and art.'

He flags down two more martinis, even though your second has yet to run dry.

'I envy you,' he says. 'What are you—twenty-one?'

'Twenty-four.'

'Twenty-four. Your whole life ahead of you. You're single, right?'

First you say no, and then yes. 'Yes. Single.'

'You've got it made,' he says, although he has just informed you that the world you are going to inherit will have neither good beef nor good writing. 'My liver's shot,' he adds. 'My liver's gone to hell and I've got emphysema.'

The waiter comes with the drinks and asks about Alex's steak, if there is anything wrong, if he would prefer something else. Alex says there's nothing particularly wrong with it and tells him to take it away.

'You know why there's so much homosexuality now?' he says after the waiter is gone.

You shake your head.

'It's because of all the goddamned hormones they inject into the beef. An entire generation's grown up on it.' He nods and looks you straight in the eye. You assume a thoughtful, manly expression. 'So, who are you reading these days?' he asks. 'Tell me who the young hotshots are, the up-and-comers.'

You mention a couple of your recent enthusiasms, but presently his attention drifts away and his eyelids flutter. You revive him by asking about Faulkner, with whom he shared an office in Hollywood for a couple of months in the forties. He tells you about a high-speed three-day carouse soaked with bourbon and studded with bons mots.

Alex hardly notices when you say goodbye to him on the sidewalk. His nose is pointed in the direction of the office, his eyes glazed with alcohol and memories. You are a little glazed yourself and a walk is absolutely necessary by way of clearing the head. It's early. There is still time. You are standing at the corner of Walk and Don't Walk—staring at Mary O'Brien McCann, the Missing Person poster girl—when somebody taps you on the shoulder.

'Hey, man, wanna buy a ferret?'

The guy is about your age, acne scars, skittish eyes. He is holding a leash attached to an animal that looks not unlike a dachshund in a fur coat.

'That's a ferret?'

'Guaranteed.'

'What does he do?'

'Makes a great conversation piece. You'll meet a lot of chicks, I'm telling you. You got any rats in your apartment, he'll take care of that. His name's Fred.'

Fred is an elegant-looking animal, apparently well behaved, though you have been known to be deceived by first appearances—witness the Austin Healey you bought with a junkyard under the hood and the genuine Cartier watch. Or the time you picked out a wife. It occurs to you that this would be the perfect mascot for the Department—a real live ferret for the fact finders. You don't really need a pet, you can't even take care of yourself, but perhaps Fred would be the ideal companion for Clara. A parting gift; a token of your affection.

'How much?'

'A hundred.'

'Fifty.'

'All right, eighty-five. My lowest.'

You tell him you'll have to shop around. He gives you a business card with the name of an adult magazine shop. 'Ask for Jimmy,' he says. 'I got boas and monkeys, too. My prices can't be beat. *I'm* insane.'

You walk across town, east on Forty-seventh, past the windows of the discount jewelry stores. A hawker with an armful of leaflets drones in front of a shop door: 'Gold and silver, buy and sell, gold and silver, buy and sell.' No questions asked on the buying end, you presume. Chain-snatchers welcome. You stop to admire an emerald tiara, the perfect gift for your next queen for a day. Fantasy shopping. Of course, when you have money you will not stop here. You're not going to wow your dream girl with a jewelry box that reads Gem-O-Rama. You'll head straight for Tiffany or Cartier. Sit in a chair in the president's office and have them fetch the merchandise for your inspection.

Hasidim hurry up and down the street, holding their hats, stopping to confer with one another, taking care not to eyeball the women in miniskirts. You examine the wares in the window of the Gotham Book Mart, and take note of the sign: WISE MEN FISH HERE.

At Fifth Avenue you cross and walk up to Saks. You stop in front of a window. Inside the window is a mannequin which is a replica of Amanda—your wife, the model. To form the cast for the mannequin, Amanda lay face down in a vat of latex batter for ninety minutes, breathing through a straw. You haven't seen her in the flesh since she left for the last trip to Paris, a few days after she did the cast. You stand in front of the window and try to remember if this was how she really looked.

64

LES JEUX SONT FAITS

You met her in Kansas City, where you had gone to work as a reporter after college. You had lived on both coasts and abroad; the heartland was until then a large blank. You felt that some kind of truth and American virtue lurked thereabouts, and as a writer you wanted to tap into it.

Amanda grew up smack in the heart of the heartland. You met her in a bar and couldn't believe your luck. You never would have worked up the hair to hit on her, but she came right up and started talking to you. As you talked you thought: *She looks like a goddamned model and she doesn't even know it.* You thought of this ingenuousness as being typical of the heartland. You pictured her backlit by a sunset, knee-deep in amber waves of grain. Her lanky, awkward grace put you in mind of a newborn foal. Her hair was the color of wheat, or so you imagined; after two months in Kansas you had yet to see any wheat. You spent most of your time at zoning-board meetings duly reporting on variances for shopping malls and perc tests for new housing developments. At night, because your apartment was too quiet, you went to bars with a book.

She seemed to think you came from Manhattan. Everyone in Kansas thought you came from New York City, whether you said Massachusetts, New England, or just East Coast. She asked about Fifth Avenue, The Carlyle, Studio 54. Obviously, from her magazine reading she knew more about these places than you did. She had visions of the Northeast as a country club rolling out from the glass and steel towers of Manhattan. She asked about the Ivy League, as if it were some kind of formal organization, and later that night she introduced you to her roommate as a member of it.

Within a week she moved in with you. She was working for a florist, and thought she might eventually like to attend classes at the university. Your education daunted and excited her. Her desire to educate herself was touching. She asked you for reading lists. She talked about the day your book would be published. All your plans were aimed at Gotham. She wanted to live on Central Park and you wished to join the literary life of the city. She sent away for the catalogues of universities in New York and typed the résumés which you sent out.

The more you learned of Amanda's early life, the less surprised you were at her desire to start afresh. Her father left home when she was six. He did something on oil rigs, and the last Amanda heard he was in Libya. She got a Christmas card with a picture of a mosque. When she was ten she moved with her mother to a cousin's farm in Nebraska. It was not much of a home. Her mother married a feed-and-grain salesman, and they moved to K.C. The salesman wasn't home often and, when he was, he was either abusive or amorous to both mother and daughter. Amanda had to look after herself; you gathered her mother didn't much care about her. She left home when she was sixteen and moved in with a boyfriend, who lasted until a few months before she met you. He left a note explaining that he was moving to California.

Hers was a childhood grimmer than most, and whenever you were inclined to find her lacking, you reminded yourself to give her credit for endurance.

In the eight months you lived together in Kansas City you visited her mother only once. Amanda was skittish and snappy on the way out. You pulled up to a trailer home on a treeless street. She introduced her mother as Dolly. The feed-and-grain salesman, you surmised, was no longer in the picture. There was tremendous tension in the cramped living room. Dolly chain-smoked Kools, flirted with you, and tossed offhand jabs at Amanda. You could see that Dolly was used to trading on her looks and that she loathed and envied her daughter's youth. The resemblance between the two was strong, except that Dolly had a bust—a difference she alluded to several times. You could tell Amanda was ashamed of her, ashamed of the velvet painting on the wall and the unwashed dishes in the sink, ashamed that her mother was a beautician. When Dolly went to the bathroom— 'to freshen up,' as she put it—Amanda picked up the souvenir Statue of Liberty on top of the television set and said, 'Look at this. It's my mother all over.' She seemed afraid that you would think it was her possession, her taste, afraid that you would identify her with Dolly.

Two years later Dolly was invited to the wedding

back East. Amanda was relieved when she couldn't make it. Her father's invitation was Returned to Sender bearing a collection of Arabic postmarks, Address Unknown. There was no bride's side at the church, no one except a distant, aged aunt and uncle to indicate that Amanda's past extended farther back than the day she arrived with you in New York. That seemed to be just how she wanted it.

If your parents were not thrilled with the living-together arrangement, they went out of their way to give her a home when you returned to the East Coast. Your mother never turned away a stray dog, or heard about the plight of children in other parts of the world without volunteering her time or reaching for her checkbook, and she greeted Amanda as if she were a refugee. Amanda's need to belong was part of her attraction. It was as if you came across one of those magazine ads—'You could turn the page, or you could save a child's life'— and the child in question was *right there*, charming and eager to please. Long before the wedding she took to calling your parents 'Mom and Dad,' and the house in Bucks County 'home.' You were all suckered. Your father once asked you if you didn't think the vast difference in your backgrounds might be a problem in the long haul, the only expressed reservation you remember.

Before you had given the subject much thought, there was on all sides the imminent assumption of marriage. After two years of living together, it seemed the thing to do. You were uneasy—had you lived enough of your life yet?—but your scrutiny of the situation yielded no decisive objections. Amanda was desperate for it. She was always saying she knew you would leave her some-day, as if you had to behave like all the other swine in

68

her life, and apparently she thought that marriage would delay or perhaps even cancel your flight. You did not feel that you could open quite all of your depths to her, or fathom hers, and sometimes you feared she didn't have any depths. But you finally attributed this to an unrealistic, youthful idealism. Growing up meant admitting you couldn't have everything.

The proposal was not entirely romantic. It came about after you had stayed out late with some friends at a party Amanda did not choose to attend. You crept in toward dawn and found her awake watching TV in the living room. She was furious. She said you acted like a single man. She wanted someone who would make a commitment. She didn't want the kind of bum her mother kept bringing home. Your guilt was aggravated by a headache. The sun was coming up and you felt that she was right. You were a bad boy. You wanted to amend your life. You wanted to make it up to Amanda for the shitty life she had had as a kid. You told her you would marry her, and, after sulking *de rigueur*, she accepted.

You arrived in New York with the question of what Amanda was going to do. She had talked about college, but lost interest when it came time to fill out the applications. She wasn't sure what she wanted to do. For several months she watched TV.

People were always telling Amanda she could be a model. One day she stopped in at one of the agencies and came home with a contract.

At the start she hated modeling and you took this as a sign of character. It was okay by you as long as she didn't take it seriously. When she started bringing home all this money it seemed even more okay. Once a week she said she was going to quit. She hated the photographers, the hustlers and the hype. She hated the *models*. She felt guilty making all this money on her looks, in which she didn't believe anyway. You asked her if she thought being a secretary was fun. You told her to stick with it long enough to salt away some money, and then she could do whatever she wanted.

You thought it was kind of kinky that she was doing this as long as she was slumming, as long as she wasn't really a model. You both joked about the *real* models, the ones who developed ulcers over pimples and thought menopause set in at twenty-five. You both despised people who thought an invitation to X's birthday bash at Magique was an accomplishment equal to swimming the English Channel. But you went to X's birthday bash anyway, with your tongues in your cheeks, and while Amanda circulated you snorted some of X's very good friend's private stash of pink Peruvian flake in the upstairs lounge.

Her agent used to lecture her, telling her that as a professional she had to take it more seriously, stop getting ten-dollar haircuts and start going to the right places. Amanda was amused. She did a fine imitation of this agent, a modeling star of the fifties who had the manner of a dorm mother and the heart of a pimp. Over the months, though, you started eating at better restaurants and Amanda started getting her hair cut on the Upper East Side.

The first time she went to Italy for the fall showings, she cried at the airport. She reminded you that in a year and a half you had never spent a night apart. She said to hell with it, she would skip Italy, screw modeling. You convinced her to go. She called every night from Milan. Later on these separations did not seem so traumatic. You postponed your honeymoon indefinitely because she had to do the spring collections three days after the wedding.

You were busy with your own work. There were nights you got home after she was asleep. You looked at her across the breakfast nook in the morning and it often seemed that she was looking through the walls of the apartment building halfway across the continent to the plains, as if she had forgotten something there and couldn't quite remember what it was. Her eyes reflected the flat vastness of her native ground. She sat with her elbows on the butcher-block table, twisting a strand of hair in her fingers, head cocked to one side as if she were listening for voices on the wind. There was always something elusive about her, a quality you found mysterious and unsettling. You suspected she herself couldn't quite identify the longing that she variously attached to you, to her job, to having and spending, to her missing father, and that she had once attached to the idea of getting married. You *were* married. And still she was looking for something. But then she would cook you a special dinner, leave love notes in your briefcase and your bureau drawers.

A few months ago she was packing for a trip to Paris when she began to cry. You asked her what was wrong. She said she was nervous about the trip. By the time the cab arrived she was fine. You kissed at the door. She told you to water the plants.

The day before she was due home, she called. Her voice sounded peculiar. She said she wasn't coming home. You didn't understand.

71

'You got a later flight?'

'I'm staying,' she said.

'For how long?'

'I'm sorry. I wish you well. Really I do.'

'What are you saying?'

'I'm going to Rome for *Vogue* next week and then Greece for location work. My career is really taking off over here. I'm sorry. I don't mean to hurt you.'

'Career?' you said. 'Since when is modeling a fucking *career?*'

'I'm sorry,' she said. 'I have to go now.'

You demanded an explanation. She said she had been unhappy. Now she was happy. She needed space. She said goodbye and promptly hung up.

After three days of transatlantic telexes and calls you located her in a hotel on the Left Bank. She sounded weary when she picked up the phone.

'Is there another man?' you asked. This was the track your mind had followed for three sleepless nights. That wasn't the point, she said, but yes, there was. He was a photographer. Probably the sort who called himself an *artist*. You couldn't believe it. You reminded her that she had said that they were all fags.

She said, '*Au contraire*, Pierre,' ripping the last strained tissues that held your heart intact. When you called again later she had checked out.

A few days afterward, a man purporting to be her lawyer called. The easiest thing all around, he said, would be for you to sue his client for sexual abandonment. Just a legal term, he said. His client, your wife, would not contest anything. You could split the possessions fifty-fifty, although she drew the line at the sterling and crystal. You hung up and wept. *Sexual Abandon-*

ment. He called again a few days later to announce that the car and the joint checking account were yours. You said you wanted to know where Amanda was. He called back and asked how much money you would settle for. You called him a pimp. 'I want an explanation,' you said.

This was months ago. You haven't told anyone at work. When they ask about Amanda you say she's fine. Your father doesn't know. When you talk to him on the phone you tell him everything is swell. You believe your filial duty is to appear happy and prosperous. It is the least you can do for him after all he's done for you. You don't want him to feel bad, and as it is, he has plenty to worry about. Then, too, you feel that spilling the beans would be irrevocable. He would never be able to forgive Amanda. As long as there is a chance she might still return, you don't want him to know about her treachery. You want to tough it out on your own. You plead work, commitments, parties with Nobel Prize-winners as your reasons for staying in the city, even though home is only two hours away. Sooner or later you will have to go, but you want to put it off as long as possible.

You stand in front of Saks Fifth Avenue and stare at the mannequin. Sometime last week, when you started shouting at it, a policeman came over and told you to move along. This is just how she looked at the end, the blank stare, the lips tight and reticent.

When did she become a mannequin?

Back at the office, your resolution to pursue the facts of the recent French elections has staled. A little nap in one of the upstairs offices would be the thing. But you've got to hang in there. You make yourself a cup of instant espresso with four tablespoons of Maxim. Megan tells you there have been three calls for you: one from the president of the Polar Explorers, one from France and another from your brother Michael.

You go into Clara's office to snag the page proofs but they're not on the desk. You ask Rittenhouse about this, and he tells you that Clara called and asked to have the proofs delivered to Typesetting. She also told him to messenger a photocopy down to her apartment.

'Well,' you say, not sure whether you are horrified or relieved. 'That's that, I guess.'

'Do you have any last-minute changes?' Rittenhouse asks. 'I'm sure there's time for some last-minute changes.'

You shake your head. 'I'd have to go back about three years to make all the necessary changes.'

'I don't suppose you remembered that bagel,' Megan says. 'Not to worry. I'm not really hungry anyway. I shouldn't be eating lunch.'

You apologize. You beg her pardon. You tell her there are so damn many things on your mind. You have a bad memory for details. You can tell her the date of the Spanish Armada, but you couldn't even guess at the balance of your checkbook. Every day you misplace your keys or your wallet. That's one of the reasons you're always late. It's so hard just getting in here every morning, let alone remembering all that you're supposed to do. You can't pay attention when people talk to you. So many little things. The big things—at least the big things declare open combat. But these details . . . When you are engaged, life or death, with the main army—then to have these niggardly details sniping at you from the goddamned trees . . .

74

'I'm so sorry, Meg. I'm really, really sorry. I'm just fucking everything up.'

Everyone is looking at you. Megan comes over and puts her arm around your shoulders. She strokes your hair.

'Take it easy,' she says. 'It's only a bagel. Sit down, just sit down and relax. Everything's going to be all right.'

Somebody brings you a glass of water. Along the windows, the potted plants form a jungle skyline, a green tableau of the simple life. You think of islands, palm trees, food-gathering. Escape.

COMA BABY LIVES!

Everyone is so kind. They all want to cover for you, take care of the work on your desk. You have been inclined of late to underestimate the goodness of the race. But Megan, Wade, Rittenhouse—they want you to relax, go home. You don't want to go home. Your apartment is a chamber of horrors. There are instruments of torture in the kitchen cabinets, rings in the walls, spikes on the bed. That place is must-to-avoid. Now that you have released your cramped grip on your responsibilities here, the office seems a quaint place, a place you love because you've already lost your lease.

You wander down to the library to browse through back issues. Marianne, the archivist, is glad to see you. She doesn't get many visitors. All day long she slices issues of the magazine into column-width strips and pastes them into file volumes by author, subject and year. She can tell you where everything is. At first she is disappointed that you are not looking for anything in particular, then amazed when you try to talk to her.

Suspicious when you ask where she lives, she gradually warms to the neutral subject of movies. She is a fiend for the comedies of the thirties and forties—Lubitsch, Capra, Cukor. 'Have you seen *Trouble in Paradise*?' she asks. Oh yes. You certainly have. 'Movies aren't what they used to be,' she says, then hints that a certain so-called film critic known to both of you has trashy taste, not to mention a filthy mouth. Marianne is loyal to the magazine but concerned about infiltrators and climbers who are trying to subvert it from within. The Druid, she worries, is getting bad advice from flatterers. Ducking into the cage of bound volumes, she comes out with 1976. She flips through the pages and puts her finger under a passage containing a four-letter word, its first appearance in the magazine. Granted, it was only fiction, granted that the author had won the National Book Award. But still . . . The dam is crumbling. She considers it an institutional imperative to maintain standards. 'If we don't say No, who will?' You find it touching, almost heartbreaking, this ethic of appearances.

'It's not just that—it's the ads,' you say. 'Look at the ads. Women doing suggestive things with cigarettes, diamonds set in cleavages, nipples everywhere you look.'

'It's everywhere,' she agrees. 'Do you know what a little boy—not eight or ten years old—said to me on the subway this morning?'

'What was that?'

'I can't even repeat it. It was unbelievable.'

You know all about unbelievable; you don't even think about it, much less repeat it.

Later you go up to the empty thirtieth-floor office of a writer on a detox sabbatical. You need a private phone.

You practice your spiel aloud, trying out a British accent. You take a deep breath and dial Amanda's agency. You don't recognize the voice on the other end. You identify yourself as a photographer and say that you are interested in working with Amanda White. Is she in New York, by any chance? The woman on the other end is clearly new, else she would not be so forthcoming with the information. Agency policy is to treat all male callers as potential rapists until proven legitimate. This voice tells you that, as a matter of fact, you are in luck, since Amanda has recently returned to New York for a couple of weeks. 'She's based in Paris, you know.' You ask if she's doing any shows; you'd like to see her on the runway before you book her. The woman mentions a show on Thursday before you hear someone in the background.

'Could I have your name, please?' the woman says, suddenly all vigilance and officiousness. You're already putting the receiver back in its cradle. Now you need only the location of the show, which a quick call to a friend at *Vogue* will provide. In your mind images of revenge and carnage do battle with scenes of tender reconciliation.

Coming back down the inside stairs, you catch a glimpse of Clara marching into the Department. You bolt up the stairs and duck into the Fiction Department Men's Room. You know you will have to face her sooner or later, so it might as well be later. Much later. Your equilibrium is fragile. Perhaps you will meet over drinks someday and laugh about this whole thing. This antic chapter of your life, 'Youthful Folly,' will follow 'Early Promise.' The magazine, ever forgiving, will be proud to claim you as one of its own. You'd gladly sleep

78

through the intervening years and wake up when this part is over. In the meantime, a truckload of Librium and a nice long coma.

You are studying your face in the mirror when the door is opened by Walter Tyler, the travel editor. It's hard to know how to greet Tyler, whether he will stand on the dignity of his position and New England lineage or be just another guy who likes the Yankees. Either way, he'll be offended if you guess wrong. Sometimes the sound of his Christian name in an underling's mouth is sacrilege to his ears. At other times his sense of hale fellowship is offended by a formal address. So this time you nod and say hello.

'I've always wanted to ask someone from Fact,' he says as he takes up his position in front of the urinal, 'does Clara piss in the Men's Room or the Ladies'?'

Now you've got the cue. 'I don't believe she pisses.'

'Marvelous,' he says. It's taking him a while to get going at the urinal. To fill in the silence he asks, 'So how do you like it down there?' as if you had joined the staff last week.

'All in all, I'd rather be in Fiction.'

He nods and tends to business for a while, then says, 'You write, don't you?'

'That seems to be a matter of opinion.'

'Hmmmm.' He shakes and zips. At the door he turns and fixes you with a serious look. 'Read Hazlitt,' he says. 'That's my advice. Read Hazlitt and write before breakfast every day.'

Advice to last a lifetime. Your advice to Walter Tyler is to give it an extra shake or two if he wants to return to his office with dry chinos.

You make for the elevator. Some troll you have never

seen sticks his head out of an office door and immediately retracts it. Rounding the corner, you narrowly miss running down the Ghost.

The Ghost cocks his head to one side, peering, his eyelids fluttering. You say good afternoon and identify yourself.

'Yes,' he says, as if he knew all along who it was. He likes to give the impression that his reclusiveness is an advantage, that he knows more than you could ever expect to. You've only seen him once before, this legend, this man who has been working on a single article for seven years.

You excuse yourself and slide past. For his part, the Ghost glides away silently, as if on wheels. You escape the building without incident. Your jacket, small ransom, is back in the Department.

It is a warm, humid afternoon. Spring, apparently. Late April or early May. Amanda left in January. There was snow on the ground the morning she called, a whiteness that turned gray and filthy by noon and then disappeared down the sewer grates. Later that morning the florist called about the bouquet you ordered for her return. Everything becomes symbol and irony when you have been betrayed.

You slip into a bar on Forty-fourth, a nice anonymous Irish place where no one has anything on his mind except drinking and sports. On a big video screen at the far end of the long wooden bar is some kind of sporting event. You take a stool and order a beer, then turn your attention to the screen. Basketball. You didn't realize basketball was in season this time of year, but you like the soothing back-and-forth movement of the ball. The guy sitting next to you swivels and says, 'Those fucking bums don't know how to handle the full court press.'

You nod and fill your mouth with beer. He seems to expect a response, so you ask him what period it is.

He looks you up and down, as if you were carrying a volume of poetry or wearing funny shoes. 'Third *quarter*,' he answers. Then he turns away.

You keep meaning to cultivate an expertise in spectator sport. More and more you realize that sports trivia is crucial to male camaraderie. You keenly feel your ignorance. You are locked out of the largest fraternity in the country. You'd like to be the kind of guy who can walk into a bar or an eatery and break the ice with a Runyonism about the stupidity of a certain mid-season trade. Have something to hash out with truck drivers and stockbrokers alike. In high school, you went in for lonewolf sports—tennis and skiing. You're not really sure what a zone defense is. You don't understand the sports metaphors in the political columns. Men don't trust a man who missed the Super Bowl. You would like to devote a year to watching every athletic event on ABC and reading all fifty-two issues of *Sports Illustrated*. In the meantime your strategy is to view one playoff game in each sport so as to manage remarks like, 'How about that slap shot by LaFleur in the third period against Boston?' Third quarter?

It's five-twenty and raining when you leave the bar. You walk down to the Times Square subway station. You pass signs for GIRLS, GIRLS, GIRLS, and one that says YOUNG BOYS. Then, in a stationery store, DON'T FORGET MOTHER'S DAY. The rain starts coming down harder. You wonder if you own an umbrella. You've left so many in taxis. Usually, by the time the first raindrop hits the street, there are men on every corner selling umbrellas. Where do they come from, you have often wondered, and where do they go when it's not raining? You imagine these umbrella peddlers huddled around powerful radios waiting for the very latest from the National Weather Service, or maybe sleeping in dingy hotel rooms with their arms hanging out the windows, ready to wake at the first touch of precipitation. Maybe they have a deal with the taxi companies, you think, to pick up all the left-behind umbrellas for next to nothing. The city's economy is made up of strange, subterranean circuits that are as mysterious to you as the grids of wire and pipe under the streets. At the moment, though, you see no umbrella vendors whatsoever.

You wait fifteen minutes on the downtown platform. Everywhere you look you see the Missing Person. An announcement is made that the express is out of service. The tunnel smells of wet clothing and urine. The voice comes over the speaker again to say that the local will be delayed twenty minutes because of a fire on the tracks. You push through the crowd and ascend to the street.

It is still raining. Getting a cab is a long shot. Knots of people on every corner wave their arms at the passing traffic. You walk down Seventh to the bus stop, where some twenty souls huddle in the shelter. A bus packed with grim faces goes by and doesn't stop.

An old woman breaks from the shelter and chases her ride. 'Stop! You stop here!' She whacks the rear of the bus with her umbrella.

Another bus pulls over and disgorges passengers. The sheltered mob clutch umbrellas, purses and briefcases, prepared to fight for seats; but once the bus unloads it's nearly empty. The driver, a massive black man with sweat rings under his arms, says, 'Take it easy,' and his voice commands respect.

You sit down up front. The bus lurches into traffic. Below Fortieth Street the signs on the corners change from Seventh Avenue to Fashion Avenue as you enter the garment district. Amanda's old stomping grounds. Above Forty-second they sell women without clothes and below they sell clothes with women.

At the Thirty-fourth Street stop there is a commotion at the door. 'Zact change,' the bus driver says. A young man standing by the change box is trying to work his hand into the pockets of his skin-tight Calvin Kleins. Peach Lacoste shirt, a mustache that looks like a set of plucked eyebrows. Under one arm he clutches a small portfolio and a bulky Japanese paper umbrella. He rests the umbrella against the change box. 'Step aside,' the bus driver says. 'People getting wet out there.'

'I know all *about* wet, big guy.'

'I just bet you do, Queenie.'

Finally he gets his change together and deposits the coins one at a time, with flourishes, and then cocks his hip at the bus driver.

'Move to the rear, Queenie,' the bus driver says. 'I know you know how to do that.'

The young man walks down the aisle with burlesque movements of the hips and wrist. The bus driver turns and watches him go. When he gets all the way back, the driver picks up the Japanese umbrella he left behind. The driver waits until it is quiet and then says, 'Hey, Tinker Bell. You forgot your wand.'

Everyone watching titters and guffaws. The bus hasn't moved.

Tinker Bell poses at the back of the bus, narrowing his

83

eyes and scowling. Then he smiles. He walks back up the aisle, putting everything he's got into it. He reaches the front and picks up the umbrella. He raises it over his head and brings it down gently on the driver's shoulder, as if he were bestowing knighthood. He does this three times, saying, in a cheery falsetto voice, 'Turn to shit, turn to shit, turn to shit.'

At your apartment building you discover that you have no keys. They're in the pocket of your jacket, which is back in the Department of Factual Verification. Much as you dislike your apartment, it has a bed in it. You want to sleep. You have attained that fine pitch of exhaustion which might make it possible. You've been thinking about that packet of instant cocoa in the kitchen, *Family Feud* on the TV. You were even thinking you might take some Dickens to bed with you. Run your mind over someone else's pathetic misadventures for a change.

An image of yourself curled up on the sidewalk next to a heat vent with the other bums yields to the slightly less grim prospect of asking the super for the spare set of keys. The super, a huge Greek, has glared at you ever since you forgot to pay the customary tribute of cash or booze for Christmas. His wife is no less formidable, being the one who wears the mustache in the family.

Fortunately, the man who answers the door is one of the cousins, a young man whose lack of English and dubious visa status make him eager to oblige. You mime the problem and within minutes you are at your door with the spare set. An envelope with the logo of Allagash's employer, an ad agency, is taped to the door. Inside, a note:

84

Coach:

Having this messengered to your digs after numerous calls to reputed place of employ. Don't you keep office hours anymore? It's tiresome, God knows, but one should try to keep up appearances and also be accessible in case of emergencies like present one. To be brief:

A long-anticipated tryst with the libidinous Inge—pin-up Queen manquée—is endangered by visit of cousin from Boston branch of family. I know what you're thinking: A Boston branch of the Allagash clan? But every family has its dark secrets. Said cousin is doing academic gig at NYU and laying over at the Allagash pad. Must be entertained in grand manner. A well-bred young woman, something of an intellect, who would not be charmed by some junior account exec with toothpaste market surveys on the brain. This assignment calls for nothing less than a speaker of French, a reader of *The New York Review of Books* and that inexpressible guileless charm with which your name is synonymous. Don't let me down, Coach, and everything I possess, including a portion of Bolivia's finest, not to mention my undying gratitude and fealty, is yours. Have taken liberty of informing cousin, one Vicky Hollins, that you will be meeting her at the Lion's Head at seven-thirty, to be joined by self and Inge at earliest possible convenience. Described you as cross between young F. Scott Fitz-Hemingway and the later Wittgenstein, so dress accordingly.

Yrs. in Christ, T.A.

P.S. Should you get lucky with cousin or inflict rare social disease this office will deny all knowledge of your actions.

The presumption of Allagash appalls you. When you call his office to decline the invitation, he has already left. Well, it's his cousin and his problem. The thought of the Allagash genes and the Boston climate is a frightening one. His brief description suggests a prig, a wearer of plaid tartan skirts, a former contender on the green New England hockey fields and a noncontender in the Looks Department. Born into the manner that Clara has been faking ever since she went to Vassar. You will unplug the phone and say you never got the letter.

You switch on the tube and throw yourself on the couch. Much fun on *Family Feud*. Ten grand rides on a question about garden tools; Richard Dawson flexes his eyebrows. But you keep glancing at the clock. By seven-twenty you are on your feet, pacing between the two rooms, kicking your laundry into the corners. If you know Tad, he won't even make it to the Lion's Head and the poor girl will be left to the slender mercies of all those aspiring actors and failed writers. A few friendly drinks with her wouldn't kill you. You throw on a jacket and head out.

You arrive ten minutes late. It's two deep along the bar and no sign of Allagash. No sign of anybody wearing a plaid tartan skirt and Allagash features.

In the middle of your beer you spot a woman standing alone beside the coatrack, holding a drink and reading a paperback. She looks up from time to time and then returns to her reading. You watch her eyes as they move around the room. Her face is intelligent. The hair is somewhere between strawberry and gold, you can't tell in this light. That she could be the Boston Allagash is too much to hope. Boots, jeans and a black silk shirt. Not a patch of madras or tartan on her.

The hell with Allagash and his race. You would like to speak to this woman, ask her if she's eaten dinner. Perhaps she is the one who could make you forget your cares and woes, start eating breakfast, take up jogging. You edge in closer. The book in her hand is Spinoza's *Ethics*. No flies on that. She looks up again and you catch her eye.

'We don't get many Rationalists in here,' you say.

'I'm not surprised,' she says. 'Too dark.' Her voice is like gravel spread with honey. She holds a smile just long enough to encourage you and then returns to her book. You wish you could remember something about Spinoza, besides the fact that he was excommunicated.

Allagash appears in the door. You consider hiding out in the Men's Room, but he spots you and comes over. Tad shakes your hand. Then he plants a kiss on the philosopher's cheek.

Introductions, brief confusion about whether everyone has met. Allagash tells you, with a deprecating roll of his eyes, that Vicky is studying Philosophy at Princeton. He introduces you as a literary cult celebrity whose name has not yet reached the provinces.

'Hate to dash out again. But I said seven-thirty and Inge thought I said ten. So she's still in *media* dress, as we say. Got to get crosstown and pick her up. But let's by all means meet for dinner.' He consults his watch. 'Let's say nine-thirty. Better make it ten. Ten o'clock at Raoul's. Don't forget.' He slips a glass vial into your

87

pocket while he's kissing Vicky. Then he's gone in a wake of camel's hair.

Vicky seems confused by her cousin's hospitality. 'Did you catch all that?'

'More or less.' You know you will not see Tad for the rest of the night.

'He said seven-thirty and his date thought he said ten?'

'It's a common mistake.'

'Well,' she says, putting her book in her purse. This could have been a very awkward situation, but she's taking it in stride. 'What now?'

Allagash has bribed you with a piece of the rock. You could invite her back to your place to share the booty, but somehow you think not. Although you suppose she would appreciate it, you'd like to see if it's possible to get through an evening without chemicals for a change. Hear yourself and another person talk without Speedy Gonzales South American accents.

You ask her if she wants to stay for another drink, and she asks what you want to do. Eventually you ascend the stairs to the street. You think of Plato's pilgrims climbing out of the cave, from the shadow world of appearances toward things as they really are, and you wonder if it is possible to change in this life. Being with a philosopher makes you think.

You linger at the edge of Sheridan Square to watch an acrobat ride a unicycle across a tightrope strung between the fences. A teenager in the crowd turns to Vicky and says, 'He did that between the towers of the World Trade Center.'

'Can you imagine,' a woman asks.

'Sounds like my job,' you say.

When the acrobat passes the hat you throw in a buck. You walk west, without any firm destination in mind. Vicky is telling you about her work. She's in her third year of graduate school, came in for an NYU conference at which she will read a rebuttal to an article entitled: 'Why There Are No People.'

The evening is cool. You find yourself walking the Village, pointing out landmarks and favorite townhouses. Only yesterday you would have considered such a stroll too New Jersey for words, but tonight you remember how much you used to like this part of the city. The whole neighborhood smells of Italian food. The streets have friendly names and cut weird angles into the rectilinear map of the city. The buildings are humble in scale and don't try to intimidate you. Gay giants stride past on hypertrophied thighs, swathed in leather and chains, and they do intimidate you.

Vicky stops in front of an antique shop window on Bleecker and points to a wooden carousel horse, painted red and white, mounted on a pedestal. 'I'd like to have the kind of house someday where a carousel horse wouldn't be out of place in the living room.'

'How about a jukebox?'

'Oh, definitely. There's always room for a jukebox. And maybe a pinball machine. A really old one with Buck Rogers stuff.'

As you resume your walk she describes the house in which she grew up. A rambling Tudor affair on the shore in Marblehead, which started out early in the century as a summer house and, despite the formal dining room, never quite lost its wet-towel ambience. There were empty rooms to play in, and a closed alcove under the stairs which no one could enter without her permission.

89

Pets galore. A gazebo where the four girls had tealess tea parties presided over by Vicky's eldest sister. Their father kept chickens in the boathouse and spent years trying to bring a vegetable patch to life. Every morning he woke up at five and went for a swim. Mother stayed in bed till her daughters and the pets gathered in her room.

What she tells you is enhanced by the increasing animation of her gestures and facial expressions and becomes a vivid image of this childhood Arcadia. You notice for the first time that she has freckles. You didn't know they still made them. You imagine her as a child carrying a bucket of sand down to the beach. You see yourself watching from the bluff, through a time warp, saying: *Someday I will meet this girl*. You want to watch over her through the interval, protect her from the cruelty of schoolchildren and the careless lust of young men. The irrevocable past tense of the narration suggests to you some intervening tragedy. You suspect a snake in the vegetable garden.

'Your parents?' you say.

'Divorced three years ago. Yours?'

'Happy marriage,' you say.

'You're lucky.'

Lucky is not the word you would have chosen, except maybe out of a hat.

'Do you have any brothers or sisters?' she asks.

'Three brothers. The youngest are twins.'

'That's nice. Symmetrical, I mean. I've got three sisters. Boys were very mysterious to us.'

'I know what you mean.'

'Listen. Do we have to meet Tad later?'

'Tad has no intention of meeting us. Or, rather, he has good intentions, but he won't be there.'

'Did he tell you that?'

'No, it's just that I know him. Tad is always on his way, but he seldom arrives.'

'What did he tell you about me?' she asks, after you have been seated in the courtyard of a café on Charles Street. She has a conspiratorial smile. She seems to think that your allegiance to Tad will crumble before this new intimacy.

'Not much,' you say.

'Come on.'

'He tried to build you up. I was expecting a field hockey player with monogrammed knee socks and thick glasses.'

She does not press for the compliment. Just smiles and looks down at the menu.

You tell her what a good guy Tad is. You like his energy and his style—*joie de vivre, je ne sais quoi, savoir-faire, sprezzatura.* You are nearly sincere. Having a cousin like Vicky tips the scales in his favor. You are inclined to cut him some slack. Not necessarily the man for a heart-to-heart, but indispensable in a party situation. You tell her that Tad has been a good friend in time of need. If not exactly sensitive, then generous in his own careless way. 'Are you two very close?' you ask.

'I think he's an ass,' she says.

'Exactly.' Everything she says is right. She's got you in the palm of her unclenched hand. You love the way she raises her water glass to her lips, the ease she has with her hands and mouth. You are afraid you are staring too intently into her eyes, even though this intimacy does not appear uninvited.

'What's your job like?' she says. 'I guess I should be pretty impressed.'

'Please don't be. I don't like it much. I don't think they much like me.'

'I know people who would kill for a job like that.'

You'd rather she wasn't too impressed with a job you may not have the next time you see her. You wish that no one, including yourself, had ever been impressed. You wince to think of all the self-aggrandizement you have heaped on this subject. You describe for her the tedious procedure of factual verification, the long hours over dictionaries, phone books, encyclopedias, government pamphlets. You tell her how you were reprimanded for suggesting stylistic changes.

'I've only known you a couple of hours,' Vicky says, 'but it doesn't seem to me like your kind of job.'

'I don't think it is.'

Standing on the corner of West Fourth Street and Seventh Avenue, you are ostensibly waiting for a cab to take Vicky back to Tad's apartment. Empty cabs keep rolling past and you and Vicky continue to talk. You have talked about work, money, Cape Cod, breakfast cereals and the Mind-Body Problem. You have already written down her address and phone number in Princeton. Walking back from the restaurant, she took your arm and you have been holding hers ever since. You feel that passing males—at least the heteros—look on with envy. You consider performing an act of inspired madcappery at her behest: stealing the hat from a policeman, or the handcuffs from one of the gay caballeros of Christopher Street. Maybe climb a lamppost and wave her scarf from the top.

'*Now* I *really* have to go,' she says.

'I wish you didn't.'

'Me too.' She steps forward and kisses you. You return the kiss and prolong it. Time passes. You become aroused. You consider asking her back to your apartment, and think better of it. You want to leave this flawless evening intact. Already you are thinking of the walk home, the review of details and nuances in bed before you sleep, of the phone call which you have promised to make tomorrow morning. You are thinking that Clara Tillinghast can go to hell because tonight you are happy.

PYGMIES, FERRETS AND DOG CHOW

Over coffee and eggs you read both *Times* and *Post*, including sports pages. Coma Mom is fading fast. Boston wins on the basketball court, loses in baseball. The waitress has filled your cup six times and it's only eight-thirty. At six-thirty you woke like a man accustomed to the hour, feeling a clarity compounding the exhilaration from your night with Vicky and the dread of your morning with Clara. You called the former when you woke up. She told you Tad never made it home and that she slept very well once she convinced the doorman she was a legitimate visitor. You want to call her again, maybe tell her all about your breakfast.

You're at the office by nine-thirty. Meg's already there. She looks embarrassed when she sees you. You can guess what happened yesterday after Clara returned. By now everybody has the story of your incompetence. You don't bother to ask.

Meg, though, can't bear the suspense. She comes over to your desk and says, 'Clara's in a rage. She says the

French piece is a mess but it's too late to pull it from the issue. There was a big pow-wow last night to decide what to do.' You nod your head. 'What happened?' she asks, as if an easy answer had inexplicably eluded her.

Rittenhouse comes in and performs his customary greeting, which falls somewhere between a nod and a full bow. You will miss his bow ties and his Edwardian bookkeeper manner. After hanging his scarf and derby on the coatrack he joins Megan at your desk, looking even more grave and mournful than usual.

'We're talking about the French piece,' Megan says.

Rittenhouse nods. 'I think the way they changed the schedule was disgraceful. Although they must have had their reasons.'

'You didn't have nearly enough time,' Megan says. 'Everybody knows his research is slipshod.'

'We're behind you all the way,' Rittenhouse says.

There's not much comfort in this, but you appreciate the thought.

Wade saunters in and stops in front of your desk. He looks at you and clicks his tongue. 'What kind of flowers do you want on your grave? I already have the epitaph: *He didn't face facts.*'

Megan says, 'Not funny, Yasu.'

'Well, Jesus. Even Lear had a clown.'

'This could've happened to any of us,' Megan says. 'We've got to stick together.'

You shake your head. 'It's my own damn fault. I dug my own grave.'

'You didn't have enough time,' Megan says. 'It was a sloppy article.'

'We've all seen errors slip through the net,' Rittenhouse adds.

'How bad could it be?' Megan asks. 'You got most of it done, didn't you?'

'I really don't even know,' you say. They're wondering: *Could this happen to me?* and you would like to reassure them, tell them it's just you. They're trying to imagine themselves in your shoes, but it would be a tough thing to do. Last night Vicky was talking about the ineffability of inner experience. She told you to imagine what it was like to be a bat. Even if you knew what sonar was and how it worked, you could never know what it feels like to have it, or what it feels like to be a small, furry creature hanging upside down from the roof of a cave. She said that certain facts are accessible only from one point of view—the point of view of the creature who experiences them. You think she meant that the only shoes we can ever wear are our own. Meg can't imagine what it's like for you to be you, she can only imagine herself being you.

You want to thank them for their concern, yet you could never truly explain how this fiasco came about.

The group disperses. It's coming up on ten o'clock. You don't have anything to do. Your hands move around the desk collecting paper clips and pens, rearranging stacks of paper. The Druid sneaks past the door. His eyes meet yours and then he looks away. You feel a touch of heat in the cheeks. His renowned manners have failed him. That is something, at least. Tell your children you were the only man in history snubbed by the Druid.

On your desk is a short story that you have been wanting to read. You follow the lines of print across the page, and it's like driving on ice with bald tires; no traction. You get up and fix yourself a cup of coffee. The others are hunched over their desks. In the quiet you can hear the scratching of pencil lead on paper and the hum of the refrigerator. You go to the window and look down on Forty-fifth Street. Maybe you can spot Clara on her way in and let her have it with a flower pot. Although the pedestrians are indistinct, you can make out a man sitting on the sidewalk playing a guitar. You open the window and stick your head out, but the traffic noise covers the music. Someone taps your hip. Wade is pointing toward the door, where Clara is standing.

'I would like to see you in my office immediately.'

Wade whispers, 'If I were you I would've jumped.'

From the window to Clara's office is a very short distance. Much too short. You are there. She slams the door from the inside, takes the seat in front of the desk and stares you down. She doesn't ask you to sit, so you do. This is shaping up even worse than you anticipated. Still, you feel a measure of detachment, as if you had suffered everything already and this were just a flashback. You wish that you had paid more attention when a woman you met at Heartbreak told you about Zen meditation. Think of all of this as an illusion. She can't hurt you. Nothing can hurt the samurai who enters combat fully resolved to die. You have already accepted the inevitability of termination, as they say. Still, you'd rather not have to sit through this.

'I would like to know what happened.'

A dumb question. Far too general. You draw a good breath. 'I screwed up.' You might add that the writer of the piece in question really screwed up, that you improved the thing immeasurably, and that the change of scheduling was ill-advised. But you don't.

'You screwed up.'

You nod. It's true. In this case, however, honesty doesn't make you feel a whole lot better. You're having trouble meeting her glare.

'May I be so bold as to ask for a little elaboration? Really, I'm interested.'

Sarcasm now.

'Just *how* did you screw up, exactly?'

More ways than you can say.

'Well?'

You're already gone. You are out the window with the pigeons. You try to alleviate the terror by thinking how ridiculous her French braids look, like spinnakers on a tugboat. You suspect that deep down she enjoys this. She's been looking forward to it for a long time.

'Do you realize just how serious this is?' she demands. 'You have endangered the reputation of this magazine. We have built a reputation for scrupulous accuracy with regard to matters of fact. Our readers depend on us for the truth.'

You would like to say, Whoa! Block that jump from facts to truth, but she is off and running.

'Every time this magazine goes to press that reputation is on the line, and when the current issue hits the stands you will have compromised that reputation, perhaps irretrievably. Do you know that in fifty years of publication there has only been one printed retraction?'

Yes, you know.

'Have you considered that everyone on the staff will suffer as a result of your carelessness?'

Clara's office is none too large under the best of circumstances, and it is getting smaller by the minute. You raise your hand. 'Can I ask what errors you have found?'

She has the list ready to hand: Two accents reversed, an electoral district in central France incorrectly identified as northern, a minister ascribed to the wrong department. 'This is just what I've been able to find so far. I'm scared to death of what I'll uncover as I go along. The proofs are a mess. I can't tell what you've verified and what you haven't. The point is, you have not followed standard procedure, which by this time should be second nature to you, which procedure is thoroughly outlined in your manual, which procedure is the net result of many years of collective labor, and proper application of which ensures that, insofar as possible, errors of fact do not appear in this magazine.'

Clara is red in the face. Although Wade claims she has recently taken up jogging, her wind is lousy.

'Do you have anything to say for yourself?'

'I don't think so.'

'This isn't the first time. I've given you the benefit of the doubt before. You seem unable to perform the duties required for this job.'

You're not about to take issue with anything she says. You would confess to all of the crimes detailed in the *Post* today in exchange for an exit visa. You nod your head gravely.

'I'd like to hear what you have to say.'

'I assume I'm fired.'

She looks surprised. She drums her fingers on the desk and glowers. You're pleased that her hands are shaking. 'That's correct,' she says at last. 'Effective immediately.'

'Anything else?' you say, and when she doesn't answer you stand up to go. Your legs are trembling, but you don't think she notices.

'I'm sorry,' she says as you open the door.

In a stall of the Men's Room you wait for composure to return. Despite your relief, and your feeling that you got no worse than you expected, your hands are twitching to the beat of your knees. Pointlessly exploring your pockets, you come up with a small glass vial, Tad's gift. In terms of improving your mood, this might be just what the doctor ordered. Or precisely not; bad medicine.

You shake a healthy snort onto the back of your hand. Lifting hand to face, you lose your grip on the vial, which drops with sickening accuracy into the toilet bowl, bounces once against the porcelain and then submerges with an insolent splash that resembles the sound of a very large brown trout spitting out the hook of a very small and painstakingly presented dry fly.

Maybe this isn't your day. You should've checked your horoscope in the *Post*.

Huddled around Rittenhouse's desk, the others fall silent when you return.

'Well?' Megan says.

Though your knees are still shaking, you have this strange feeling of omnipotence. You could dive out the window and fly over the rooftops. You could pick up your desk with one hand. Your former colleagues carry the stamp of oppression on their brows.

'It's been nice working with you.'

'They didn't,' Megan says. 'They couldn't.'

'They did.'

'What exactly did she say?' Rittenhouse asks.

'The gist of it is that I'm fired.'

'They can't do that,' Megan says.

'Perhaps we could take your case to the employee arbitration committee,' Rittenhouse says. 'As you know, I'm a member of the committee.'

You shake your head. 'Thanks, but I don't think so.'

'Well, at least they could allow you to resign if that's what you want to do,' Wade says.

'It doesn't matter,' you say. 'It really doesn't.'

They want to hear exactly what was said, and you oblige them as well as you can. They advise you to make a stand, appeal the decision, ask for clemency, plead special circumstances. They are not convinced that you'd rather switch than fight. Clara does not reappear. Wade thinks you ought to seize this opportunity for a dramatic parting gesture. He suggests hanging a moon in the Druid's office. When Megan asks what you're going to do now, you say you don't know.

'No point in sticking around here. I'll pick up my things tomorrow.'

'Can we have lunch tomorrow?' Megan asks. 'I'd really like to talk to you.'

'Sure. Lunch tomorrow. I'll see you then.'

You shake hands all around. Megan catches you at the elevator. 'I forgot to tell you. Your brother Michael called again. He sounds really eager to talk to you.'

'Thanks. I'll call him. Thanks for everything.'

Megan puts her hands on your shoulders and kisses you. 'Don't forget lunch.'

Down on the street, you clamp your sunglasses to your face and wonder where to go. An old question, it seems to come up more and more frequently. You've lost whatever bravura you possessed a few minutes ago. It's just beginning to sink in that you have lost your job.

You are no longer associated with the famous magazine where, in time, you might have become an editor or a staff writer. You remember how excited your father was when you got the job, and know how he's going to feel when he hears you have been fired.

You go over and listen to the sidewalk guitarist. He's playing blues, and every phrase is aimed directly between your third and fourth ribs. You listen to 'Ain't Got No Home,' 'Baby Please Don't Go,' 'Long Distance Call.' You turn away when he starts into 'Motherless Children.'

On Forty-second near Fifth a kid falls into stride beside you.

'Loose joints. Genuine Hawaiian sens. Downers and uppers.'

You shake your head. The kid looks all of thirteen.

'Got coke. Got coke if you wannit. Uncut Peruvian flake. Closest you're gonna get to God these days.'

'How much?'

'Fifty dollar the half.'

'Half what? Half borax and half mannitol?'

'Pure stuff. Uncut.'

'Sure thing. Thirty-five.'

'I'm a businessman. Not a fie-lanthropuss.'

'I can't do fifty.'

'Forty-five. You're robbing me.'

You follow the kid into the park behind the library. Look both ways before you enter. His brother may be waiting with a baseball bat. Two elderly male civilians are throwing bread at the pigeons. The kid leads you over to a big tree where he tells you to wait. Then he runs to the other side of the park. You can't believe you're doing this. Encouraging juvenile delinquency.

Wasting your money on street toot. The kid comes running out from behind the fountain.

'I want a taste.'

'Shit,' he says. 'Who you think you are—John DeLorean? You be buying a half. I'm telling you it's good.'

The classic standoff. His salesman's smile is disappearing. You suddenly realize you are about to be ripped off, but you hang onto the hope of a buzz.

'Let me see it at least.' He walks behind the tree and opens the packet. You're buying some kind of white powder and the weight looks about right, not that this means much. You give him the money. He stuffs it in his pocket and backs off, watching you as he retreats.

As long as you are relatively secluded you figure you'll try some. You use your office key for a spoon. The first taste is like Drano. The second time you're ready for it, and it's not so bad. Still, it feels like your nose is emitting sparks. Whatever the stuff is, you hope it's not lethal. You hope there's something South American in the mix. After bumping yourself up again you fold the packet. You *think* you can feel a lift coming on. You want to go somewhere, do something, talk to someone, but it's only eleven-thirty in the morning and everyone else in the world has a job.

Much later, near midnight, you return to the office. Tad Allagash is with you. You are both in high spirits. You have decided that you are better off without that pissant job, that it is a good thing you got out when you did. A longer tenure in the Department of Factual Verification would have eventually resulted in an incurable case of anal retentiveness. You're well shut of the place. This conclusion does not absolve Clara Tillinghast of her many crimes against humanity, and particularly against you. Tad casts it as a matter of honor. In his part of the country these matters are settled with horsewhips and ivory-headed canes. He says the caning and horsewhipping of libelous editors has a long, dignified history. The present case, however, calls for something more subtle. The better part of the night has been devoted to devising and executing the proper response. Part of the plan involved getting in touch with Richard Fox, the hatchet man, and telling him some of the nasty secrets to which you have become privy after two years at the magazine. You were inclined to let it slide, but Tad appealed to your fighting spirit. He placed the call and got Fox's answering service. He left a message, calling himself Deep Shoat, an inside source, and promised major revelations. He left Clara's number. You proceeded to phase two.

The nightwatchman nods at your employee ID card and tells you to sign the book. You sign in as Ralph Kramden and Ed Norton. Tad explains that your errand is urgent; First Amendment issues are at stake. The watchman is used to writers coming and going at strange hours, and doesn't have the energy to worry about two more drunks. He points to the freight elevator and then goes back to his wrestling magazine. He doesn't even ask about the suitcase.

When the elevator begins to ascend, shrill, birdlike noises issue from the bag. The sound of the animal's distress gives you pause. This is probably a bad idea. You're not particularly worried about Clara, but you feel sorry for Fred the Ferret in his role of unwitting accomplice.

'*Pas de* sweat,' Tad says. 'This is almost too easy.

Maybe we should have tried for the wolf cub.' Initially Tad wanted to get hold of a bat, but when you mentioned the ferret his eyebrows climbed his forehead in delight.

The door opens on the twenty-ninth floor. You both stand inside the elevator, listening. It's quiet. Tad looks at you inquisitively. You nod and step out into the reception area. Tad follows. The whoosh of the elevator doors sounds like a passing freight train. There is a hollow echo of cables and gears, and then it's quiet again. Tad leans over and whispers in your ear, 'Take no prisoners.'

You lead the way down the hall, carrying the suitcase. Up to the corner all the offices are dark, but you remain anxious. The Druid is known for his insane hours and you briefly picture yourself turning the corner and facing him. You would die of mortification. Still, the challenge of the caper has got your adrenaline going. No thrills without chills. The forty-five-degree mirror at the corner shows no lights on farther up.

Clara's door is locked, but that's no problem. You have a key to the Department office, and a key to her office is hidden behind—what else?—volume K of the *Encyclopaedia Britannica*. It's the work of a moment.

You let yourselves into Clara's office and close the door. 'They entered the lair of the dragon,' Tad whispers. You turn on the light. 'You call this an office?' he says. 'It looks like an uppity maid's room.'

Now that you're here, you're not quite sure what to do. The ferret is scratching wildly inside the suitcase.

'Where's the leash?' you ask.

'I don't have it.'

'I gave it to you.'

'We don't need the leash. It'll be a better surprise to have the sucker pop out from a desk drawer.'

Tad lays the suitcase on the floor and flips the latches, then stands back. 'Let him out,' he says. You lift the top. Things happen quickly after that. The animal sinks its teeth into your hand. You jerk your arm away. There's a foot of ferret still attached. The pain is terrific. You shake your arm savagely, flinging the thing toward Tad. Fred tears a swath out of Tad's pants leg before landing on the floor, careening around the room, upsetting boxes and finally holing up in the bookshelf behind a row of bound volumes of *Scientific American*.

Your hand is on fire. It is connected by red-hot wires to your brain, which is throbbing inside your skull. You shake your arm, spattering little red droplets on the walls. Tad's face is white. He leans down and gingerly examines the tear in his pants just below the crotch.

'Good Christ! One more inch . . .'

He is interrupted by a thump on the door.

'Oh, Jesus!'

There is another thump and then a hoarse voice: 'Open up! I know you're in there.'

You recognize the voice—it could be worse—and put a finger to your lips. Taking a pencil and pad from Clara's desk, you clumsily write, with your uninjured left hand, *Is the door locked?*

Tad gives you a search-me look.

There is a steady wheezing outside the door and another knock. The doorknob turns one way and then the other. Allagash is poking your arm and mouthing frantic interrogatives. The latch clicks and the door swings open. Alex Hardy stands in the doorway. He nods his head gravely as if you were the very two people he expected to find in Clara's office at midnight. You are trying to devise a quick story that will wash. Tad is brandishing a yardstick that he found behind the door.

'You gave us a scare, Alex. I couldn't imagine who would be wandering around here at this time of night. I was just looking for my wallet. I was in here this morning . . .'

'Pygmies,' Alex says.

Tad looks at you inquisitively. You shrug.

'I am surrounded by pygmies.'

You now see that Alex is stupendously drunk. You wonder if he recognizes you.

'I knew the giants,' he says. 'I worked with the giants. The guys whose words went out into the world and kicked ass. Okay, girls too. Women, whatever. I'm talking about ambition. I'm talking about talent. Not like these precious turds around here. These goddamned pygmies.' Alex thumps his fist on the wall. The ferret leaps out from hiding and bolts for the door. It snakes its way between Alex's legs. Alex tries to get out of the way. The ferret's claws scrabble on the linoleum. Alex struggles for equilibrium, grabbing first at the door frame, then, as he starts to fall, at the coatrack, and finally at a bookshelf which goes down with him. The top hooks of the falling coatrack narrowly miss Tad's face. Alex is sprawled on the floor in a heap of books. You're not sure how hard he hit.

'Let's get out before he comes to,' Tad says.

'I can't leave him like this.' You crouch down and check him out. He's breathing; already the office smells like liquor.

'Come on. Do you want to *explain* what we're doing here? Let's go.'

You clear some of the books from Alex's chest and stretch his legs out. Down the hall a phone starts ringing.

'He's fine, for Christ's sake. We're dead meat if we get caught in here.'

'Get the suitcase,' you say. You take the cushion from Clara's chair and put it under Alex's head. His feet are sticking out the door so you can't close it. The elevator takes days to arrive and makes a racket like an All Points Bulletin.

In the lobby, the watchman is still absorbed in his magazine. You keep your hand in your jacket pocket while he unlocks the door to the street. Outside, you both break into a sprint.

Neither of you speaks a word until you're in the cab. At Tad's place you wash and examine the wound while he changes his pants. At first you're concerned. You're trying to remember the last time you had a tetanus shot when suddenly you think of rabies. The signature of the teeth is clearly visible between your thumb and index finger. The punctures are deep but not wide. Tad assures you that stitches aren't necessary. He says that if the animal was rabid, it would not have been so friendly before you put it in the suitcase. He pours a glass of vodka over the wound. You're eager to be reassured. You don't want to go to the hospital. You hate hospitals and doctors. The smell of denatured alcohol nauseates you. Then you think of Alex. Maybe he suffered a concussion. Only the *Post* could make this funny: FAULKNER FRIEND FALLS AFOUL OF FURRY FIEND.

'He's just sleeping off his drunk,' Tad says.

'Let's hope.'

'Love to be there in the morning when the gang starts coming in for work.'

Tad gets some cotton pads and adhesive tape from the medicine cabinet and then cuts some lines on the table while you fuss with the first aid.

With the application of anesthetics, the pain and guilt recede and the episode becomes a source of hilarity. 'Giants,' Tad says. 'Fucking giants. I'm thinking, Who is this dwarf calling me a goddamned pygmy? Then— boom. Fred the Ferret to the rescue. *De casibus virorum illustrium*, as we used to say in Latin class.'

'Say what?'

'Something about the fall of famous men.'

Tad suggests taking the show on the road. He says it's early yet. You say it's not that early, and he points out that it's not as if you had a job to wake up for in the morning. This is a convincing point. You agree to one drink at Heartbreak.

In the cab on the way downtown, Tad says, 'Thanks for taking Vicky off my hands. Inge is eternally grateful.'

'My pleasure.'

'Really? Got lucky, did you?'

'None of your business.'

'Are you serious?' He leans over and looks into your face. 'You are serious. Well, well. To each his own.'

The cabby swerves between lanes, muttering in a Middle Eastern language.

'Anyway, it's nice to see you getting over this Amanda deal. I mean, she wasn't hard to look at. God knows. But I don't see why you felt like you had to marry her.'

'I've been wondering that myself.'

'Weren't you suspicious when you saw the sign on her forehead?'

'Which sign was that?'

'The one that said, *Space to Let. Long and Short Term Leasing*.'

'We met in a bar. It was too dark to read.'

'Not so dark that she couldn't see you were her ticket out of Trailer Park Land. Bright lights, big city. If you really wanted to do the happy couple thing you shouldn't have let her model. A week on Seventh Avenue would warp a nun. Where skin-deep is the mode, your traditional domestic values are not going to take root and flourish. Amanda was trying to get as far from red dirt and four-wheel drive as she could. She figured out she could trade on her looks farther than she got with you.'

For Tad, Amanda's departure was not only not surprising but inevitable. It confirmed his world view. Your heartbreak is just another version of the same old story.

Toward dawn you are riding around in a limo with a guy named Bernie and his two assistants. The assistants are named Maria and Crystal. Crystal is in the back seat with one arm around you and the other around Allagash. Bernie and Maria are facing you from the jump seats. Bernie runs his hand up and down Maria's leg. You're not sure if Tad knew these people before tonight or if they are new friends. Tad seems to think he knows of a party somewhere. Maria says she wants to go to New Chursey. Bernie puts a hand on your knee.

'This is my office,' he says. 'So what do you think?'

You're not sure you want to know what line of work Bernie is in.

'You got an office like this?'

You shake your head.

'Of course you don't. You got Ivy League written all

110

over you. But I could buy you and your old man and his country club. I use guys like you in your button-down shirts to fetch my coffee.'

You nod. You wonder if he's hiring this week and how much it pays.

'You're wondering where the rest of my operation is, right?'

'Not really,' you say.

Tad is disappearing inside Crystal's dress.

'You'd like to know, wouldn't you?' Bernie says. 'You know what? I'm going to tell you. It's down on the Lower East Side, Avenue D and the Twilight Zone. Not too far from where my old *Bubbie* and *Zadie* ruined their health in a sweatshop so their kids could move out to Scarsdale and Metuchen. It's spics and junkies now. I'll show you. I'll even tell you how we move the product. You want to know?'

'I don't think so.'

'Smart. You're a smart boy. I don't blame you for not wanting to know. You know what happens to people who know too much?'

'What's that?'

'They become dog chow. Fucking Purina Dog Chow.'

Tad looks up. 'We handle that account at the agency.'

You ask yourself: How did I get here? The hand that Fred bit throbs painfully. You wonder if it's rabies. You wonder if Alex is all right.

'Used to be,' Bernie says, 'this was your basic grease-ball sector of the economy. You're dealing with your South American spics and your New Jersey dago element. It was an up-and-down scene—all these Latin types with long knives and short tempers—but there was a lot of room for the entrepreneurial spirit. Now we're seeing a different kind of money moving into the neighborhood. I'm talking to three-piece bankers with P.O. boxes in Switzerland. That's one of the things that's happening to this business. But these guys I can deal with. All they want is a good return on their money. Simple. What I'm scared of is my brother Jews—the Hasidim. They're moving in in a big way, crowding out the independent. It's more lucrative than diamonds—hey, they're not stupid. They know an opportunity when they see one. They're all set up for something like this. Liquid capital, world-wide organization, secrecy and trust. How can they lose? I'm telling you, most of the blow in the country already has a Yiddish accent.'

'You mean the guys with the black hats and funky sideburns?' Tad says.

'Believe me,' Bernie says, 'it ain't like they can't afford a haircut. So what do you think of the Yankees this year?'

'Looking good for a pennant,' Tad says.

You bail out at the next red light, claiming car sickness. You are halfway up the block when Bernie calls out—'Hey, you! Don't forget. Dog chow.'

O COUTURE!

Your interest in clothing doesn't normally take you beyond Brooks Brothers and J. Press—and at the moment there seems to be a little credit trouble at both establishments. But this morning you are waiting to enter the ballroom of the Waldorf-Astoria, where a fashion designer is showing his fall line. You copped an invitation from your friend at *Vogue*. He owes you for the time he took your Austin Healey out to Westchester and plowed it into a ten-point buck. You know people who have been hunting for twenty years and have never seen ten points on one deer. The car ended up in a junk-yard outside of Pleasantville. You don't know what happened to the deer, and it's hard to say what happened to the insurance money except that it was gone in two weeks.

At the door, a tall woman with silver hair scrutinizes your invitation. On either side of the door, two large black men in turbans stand with their arms folded across their chests. They are supposed to be Nubian slaves or something. Only an Italian fashion designer could get away with this. The woman seems to be an ethnic group unto herself. She has no eyebrows or eyelashes and her hairline is extremely high, not far from the top of her skull. Was she in an accident, or is she just chic? She is staring at your homemade bandage, which this season is gray and spotted.

'Mister . . .'

'Allagash,' you say, pulling yourself up into military posture. It's the first name that comes to mind. You're not about to use your own.

'From *Vogue*?' she says.

'Since last week.'

She nods and returns your invitation. She narrows her eyes and wrinkles her nose as if to say she will feed you to the giant Nubians if you're lying.

You spot the bar and it appears to be open. The veteran department-store buyers are huddled in the vicinity, clutching glasses. They look like they would rather be in Florida. It could be a mistake to start in at the bar right away; indeed, by any reasonable standard of conduct it is a mistake to be here at all, using someone else's name, with a vague notion of disrupting the proceedings.

You excuse your way up to the bar and order vodka. 'With ice,' you say, when the bartender asks how you want it. 'And one for my date,' you add.

With your two drinks in your hands, you move away from the bar and strike a determined pose in the middle of the crowd, looking around the room with furrowed brow as if you were searching for your very good friend the Revlon Girl. You don't want to be too conspicuous. There is a slim chance that one of Amanda's friends will recognize you and sic the giant Nubians on you before you have had a chance to do whatever it is you are here to do. This, you realize, is how the terrorist feels as he waits in the crowd with the bomb in his briefcase, believing that everyone can look through a window in his head and see murder on his mind. Your knees are shaky. You drink one of your two drinks. Alas, you would not make a very good terrorist. Then you remember seeing a briefcase standing beside the bar and a small flash of cognition, coincident with the first tingle of alcohol, flickers in your brain.

You walk back to the bar. The briefcase is still there. The owner appears to be the balding man with the Bain de Soleil complexion talking to two Oriental girls. His back is turned to the briefcase. You lean against the bar on your elbows, looking bored.

'Can I get you something?' the bartender inquires. He frowns when you say no, and you think there is a trace of suspicion in the way he looks you over before turning away.

'I don't know how to sail the damn thing,' the balding man says. 'I pay some Greeks to do that.' The girls consult, putting their heads together, and then they laugh. Apparently they took a vote. He is telling them about islands when you slip away with the briefcase. *Pas de* sweat.

You take a seat on the near side of the runway, in the middle of a middle row, thinking that once the show gets underway you want to be as inaccessible as possible. You stash the briefcase under the seat and cover it with your jacket. Your plan is beginning to congeal.

An eddy in the crowd ripples out from the door, a sense of waters being parted. Flashbulbs ignite. Finally you see the cause of the excitement: a face that brings to mind a line of cosmetics, a Cola and recent shocking revelations in supermarket tabloids. It's the famous actress/model on a busman's holiday. She's wearing faded jeans, a sweatshirt and a yachting cap, as if to say: 'I can look terrific with both hands tied behind my back.' You know for a fact, or at least you have it on good authority from Amanda, who once did location work with her, that she is a martyr to the search for the perfect nose. She has had no less than seven reconstructive operations and she's still not happy. She refuses to be photographed in profile. You can think of better ways to traumatize the nasal cartilage. From this distance, the nose looks unexceptional and the rest strikes you as bland. You judge her to be about five-five, not tall enough for runway work. She's got too much chest for couture.

Amanda is, or was, a perfect eight: hips thirty-four, waist twenty-three, bust thirty-three. You also know her shoe, glove and ring sizes. Clara would be proud. You have all the numbers. Factoring in the cheekbones, which a photographer once described as 'neo-classical,' they add up to a hundred and fifty dollars an hour.

People are taking their seats. A woman in a pink gown comes out onto the runway, apparently the mistress of ceremonies. She smiles and nods, mouthing little greetings, and walks out to the lectern at the runway's edge. Your hands are beginning to shake and you decide on a booster shot. You buck the flow of the crowd and race for the bar. People are looking at you and you are afraid they know your every thought. You brace yourself with the fact that you looked at Amanda every day for almost three years and you don't have the ghost of a clue what was going on in her mind. She showed all the vital signs and made all the right noises. She said she loved you.

The lights are dimmed, and the woman in pink begins to explain the reason we are here today. She says something about a Revolution in Taste. This fashion designer has the same name as a famous Renaissance painter, and she thinks it is not too much to compare the impact of his work in couture with that of the Old Master in painting. Meanwhile, the bartender tells you that the bar is closed until after the show, but he makes an exception for you and your ten-dollar bill. He is about your age. You want to tell him about Amanda. Instead you say, 'Lots of jewelry in this crowd. I don't see much in the way of security.'

He looks at you. 'They're around,' he says with conviction. You tell yourself, nice move. You thought that your phrasing cleverly disguised your real interest in the security question, but now he has you pegged for a jewel thief, which in his eyes may be even worse than a sexually abandoned husband. If only your hands would stop shaking. He is looking you over; it is obvious he doesn't like what he sees. He is going to call the Pinkertons, or the giant Nubians, at any minute. They will beat the soles of your feet until you admit everything. Amanda will watch your inglorious exit and think, So this is what he has come to.

'My girlfriend was just a little worried about her necklace,' you say to the bartender. 'Maybe I should bring her a drink, too, while I'm up.'

He doles a few fingers into another glass. 'Skip the ice,' you say. His look is frosty. 'Her husband wouldn't be too thrilled if she came home without her necklace.'

117

You wink. 'He thinks she's playing bridge.' Why are you saying these things?

You look back over your shoulder as you head for your seat. The bartender is signaling someone. You slide past all the knees, apologizing and spilling. The pink lady is talking about Bold New Looks. The first model comes out as you take your seat. She is black and tall as a Zulu. The pink lady describes her outfit, emphasizing the ruffles and their importance to the new elegance.

Amanda is the third model out. At least you think it's Amanda. With the makeup and the pulled-back hair, you can't be absolutely certain. The walk is stylized, but you think you recognize Amanda's signature sway and rhythm. She takes her spin on the runway and then she's gone. You didn't have time to think. You can't decide if it was really her. You remember your friends used to say they had seen her in the *Times* magazine or somewhere when it was actually another model. Sometimes they brought you pictures they had clipped and you would think it was funny—the pictures looked nothing like Amanda. But since she left, you have had the same trouble identifying her face. You have gone back through her portfolio and tried to make a composite that matches the image in your memory. The photos all look slightly different. Her agent said she could do any look—temptress, businesswoman, girl next door. A designer who used her all the time said she had plastic features. You begin to suspect that all of your firm beliefs about Amanda were no more substantial than the images she bodied forth under the klieg lights. You saw what she was selling then; you saw what you wanted to see.

You clutch the edge of your seat and wait for her next

appearance. You have your plan worked out, more or less. You will confront her when she comes out again. If they try to stop you, you will tell them the briefcase is full of high explosives, that you will blow the place into orbit if anybody comes near you. The Zulu comes out again in a new outfit. Then another model. The next one should be Amanda, but it's a brunette. You panic. She has seen you. She won't come out again. But the next model is Amanda, or the woman you think is Amanda. As she advances down the runway, you stand up. The pink lady is enthusing about pleats. You want to shout Amanda's name, but your voice is gone. People are beginning to look at you. A small clicking sound is coming from your throat. Finally you hear your voice: 'A-man-da!'

She keeps walking. She walks to the end of the runway and pirouettes in a way that flares the skirt of her dress. She walks down one arm of the T, turns and walks down the other. When she is almost directly in front of you, she turns and looks at you. It is a look that could carry either hatred or indifference. You want to ask for an explanation. She turns away and retraces her steps down the runway as if nothing had happened. Whoever she is, she is a professional. Whoever she is, you don't know her.

The pink lady is asking you to please sit down. People are turning in their seats to look at you. They are saying *Sit down!* and *What does he want?* A photographer up front snaps your picture just in case you turn out to be news. You imagine the *Post*'s caption: SEXUALLY ABANDONED HUBBY GOES BERSERK. Two large men in suits are hurrying down the aisles. The wires hanging from their ears probably connect earplugs with small transmitter-receivers. But it is more interesting to consider the possibility that the men could be robots. How do you know that the terrified-looking woman sitting next to you is actually feeling what you would call terror? If you were to step on her foot she would cry out, but how do you know she would *feel* what you call pain? You could observe one of these robots for years and never know. You could even be married to one.

The robot men are coming down the row of seats to get you, one from either side. You applaud this clever and efficient maneuver. Someone has turned up the music on the sound system, perhaps to cover the noise of your apprehension. You do not resist as one of the men with a wire hanging out of his ear takes your arm and says, 'Let's go.' You follow him down the row of seats and apologize to the people whose knees you are bumping. Once he gets you into the main aisle, he grips your arm uncompromisingly.

The two robots escort you out through the lobby. You are temporarily engulfed by a band of Japanese tourists following a guide with a pink flag and ideographic lapel badge. Your escorts are talking into microphones attached to their sleeves. 'Agitator apprehended. Proceeding to lobby.' Before shoving you out the door, one of the men leans down and says, 'We don't want to see you here again.'

It is a blue, sunny day—much too sunny for you, thanks. Fortunately, for once you have not forgotten your Ray-Bans. The lunchtime crowd churns Park Avenue. You expect people to gaze at you, horror-stricken, yet nobody pays any attention. On the corner a fat man in a Yankees cap is selling pretzels from a push-cart. A woman in a fur coat holds her right arm erect, hoping to conjure a taxi. A bus roars past. Cautiously, as if you were entering a swimming pool for the first time in years, you ease yourself into the ranks of pedestrians.

'Things happen, people change,' is what Amanda said. For her that covered it. You wanted an explanation, an ending that would assign blame and dish up justice. You considered violence and you considered reconciliation. But what you are left with is a premonition of the way your life will fade behind you, like a book you have read too quickly, leaving a dwindling trail of images and emotions, until all you can remember is a name.

LINGUINE AND SYMPATHY

After dark you return to the scene of your former crimes to gather up loose odds and ends. Since the magazine went to press this morning, you can assume everyone will have gone home. You feel strange walking into the building, an infidel penetrating the temple. Your hangover from the Waldorf doesn't help.

As you come out of the elevator on twenty-nine, the first person you see is the Ghost. The elevator doors close behind you.

He stands in the middle of the reception area, head tilted to one side like a robin listening for worms, and says hello.

You feel compelled to turn around and run. Your mere presence seems shameful, especially after last night. The longer you wait, the harder it becomes to speak. It's as if he's deaf and you're dumb.

'Evening,' you say in a weird, flickering voice.

He nods his head. 'I'm sorry to hear you're leaving us,' he says. 'If ever you need a good reference . . .'

'Thank you. Thanks very much.'

'Goodbye.' He turns and rolls off toward Collating. More than anything yet, this strange encounter makes you feel the sadness of leaving.

You check the mirror at the corner of the hall. Clara's door is closed and dark, as is the door which leads to the secret chambers of the Druid. There's a light on in Fact. You proceed cautiously.

Megan is at her desk. She looks up when you come in, goes back to her reading.

'Remember me?'

'I remember something about a lunch date.' She keeps her eyes on her desk.

'Oh, no. I'm sorry.'

She looks up. 'You're always sorry.'

'There was this thing I had to do.'

'A sweet young thing?'

'An old thing gone sour.'

'I have feelings, too, you know.'

'Damn it, I'm sorry.'

'I know you've had a lot on your mind lately,' Megan says.

'How about dinner?'

'One more meal with you could be the death of me.' She's smiling now.

'Just let me pack up my things here. Won't take a minute.'

Once you open the drawers of your desk you realize it could take all night. There is a vast quantity of flotsam: files, notebooks, personal and business correspondence, galleys and proofs, review books, matchbooks, loose sheets with names and phone numbers, notes to yourself, first drafts of stories, sketches and poems. Here, for instance, is the first draft of 'Birds of Manhattan.' Also the 'U.S. Government Abstract of Statistics on Agriculture, 1981,' indispensable in researching the three-part article on the death of the family farm, and on the back of which you have written the name Laura Bowman and a telephone number. Who is Laura Bowman? You could dial the number and ask for her, ask her where she fits into your past. Tell her you are suffering from amnesia and looking for clues.

In the top drawer you discover two empty rectangular packets. Actually, one of them is not quite empty; inside the black paper is a fine dusting of white. You scrape it onto the desk with a credit card, using the edge of the card to rake up two clean lines. You look over at Megan. She's reading. You could quietly hoover the lines and she'd never know the difference. You extract a bill from your wallet and roll it into a tight cylinder between thumb and forefinger. One apiece isn't going to do much for either of you. On the other hand, two won't do much for you, either; one will make you want another, and another will only initiate a chain reaction of desperate longings. Is this self-knowledge? In any case, you want to do something nice for Megan. For her it might be a treat, something out of the ordinary.

'Meg. Come over here a minute.' Now you are committed.

You hold out the bill. She raises her eyebrows.

'This will make you forget you didn't eat lunch.'

'What is it?'

'The powder that made Bolivia famous.'

She lifts the bill tentatively to her nose and bends over the desk.

124

'Do the other one, too,' you say when she offers you the bill.

'Are you sure?'

'Sure.' You just wish she would hurry up and finish it off.

Meg twists her nose like a rabbit and sniffles. 'Thanks.'

You shovel the contents of the top drawer onto the desk and wonder how, exactly, to deal with all this paper. Some of it may be significant. Most of it is junk. How do you tell the difference?

'We had some trouble here this morning,' Megan says. She sits down on the edge of your desk. You resist the urge to jump out of the chair and run down the hall with your jacket pulled over your head. *No comment.* All day you have been stifling the memory of your drunken-commando raid on Clara's office. You want to explain to Megan that it was a joke, you were drunk, it was Tad's idea. It wasn't really you, just a clownish alter ego over whom you have no control. You don't do things like that. You're not that kind of guy at all. If Alex were seriously hurt, though, Meg probably would have said so already. You keep your eyes fixed on a pamphlet entitled 'Manual of Factual Verification.'

'What do you mean, trouble?'

'Well, when Rittenhouse came in this morning he found Alex Hardy passed out on the floor of Clara's office.'

You find it difficult to talk. 'Really? Is he all right?'

'I don't imagine he feels terrific. He'll be fine once his blood detoxifies. He's taking the cure up at McLean's. Famous Drinking Writers' Club.'

'Didn't he hurt himself when he fell?'

'That's the strange thing. There was no sign of injury, but there was blood on the floor of Clara's office. And on the walls, too. Very peculiar.'

'Did he say anything? I mean, about what happened?'

'Nothing coherent. He said something about being attacked by pygmies.'

'They didn't call the, uh, police, did they?'

'Why would they?'

'Just wondering. Sounds to me like a weird deal all around.' You start to relax. Alex is okay and the visions of cops at your door are fading.

'Another odd thing,' Megan says. 'There was a mink in the mailroom.'

'A *mink?*'

'It was hiding in a mail bag full of rejected manuscripts. When the mail guy hoisted the bag this morning it started biting him. They had to call the ASPCA.'

'Really strange.' Poor Fred, you think.

'How are you coming?' she says, pointing at the desk.

'I think this calls for drastic measures.' You stand up and collect all the wastebaskets in the room, lining them up beside the desk. You take a book from the desk and hand it to Megan. 'Could you give this to Alex for me? Tell him it's one of the Young Turks.' She takes the book. You pull open the drawers one by one and dump the contents, entire, into the steel buckets.

'That's done. Let's eat.'

In the cab, you ask Megan where she wants to eat.

'How about my place?'

'You're going to cook?'

'You sound suspicious.'

'It just seems like a radical idea.'

'If you'd rather go out . . .'

'No. That sounds great.'

You get out at Bleecker Street. Megan takes your hand and leads you into a delicatessen. She holds up a box for your approval. 'Linguine,' she says. You nod. 'I'm going to teach you how to purchase and make a meal.' In the next aisle she introduces you to two cans of clams. Ordinarily, she says, she would use fresh clams and fresh pasta, but she doesn't want to scare you on your first lesson.

From the deli you walk toward Sixth. Megan is telling you about the difference between fresh and dried pasta. Each step takes you closer to the old apartment on Cornelia Street, where you first lived with Amanda in New York. This was your neighborhood. These shops were your shops. You possessed these streets as securely as if you held title. Now the vista is skewed slightly, someone has tilted the ground a few degrees, and everything is the same and not the same.

You pass Ottomanelli's Meats, where the corpses of small animals hang in the window: unskinned rabbits, hairless fetal pigs, plucked fowl with yellow feet. No ferrets. Amanda was always grossed out by this display. Already she was aspiring to the Upper East Side, where the butchers dress their wares in paper replicas of designer outfits.

At the corner of Jones and Bleecker a Chinese restaurant has replaced the bar whose lesbian patrons kept you awake so many summer nights when, too hot to sleep, you lay together with the windows open. Just before you moved out of the neighborhood a delegation of illiberal youths from New Jersey went into the bar with baseball bats after one of their number had been thrown out. The lesbians had pool cues. Casualties ran heavy on both sides and the bar was closed by order of the department of something or other.

Farther along, the obese gypsy Madame Katrinka beckons you to enter her storefront parlor with red velvet couch to have your fortune told. What would she have told you a year ago?

'Best bread in the city,' Megan says, pointing to Zito's Bakery. The bell over the door rings as you enter. The fragrance of the interior reminds you of mornings on Cornelia when you woke to the smell of bread from the bakery ovens, Amanda sleeping beside you. It seems a lifetime ago, but you can see her sleeping. You just can't remember what you talked about.

'White or wheat?' Megan asks.

'I don't know. White, I guess.'

'You don't know what's good for you.'

'All right, wheat. Wheat's better.'

From the bakery you proceed to the vegetable stand. Why are all the vegetables in the city sold by Koreans? Boxes of tumescent produce glisten under the green awning. You wonder if they color-coordinate the displays according to secret Oriental principles of mind control. Maybe they know that the juxtaposition of red tomatoes and yellow squash will produce in the consumer an irresistible urge to buy a bag of expensive oranges. Megan buys fresh basil, garlic, romaine lettuce and tomatoes. 'Now *there's* a tomato,' she says, holding a large red vegetable up for your inspection. Or is it a fruit?

Megan lives in a big fifties building on Charlton and Sixth. Two large cats, a Siamese and a calico, are waiting at the door. She introduces them as Rosencrantz and Guildenstern: Rose and Guildy for short, explaining that her first off-off Broadway role was Gertrude in a rock-and-roll version of *Hamlet*.

'I didn't know you were an actress.'

'My first love. But I got tired of waitressing.'

The apartment is a studio, not large, but furnished to give the impression of distinct areas. Against one wall is a double bed with patchwork quilt. In the center of the room a floral couch, and matching chairs are grouped in front of the largest window. At the other end of the room a rolltop desk is sheltered behind a row of bookcases. The tidiness of this arrangement is qualified by strident outbursts of plant life.

The cats stroke themselves on Megan's ankles while she hangs her shawl in a closet by the door. 'How about a glass of wine?' she says.

'Sure. Thanks.'

The cats follow her into the kitchen. You read the bookshelves. In the examination of personal libraries is an entire hermeneutics of character analysis. Megan has functional blond maple shelves with a little bit of everything in them. The shelves themselves are just untidy enough to suggest actual use and just neat enough to indicate respect for the equipment. The books are organized according to broad categories: a shelf of poetry, a cluster of oversized art books, a long row of *livre de poche* French novels, music and opera books, scores of thin Samuel French drama scripts, and half a shelf of memoirs of life at the magazine. The latter is an entire genre. You pull out Franklin Woolcraft's chatty volume, *Man about Town;* the flyleaf is signed: 'To Meg, who keeps me honest, with Love.' Putting the book back, you catch sight of a spine that reads *Exercise for Better Sex*.

Megan returns with two glasses of red wine. 'Give me a minute to change,' she says. 'Then I'm going to teach you how to make the world's easiest meal.'

Megan goes over to the freestanding wardrobe beside the bed. Where is she going to change? Just how casual are we here? As she digs through the wardrobe, you can't help noticing that she has a terrific ass. You have worked with her for almost two years without noticing her ass. How old is she anyway? She removes something from a hanger and tells you she'll be right back. She goes into the bathroom. The Siamese massages its head on your shin. *Exercise for Better Sex.*

Megan comes out wearing a maroon silk shirt with puffed sleeves which is not open to immediate interpretation. One less button buttoned might mean *sexy*, but what you see suggests *casually dressy*.

'Sit down,' Megan says, gesturing toward the couch.

You both sit. 'I like your place,' you say.

'It's small, but I can't afford to move.'

You hope the conversation improves. A few minutes ago you were colleagues headed out for a bite to eat. Now you are a man and a woman alone in a room with a bed.

One of the photographs on the end table beside the couch is a large glossy of a younger-looking Megan onstage with two men.

'That was my last play. *Who's Afraid of Virginia Woolf?* in Bridgeport, Connecticut.'

You pick up another picture, a boy with a fishing rod holding a trout, cabin and woods in the background.

'Old boyfriend?'

Meg shakes her head. She slides across the couch and takes the picture, studying it earnestly. 'My son,' she says.

'*Son?*'

Megan nods, looking at the picture. 'This was taken a couple of years ago. He's thirteen now. I haven't seen him in almost a year, but he's coming for a visit as soon as school lets out.'

You don't want to appear too inquisitive. This sounds like a dangerous subject. You haven't heard about a son before. Suddenly Megan seems much less scrutable than you had imagined.

She reaches across your chest to put the picture back on the end table. You can feel her breath on your cheek.

'He lives with his father in northern Michigan. It's a good place for a boy to grow up. They do boy things— hunting and fishing. His father's a logger. When I met him he was an aspiring playwright who couldn't get his plays produced. It was hard. We were broke and it seemed like everyone else had money. And I wasn't the greatest wife in the world. Jack—that's my ex-husband—didn't want his son growing up in the city. I didn't want to leave. Of course I didn't want my son to leave either, but when the decision was made I was in Bellevue stupefied with Librium. Obviously in no position to fight for custody.'

You don't know what to say. You are embarrassed. You want to hear more. Megan sips her wine and looks out the window. You wonder how painful this is for her.

'Did your husband commit you?'

'He didn't have much choice. I was raving. Manic depression. They finally figured out a few years ago it was a simple chemical deficiency. Something called lithium

131

carbonate. Now I take four tablets a day and I'm fine. But it's a little late to become a full-time mother again. Anyway Dylan—that's my son—has a wonderful stepmother and I see him every summer.'

'That's awful,' you say.

'It's not so bad. I'm okay now, Dylan has a good life. I call that a good deal. How about some dinner?'

You would rather fill in the gaps of the story, hear all the details, the shrieks and moans of Bellevue, but Megan is up and she is holding out her hand.

In the kitchen she passes you a paring knife and three cloves of garlic which you are supposed to peel. The skin is hard to remove. She explains that it's easier if you whack them a few times with the blunt edge of the knife. Then she notices the bandage. 'What happened to your hand?'

'Got caught in a door. No big deal.'

Megan goes behind you to wash lettuce in the sink. When you step back to get a better angle on the cutting board your buttocks meet. She laughs.

Megan moves around to the stove. She reaches up to an open shelf and pulls down a bottle. 'Olive oil,' she says. She pours some in a saucepan and turns on the burner. You pour yourself another glass of wine. 'Is the garlic ready?' Meg asks. You have succeeded in peeling two cloves. They look nude. 'Not too efficient, are we?' Megan says. She relieves you of the knife and strips the third clove, then chops it all up. 'Now we dump the garlic in the pan and let it fry. Meanwhile, I'll chop the basil while you open the clams. You know how to operate a can opener?'

You mostly stand and watch as Meg flashes around the kitchen. She moves you occasionally, whenever you're in the way. You like the feel of her hands on your shoulders.

'Tell me about Amanda,' Megan says over salad. You are sitting at the table in the dining alcove in candlelight. 'I get the feeling that something bad happened.'

'Amanda is a fictional character,' you say. 'I made her up. I didn't realize this until recently, when another woman, also named Amanda, shed me with a collect phone call from Paris. Do you mind if I open another bottle of wine?'

You eventually give Megan the gist of it. She says that Amanda must be enormously confused. You will drink to that.

'You've had a terrible time, haven't you?' she says. You shrug. You are looking at her breasts, trying to determine whether or not she is wearing a bra.

'I've been worried about you,' Megan says.

You move from the table to the couch. Megan says that we all project our needs onto others, and that others aren't always capable of fulfilling them. No bra, you decide.

You excuse yourself to go to the bathroom. You switch on the light and close the door behind you. The bathroom has a cluttered, homey look. Dried flowers on the toilet tank, white sheepskin on the seat. You pull back the shower curtain. Inside the shower is a shelf loaded with bottles. *Vitabath, Bath & Shower Gelée*. You like the sound of that. *Pantene Shampoo. Pantene Conditioner*. Doubtless this should not make you think of *panties*, but it does. *Lubriderm Lotion*. You pick up a luffa and rub it against your cheek, then return it to the shelf. A pink disposable razor is cradled in the soap dish.

You open the medicine cabinet over the sink: cosmetics, the usual assortment of noneuphoric home medicines. A tube of *Gynol II Contraceptive Jelly. Odorless, Colorless, Flavorless*. This is good news. On the top shelf there is a cache of prescription bottles. You remove one: 'Megan Avery; Lithium Carbonate; four tablets daily.' The second bottle is tetracycline. So far as you know you are not suffering from bacterial infection. You replace it. You score on the third try: 'Valium, as directed, for tension.' Tension you've got. You hold the bottle up to the light. Nearly full. After a brief struggle you master the childproof cap. You shake a blue tab onto your palm and swallow it. You consider. The last time you dropped a Valium you didn't even feel it. You take another. Of course, the last time you took a V, you were wired on C. Anyway. You replace the bottle, take an L and flush.

Megan is making noises with the dishes in the kitchen when you return. 'Be right out,' she says. You sit on the couch and pour another glass from the bottle on the coffee table. A bouquet with a hint of migrant-worker sweat.

'Just thought I'd get the dishes out of the way,' Megan says when she returns.

'A good policy,' you say. 'Want some more wine?'

She shakes her head. 'I'm not much of a drinker anymore.'

'That's a good policy, too.' You are feeling magnanimous.

'Are you doing any writing?' Megan asks.

You shrug your shoulders. 'I've been working on some ideas.'

'Do it,' Megan says. 'I want to see you walk back into

that place someday to pick up a check in Fiction. I want to see you walk past Clara's office into the Department. I'll have a bottle of champagne waiting.'

You don't know how Megan has come to believe in you, since you don't even believe in yourself. But you're grateful. You try to picture the scene of your triumphal return to the magazine, but instead you find yourself admiring Megan's bare feet drawn up beside her thighs on the couch.

'What will you do in the meantime? Any job prospects?'

'I've got some leads,' you say.

'I could put you in touch with a few people,' she says. 'What you've got to do is make up a good résumé— wide enough for journalism and publishing. I know an editor at Harper & Row who'd be happy to talk to you. I've already talked to Clara, and she says as far as the magazine is concerned, the parting was amicable and you'll get a good recommendation.'

You appreciate Megan's wonderful efficiency, but getting fired really wore you out and you would just as soon put the question of new employment on hold. Right now you would like to drink some more of this wine and sink a little deeper into the upholstery. You would like to show Megan how grateful you are. You reach over and take her hand. 'Thanks,' you say.

'And don't be afraid to ask for a loan to tide you over.'

'You're terrific.'

'I just want to help you get back on your feet.'

Not now, you think. You'd rather lie down. Bury your head in Megan's lap and stay there for a week or two. The bed is just a few feet away. You lean over and place your free hand on Megan's shoulder. The silk slides back and forth across her skin as you massage. No bra strap. You look into her eyes. She's a rare woman. She smiles, reaches out and strokes your hair.

'Everything's going to work out,' she says.

You nod.

Her face registers a shift of thought, and then she says, 'How's your father doing?'

'He's fine,' you say. 'He's terrific.' You pull her toward you. You slide a hand behind her head and close your eyes as your lips find hers. You press her head against the back of the couch and run your tongue along her teeth. You want to feel her tongue. You want to disappear inside her mouth. She turns her head away and tries to withdraw from your embrace. You reach a hand under her shirt. Gently, she grips your hand and holds it there.

'No,' she says. 'That's not what you want.' Her voice is calm and soothing. She is not angry, just determined. When you try to advance your hand she stops it.

'Not that,' she says. When you try to kiss her again she holds you off, but she remains on the couch. You feel like water seeking its own level, and Megan is the sea. You put your head in her lap. She strokes your hair. 'Calm down,' she says. 'Calm down.'

'Are you all right now?' Megan asks when you lift your head from her lap.

The level of the room keeps changing. All of the surfaces swell and recede with oceanic rhythm. You are not quite all right. You are somewhat wrong.

'I think maybe I'll get up and go to the, uh, bathroom.' This is you speaking. Testing: one, two, three.

Megan is helping you to your feet. She holds your elbow as she leads you to the door. 'I'll be right out here if you need me.'

The black-and-white tiles on the floor keep moving. You stand in front of the toilet and consider. Do you feel sick? Not exactly. Not yet, anyway. You might as well take a leak, though, as long as you are here. You unzip and aim for the bowl. There is a poster with some kind of print in front of you. You lean forward to read it, and then you lean back, so as not to fall forward.

You try to grab hold of the shower curtain as you go down but you can't get a grip.

'Are you all right?' Megan says from the other side of the door.

'Fine,' you say. You are mostly in the tub. Only your feet stick out, way down at the far end of your body. It's not uncomfortable, really, except that you are a little damp around the midsection. You will have to investigate this. Find the source. In a minute.

The door opens. Help is on the way.

SOMETIMES A
VAGUE NOTION

You wake up with a cat on your chest. You are on a couch, wrapped in a quilt. After a few minutes you recognize Megan's apartment. Her bed is empty. The clock on the nightstand says 11:13. That would be A.M., judging by the sunlight. The last thing you remember is an amorous lunge at Megan somewhere in the P.M.; presumably unsuccessful. You have the feeling you have made a fool out of yourself.

You sit up in bed and marvel at this strange pair of pajamas. You stand up. There is a note on the kitchen table: *Eggs, English muffins and orange juice in fridge. Your clothes are hanging in bathroom. Give a call later on. Love—Megan.*

At least she doesn't hate you. Perhaps you did not entirely disgrace yourself. Better not to think about it. You find your clothes in the bathroom. Everything is stiff and clean as if freshly laundered. The calico cat jumps up on the sink and rubs its head on your hip as you dress.

You should leave a note for Meg. You find a pen and a fat pad in which every sheet has MEMO written across the top.

Dear Meg—Thanks for the bed and board. Dinner was delicious. Now what? Should you acknowledge loss of full recall? *I guess I nodded off a little early*. The question is, what did you do before that? For that matter, what about after? What you need is an all-purpose apology. Something to cover each possible misdemeanor. *Please excuse my lapse from gentlemanly comportment. Let's get together soon, maybe for lunch*.

You rip this up. On the new sheet you write: *Dear Megan—I'm sorry. I know I'm always saying that, but I mean it. Thank you*.

The phone is ringing when you get back to your apartment. Living dangerously, you answer. It's Richard Fox, the reporter. He says he heard a rumor about your recent loss of employment. He says he liked a book review you wrote for the *Village Voice* a while back. Nobody reads book reviews in the *Voice*, but you admire the diligence exhibited by Fox's assistant in tracking the thing down. He mentions an opening at *Harper's* that might be right for you, and says that he could put in a good word. He is too kind. He wasn't nearly so friendly when you met him at the publication party for his last book.

'I met Clara Tillinghast a few weeks ago,' he says. 'No man I'd care to drink with could put up with that for long. My sources tell me she had it in for you from the start.'

'Short honeymoon, long divorce.'

'Would it be accurate to say that she is something of a bitch on wheels?'

'I think she has treads, actually. Like a Sherman tank. But it would be a tough thing to verify.'

'I guess you know I'm writing a piece on the magazine.'

'Really?'

'I was hoping you might be able to give me some background. You know—human interest, anecdotes.'

'You want smut?'

'Whatever you've got.'

A baby cockroach is working its way up the wall next to the phone. Should you crush it or let it pass?

'I was just a little worker bee. I don't think I could tell you anything of national interest.'

'Let's face it. The stagehands have the best view in the house.'

'It's a pretty dull place,' you say. Already it seems so far behind you, the office politics and the broom-closet affairs no more interesting there than elsewhere.

'Why feel loyal to them? They threw you out on your ass.'

'The whole subject just bores me.'

'Let's have lunch. Bat some ideas around. Say, Russian Tea Room at one-thirty?'

You tell him you don't have any ideas. Your information is imperfect. Everything you thought you knew turned out to be wrong. You tell him you are an unreliable source. He appeals to the public's right to know. He appeals to your sense of vengeance. He gives you his phone number in case you change your mind. You don't write it down.

You go out for a bite and the *Post*. It's almost two

o'clock. Not for the first time, you wonder why all the coffee shops in the city are run by Greeks. The take-out cups have pictures of seminude classical Greek figures.

O Attic shape . . . of paper men and maidens overwrought . . .

You spread the newspaper out on the counter and learn that Coma Baby was delivered six weeks premature in an emergency Caesarean and that Coma Mom is dead.

Coming up West Twelfth from Seventh Avenue, you see someone sitting on the steps of your apartment building. It looks an awful lot like your brother Michael. Whoa! You slow down. Then you stop. It is Michael. What is he doing here? He should be home in Bucks County. He doesn't belong here.

He sees you. He stands up, starts toward you. You turn and bolt. The subway entrance is half a block up. You take the steps two at a time, dodging the zombies trudging up the stairs. An uptown train with open doors waits at the platform. A line at the token booth. You vault the turnstile. A metallic voice issues from the speaker on the booth: 'Hey, *you*!' You dash inside as the doors close. People are staring. When the train begins to move they return to their *Post*s and their private sorrows.

Looking out the sooty windows at the receding platform and seeing Michael standing outside the turnstiles, you duck away from the window. You don't want to see him. It's not that he's a bad guy. You feel guilty of everything. Even now, a transit cop with a walkie-talkie may be striding through the cars to arrest you.

You sit down and allow the racket of the train to fill

your head. You close your eyes. Soon the noise doesn't seem like noise and the motion doesn't feel like motion. You could fall asleep.

You open your eyes and look at the ads. TRAIN FOR AN EXCITING NEW CAREER. BE AN INSTANT WINNER WITH WINGO! SOFT AND LOVELY HAIR RELAXER. BE A MODEL—OR JUST LOOK LIKE ONE.

At Fiftieth you get off and walk up the stairs to the street. Walking east, you cross abrupt thermoclines as you move between the cool shadows of tall buildings and brief regions of direct sunlight. At Fifth Avenue you stand on the corner and look over at the long row of windows fronting Saks. You cross the street to the third window down from the uptown corner.

The mannequin is gone. You count windows again. Where the Amanda mannequin had been is a new one with brunette acrylic on its head and a delicately upturned nose. You walk up and down the block, examining each of the mannequins. For a moment you think you have found it on Fiftieth Street, but the face is too angular and the nose is wrong.

You came here with a notion of demonstrating to yourself that the icon was powerless, yet you are unsettled now that it is gone. What does this mean? You decide that it has disappeared because you were through with it, and you consider this a good omen.

On Madison you pass a construction site, walled in by acres of plywood on which the faces of various rock stars and Mary O'Brien McCann are plastered. Thirty stories above you, a crane dangles an I-beam over the street beside the skeleton of a new building. From the sidewalk the crane looks like a toy, but a few months back you read about a pedestrian who was killed at this site when a cable broke. DEATH FALLS FROM SKY, the *Post* said.

You pass the Helmsley Palace—the shell of old New York transparently veiling the hideous erection of a real estate baron. A camera crew has taken over the sidewalk beside the entrance. Pedestrians submit to a woman with a clipboard who orders them to detour out into the street. 'Close-up with the mini-cam,' someone says. The crew wear their importance like uniforms. Out in the bus lane, a kid in a Blessed Mother High School sweatshirt turns down the volume on his ghetto-blaster. 'Who is it?' he asks you. When you shake your head he turns the music back up.

> *Facts are simple and facts are straight*
> *Facts are lazy and facts are late*
> *Facts all come with points of view*
> *Facts don't do what I want them to*

'Here she comes,' a voice shouts.

You keep walking, thinking briefly about the Missing Person, the one who's come and gone for good. Out into the sunlight of Fifth Avenue and the Plaza, a gargantuan white chateau rising in the middle of the island like a New Money dream of the Old World. When you first came to the city you spent a night here with Amanda. You had friends to stay with, but you wanted to spend that first night at the Plaza. Getting out of the taxi next to the famous fountain, you seemed to be arriving at the premiere of the movie which was to be your life. A doorman greeted you at the steps. A string quartet played in the Palm Court. Your tenth-floor room was tiny and overlooked an airshaft; though you could not see the city out the window, you believed that it was spread out at your feet. The limousines around the entrances seemed like carriages, and you felt that some-day one would wait for you. Today they put you in mind of carrion birds, and you cannot believe your dreams were so shallow.

You are the stuff of which consumer profiles—American Dream: Educated Middle-Class Model—are made. *When you're staying at the Plaza with your beautiful wife, doesn't it make sense to order the best Scotch that money can buy before you go to the theater in your private limousine?*

You stayed there once before, with your parents and your brothers, when your father was in between corporate postings. You and Michael rode the elevators up and down all day. The next day you were going to embark for England on the *Queen Elizabeth*. You told Michael that they didn't have silverware in England, that people had to eat with their hands. Michael started to cry. He didn't want to go to England, didn't want to eat with his hands. You told him not to worry. You would sneak some silverware into the country. Prowling the halls, you stole silverware from the room-service trays and stashed it in your suitcases. Michael wanted to know if they had glasses. You packed some just in case. At customs in Liverpool Michael began to cry again. You had warned him of the terrible penalties for smuggling. He didn't want to have his hands cut off. A few years ago you were home for the weekend and you found one of the spoons with the Plaza crest in the silverware drawer.

* * *

You walk up Fifth Avenue along the park. On the steps of the Metropolitan Museum, a mime with a black-and-white face performs in front of a small crowd. As you pass you hear laughter and when you turn around the mime is imitating your walk. He bows and tips his hat when you stop. You bow back and throw him a quarter.

At the ticket window you say you're a student. The woman asks you if you have an ID. You say you left it in your dorm and she ends up giving you the student rate anyway.

You go to the Egyptian wing and wander among the obelisks, sarcophagi and mummies. In your several visits to the Met this is the only exhibit you have seen. Mummies of all sizes are included, some of them unwrapped to reveal the leathery half-preserved dead. Also dog and cat mummies, and an infant mummy, an ancient newborn bundled up for eternity.

From the Met you walk to Tad's place on Lexington. It's a little after six. No answer to the buzzer. You decide to go for a drink and come back later. In a few minutes you are in singles' heaven on First Avenue. You start at Friday's, where you get a seat at the bar and finally succeed in ordering a drink. Prime time approaches, and the place is packed with eager secretaries and slumming lawyers. Everyone here has the Jordache look—the look you don't want to know better. Hundreds of dollars' worth of cosmetics on the women and thousands in gold around the necks of the open-shirted men. Gold crucifixes, Stars of David and coke spoons hang from the chains. Some trust in God to get them laid; others in drugs. Someone should do a survey of success ratios, publish it in *New York* magazine.

You are sitting beside a girl with frosted hair who emanates the scent of honeysuckle. She has been sneaking peeks at you in between conferences with her girlfriend. You would guess her age to be somewhere in the illegal range. Underneath her eyes she has painted two purple streaks suggestive of cheekbones. You know what's coming, it's only a matter of time. You don't know how to respond. You catch the eye of the bartender and order another drink.

'Excuse me,' the girl says. 'Do you happen to know where we could get some coke?'

'No can do.'

'I do,' she says. 'I mean, we know where we can score a gram but we don't have enough bread. You wanna go in with us, maybe? We got some ludes.'

You are not this desperate, you tell yourself. You still have some self-respect.

You wake to the voice of Elmer Fudd. 'Kill the wabbit! Kill the wabbit!' You feel like a murder victim yourself. Then you see a girl with frosted hair and puffy eyes looking down at you and you wonder if the crime isn't rape.

'What happened?'

'Nothing,' she says. 'Not a goddamn thing. Story of my life. Meet a guy at a bar and carry him home so he can pass out on my bed.'

This account of events relieves a fraction of the pain in your head. You are in a strange bed. A television shows the cartoon on the other side of the room. You discover that you are still partially clothed.

'At least you didn't puke,' she says.

'You better hope your luck holds.'

146

'Say what?'

'Where am I?'

'You're in my goddamn apartment.'

'Where might that be?'

'Queens.'

'You're kidding.'

'What's to kid?' Her face softens and she strokes your forehead. 'You wanna try again?'

'What time is it?' you say. 'I'm late for work.'

'Cool your jets. It's Saturday.'

'I work Saturdays.' You sit up in bed, extracting her hand from your hair. You feel ravaged. On the television screen, Wile E. Coyote is building an improbable contraption to catch the Road Runner. Posters on the wall depict rock groups in lurid light and kittens in soft focus.

You hear sounds coming from the next room. 'Who's that?' you say, pointing at the door.

The girl is putting a record on the turntable.

'My parents,' she says.

By the time you get back to Manhattan it is two o'clock. You feel as if you have come across oceans and mountains. The parents were watching television when you finally worked up the courage to slouch out of the bedroom. They didn't even look up.

You have never been so glad to see the inside of your apartment. You check the refrigerator for liquids. The milk is sour. You are trying to nod off on the couch when the buzzer rings.

When you punch the Listen button a voice says, 'United Parcel Service.' Possibly some kind soul has sent you a brand-new mail-order heart. The voice sounds like it is coming through layers of cloth. Where the hell is the doorman? Does UPS deliver on Saturday? Do you care? You press the Door button and go back to the couch. When the bell rings you go to look through the peephole. Michael is standing in the hall, greatly reduced in size but no less menacing. You consider the fire escape. He steps forward and pounds on the door. The fisheye peephole makes his fist seem like a monstrous appendage. Maybe if you're quiet he'll go away. He pounds again.

You open the door. Michael seems to fill the entire frame.

'Michael,' you say. You meet his eyes, which are implacable, then you look down at his feet on which there are a pair of genuine work boots of a type not usually seen in the city.

You leave the door open and walk back to the living room. He doesn't follow immediately. Presently he enters and slams the door. You stretch out on the couch. 'Take a seat,' you say. He remains standing in front of you. This is not really fair, you think, aggravating, as it does, his advantage in height.

'What the hell is going on with you?' he says. He is growing larger by the minute.

You shrug.

'I've been trying to track you down for over a week. I called your office, called here.'

'When did you get to the city?' you ask.

'And then when I take the goddamn bus down to the city and stake out your doorstep, you bolt when you see me.'

'I thought you were somebody else.'

'Don't give me that shit. I left about a hundred and

fifty messages at your office. And then yesterday I go to your office and they tell me you are no longer employed as of Wednesday. What the fuck is going on?' His fists are clenched. You would think it was *his* job you had lost.

'What did you want to see me about?'

'*I* don't *want* to see you. I'd just as soon leave you here to drown in coke or whatever it is you're doing. But Dad's worried about you and I'm worried about Dad.'

'How *is* Dad?'

'Do you care?'

You have always thought that Michael would make a great prosecuting attorney. He has an acute sense of universal guilt and a keen nose for circumstantial evidence. Although he is a year younger than you, he has appropriated the role of elder. He takes your foibles and lapses from good citizenship as personal affronts.

'Dad's in California on business. At least he was until last night. He asked me to call and make sure you got home for the weekend. Since you never answer or call back, well, here I am. You're coming home with me whether you want to or not.'

'Okay.'

'Where are you keeping the Healey?' he says.

'Little problem there. A friend of mine totaled it.'

'You let some guy wreck your car?'

'Actually, I told him just to put a few dents in it but he got carried away.'

He shakes his head and sighs. He has learned to expect no better from you. Finally he takes a seat, a good sign. He looks around the apartment, which he has never seen before, and shakes his head at the mess. Then he looks at you.

'Tomorrow is the anniversary, in case you've forgotten. One year. We're going to spread her ashes in the lake. Dad wants you to be there.'

You nod your head. You knew this was coming. You weren't watching the calendar but you could feel it coming on. You close your eyes and lean your head back against the couch. You surrender.

'Where's Amanda?' he says.

'Amanda?' You open your eyes.

'Your wife. Tall, blonde, slender.'

'She's shopping,' you say.

For what seems like a long time you sit across from each other in silence. You think of your mother. You try to remember the way she was before she got sick.

'You've just forgotten Mom completely, is that it?'

'Don't get righteous with me.'

'And Dad, who you haven't seen since Christmas.'

'How about if you just shut up.'

'You never had to exert yourself for anything and you're not about to start now. School, girls, awards, fancy jobs—it all just falls in your lap, doesn't it? You don't even have to go out and look for it. Mom and Dad certainly couldn't do enough for you. So I guess it gets pretty easy to take people for granted when you're Mr. Everything.'

'Omniscience must be a terrible burden, Michael. How do you bear it?'

'Mr. Wonderful, who galloped in from New York last year like some kind of fucking knight in his British sportscar, just in time for the dramatic finale of Mom's life. Like it was some goddamn New York party that you didn't want to be early for, God forbid.'

'Shut up.'

'Don't tell me to shut up.'

'How about if I make you shut up?'

You stand up. Michael stands up.

'I'm getting out of here,' you say. You turn away. You can hardly see your way to the door. Your eyes are dim and cloudy. You hit your knee on a chair.

'You're not going anywhere.'

Michael grabs your arm as you reach the door. You yank it away. He slams you against the doorframe and bangs your head against the metal. He's got you pinned. You jam your elbow into his belly and he lets go. You turn and punch him in the face. You punch him hard. You hit him with the hand the ferret bit and it hurts like hell. You fall backward into the hall. You get to your feet and look to see what's happened to Michael. He is on his feet. You remember thinking, *He's going to hit me.*

When you come around, you are stretched out on the couch. Your head feels truly awful. You can feel the point of contact just below your left temple.

Michael comes out of the kitchen holding a paper towel to his nose. The towel is stained with blood.

'You all right?' you ask him.

He nods. 'That kitchen faucet needs a washer. Drips like crazy.'

'Amanda isn't shopping,' you say. 'She left me.'

'What?'

'She called up from France one day and said she wasn't coming home.'

Michael scrutinizes your face to see if you are serious. Then he leans back in the chair and sighs.

'I don't know what to say,' he says. He shakes his head. 'Goddamn. I'm sorry. I'm really sorry.'

Michael stands up and comes over to the couch. He crouches down, then says, 'Are you all right?'

'I miss Mom,' you say.

THE NIGHT SHIFT

Michael is hungry and you are thirsty; a foray is proposed and seconded. All of uptown seems to be headed downtown for Saturday night. Everyone on the sidewalk looks exactly seventeen years old and restless. At Sheridan Square a ragged figure is tearing posters off the utility poles. He claws at the paper with his fingernails and then stomps it under his feet.

'What is he, political?' Michael says.

'No, just angry.'

You walk down into the Lion's Head, past all the framed dust jackets of all the writers who have ever gotten drunk here, heading for the back room where the lights are low. When you sit down, James, long-haired and black, jumps up on the table; the house cat.

'I never really liked her much, to tell you the truth,' Michael says. 'I thought she was fake. If I ever see her I'm going to rip her lungs out.'

You introduce Michael to Karen, the waitress, and she asks you how the writing is going. You order two double vodkas. She tosses down a couple of menus and ducks around the corner.

'At first,' you say, 'I couldn't believe she left me. Now I can't believe we got married in the first place. I'm just starting to remember how cold and distant Amanda was when Mom got sick. She seemed to resent Mom's dying.'

'Do you think you'd have married her if Mom hadn't been sick?'

You have made such a point of not dwelling on the incidents associated with your mother's death, almost denying that it was a consideration at all. You were living with Amanda in New York and marriage wasn't high on your list of priorities, although on Amanda's it was. You had your doubts about in sickness and in health till death do us part. Then your mother was diagnosed and everything looked different. Your first love had given notice of departure and Amanda's application was on file. Mom never said it would do her heart good to see you married, but you were so eager to please her you would have walked through fire, given your right and left arms . . . You wanted her to be happy and she wanted you to be happy. And, in the end, you might have confused what she wanted with what Amanda wanted.

Before it happened you couldn't believe you would survive your mother's death. Torn between thinking it was your duty to throw yourself on her pyre and her wish that you should not waste time mourning, you knew no reaction that satisfied both conditions. You spent so much time in anticipation that when her death came you didn't know what you felt. After the funeral it seemed as if you were wandering around your own interior looking for signs of life, finding nothing but empty rooms and white walls. You kept waiting for the onset of grief. You are beginning to suspect it arrived nine months later, disguised as your response to Amanda's departure.

Michael orders the shepherd's pie. You wave the menu away. You talk about the past and the present. You ask about the twins, Peter at Amherst and Sean at Bowdoin. Having already discussed your travails at the magazine, including your recent ferret gambit, you ask Michael about his business—restoring old houses—and he tells you it's going well. He's working on a derelict carriage house in New Hope.

'I'm going to hire out some grunt work. Maybe you'd be interested. At least it's a change of scene. Say, three or four weeks of work.'

You tell him you'll think about it. You are surprised that he would offer. Michael has long considered you incompetent. By the time he was twelve he was bigger than you. He shaped an ethic of engagement with the physical world under which your aptitudes and accomplishments were suspect.

You drink and talk. Under the spell of alcohol your differences recede. You and Michael and Peter and Sean and Dad stand against the world. The family has been fucked over, but you're going to tough it out. Forget that slut Amanda. The doctors who couldn't save your mother's life and wouldn't tell you what was going on. Clara Tillinghast. The priest who, at your mother's deathbed, said, 'We've seen some beautiful deaths with cancer.'

After many drinks Michael says, 'I need a little air.' On the way back to the apartment, you stop in on a friend who happens to have a spare half for the low, low price of sixty dollars. You feel that you are basically through with this compulsion. This time you just want to celebrate crossing the hump. You are a little drunk and you want to keep going, keep talking.

You should have told us, Michael says, sprawled out on the couch in your apartment. 'I mean, what's a family for?' He bangs his hand on the coffee table for emphasis. 'What's family for?'

'I don't know. You want to do a few lines?'

Michael shrugs. 'Why not?' He watches as you get up and take the mirror from the wall. 'What was bad for me,' he says, 'is at first I'd see her the way she was toward the end, all wasted and thin. But now I have this image I keep with me. I don't know when it was, but I came home from school one day—this was after you'd gone to college—and Mom was out back raking leaves. It was October or something and she was wearing your old ski team jacket, which was about six sizes too big.' He stops. His eyes are closed and you think maybe he has passed out. You shake some coke out onto the mirror. Michael opens his eyes. 'I remember the way the air smelled, the way Mom looked in that jacket with leaves in her hair, the lake in the background. That's the way I remember her now. Raking leaves in your old ski team jacket.'

'I like that,' you say. You can imagine it. She wore that jacket for years. Once you finished high school you didn't want any part of it and she took it up. You'd never really given it a thought, but now you feel good about it.

You cut eight lines. Michael begins to snore. You call

156

his name and then you get up and gently shake his shoulder. He turns his face into the cushions. You do two of the lines and sit back in the chair. A year ago tonight you were up until daybreak, sitting beside your mother's bed.

You thought you would faint when you came home the last time, three days before she died, and saw the ravaged form. Even the smile had shifted. After months of waffling, the doctors had admitted there was not much they could do, and agreed she could stay at home if the family would attend her constantly. When you got home, Michael and your father, who had traded twelve-hour shifts for a week, were exhausted. For the last seventy-two hours, you took the night shift, midnight to eight. You gave her the morphine injection every four hours, and tended as best you could to the symptoms of the disease.

When you first saw her, even after Michael had warned you, you wanted to run away. But the horror passed, and you were glad you could do something for her. You were glad you could be with her. But for those last hours you might never have really known her. The last few nights she was not sleeping at all, so you talked.

'Have you ever tried cocaine?' she asked that last night.

You didn't know what to say. A strange question from a mother. But she was dying. You said you had tried it.

'It's not bad,' she said. 'When I could still swallow they were giving me cocaine with morphine. To ease the depression. I liked it.'

Your mother, who never smoked a cigarette in her life, who got loopy on two drinks.

She said the morphine was good for the pain but made her drowsier than she wanted to be. She wanted to be clear. She wanted to know what was happening.

Then she said, 'Do young men need sex?'

You asked what she meant by *need*.

'You know what I mean. I should know these things. I don't have much time and there's so much I've always wondered about. I was brought up to think sex was an ordeal that married women had to endure. It took me a long time to get over that idea. I feel sort of cheated.'

You always thought your mother was the last Puritan.

'Have you slept with a lot of girls?'

'Mom, really,' you said.

'Come on. What's to hide? I wish I'd known a long time ago that I was going to die. We could've gotten to know each other a lot better. There's so much we don't know.'

'Okay, there have been some girls.'

'Really?' She lifted her head up from the pillow.

'Mother, I'm not going into details.'

'Why not?'

'It's, well, embarrassing.'

'I wish people wouldn't waste their time being embarrassed. I wish I hadn't. So tell me what it's like.'

You began to forget the way she looked then, and to see her somehow as young, younger than you had ever known her. The wasted flesh seemed illusory. You saw her as a young woman.

'Do you really enjoy it?' she asked.

'Sure. Yeah, I do.'

'You've slept with girls you're not in love with. Isn't it different if you're in love?'

'Sure, it's better.'

158

'How about Sally Keegan? Did you sleep with her?'

Sally Keegan was your High School Prom date. 'Once.'

'I *thought* so.' This verification of her intuition pleased her. 'What about Stephanie Bates?'

Later, she said, 'Are you happy with Amanda?'

'Yes, I think so.'

'For the rest of your life?'

'I hope so.'

'I was lucky,' Mom said. 'Your dad and I *have* been happy. But it hasn't always been easy. One time I thought I was leaving him.'

'Really?'

'We were human.' She adjusted her pillow and winced. 'Foolish.' She smiled.

The candor was infectious. It spread back to the beginning of your life. You tried to tell her, as well as you could, what it was like being you. You described the feeling you'd always had of being misplaced, of always standing to one side of yourself, of watching yourself in the world even as you were being in the world, and wondering if this was how everyone felt. That you always believed that other people had a clearer idea of what they were doing, and didn't worry quite so much about why. You talked about your first day of school. You cried and clutched her leg. You even remembered how her plaid slacks felt, the scratchiness on your cheek. She sent you off to the bus—she interrupted here to say she wasn't much happier than you were—and you hid in the woods until you saw the bus leave and then went home and told her you had missed it. So Mom drove you to school, and by the time you got there you were an hour late.

Everybody watched you come in with your little note, and heard you explain that you missed the bus. When you finally sat down you knew that you would never catch up.

'Don't you think everyone feels a little like that?' Then Mom told you she knew all along about the hot-water-on-the-thermometer trick, but let you pretend you were sick whenever you really seemed to need it. 'You were a funny boy. An awful baby. A real screamer.' Then she grimaced and for a moment you thought it was the memory of your screaming.

You asked her if she wanted the morphine and she said not yet. She wanted to talk, to be clear.

The window behind the headboard showed a glimmer of gray. In the other rooms your three brothers, your father, and your Aunt Nora were sleeping. Amanda was in New York.

'Was I worse than Michael and the twins?'

'Much worse.' She smiled as if she had just conferred a great distinction upon you. 'Much, much worse.' The smile twisted into a grimace and she clutched the sheet in her fingers.

You begged to give her some morphine. The spasm passed and you saw her body relax.

'Not yet,' she said.

She told you how unbearable you were as an infant, always throwing up, biting, crying through the night. 'You've never been much good at sleeping, have you? Some nights we had to take you out in the car and drive around to get you to sleep.' She seemed pleased. 'You were something else.'

She winced again and groaned. 'Hold my hand,' she said. You gave her your hand and she gripped it harder than you would have imagined she could. 'The pain,' she said.

'Please let me give you that shot.'

You couldn't stand to see her suffer much longer, felt you were about to collapse. But she told you to wait.

'Do you know what this is like?' she said. 'This pain?'

You shook your head. She didn't answer for a while. You heard the first bird of morning.

'It's like when you were born. It sounds crazy, but that's exactly what it's like.'

'It hurt that much?'

'Terrible,' she said. 'You just didn't want to come out. I didn't think I'd live through it.' She sucked breath through her teeth and gripped your hand fiercely. 'So now you know why I love you so much.' You were not sure you understood, but her voice was so faint and dreamy that you didn't want to interrupt. You held her hand and watched her eyelids flicker, hoping she was dreaming. Birds were calling on all sides. You didn't think you had ever heard so many birds.

In a little while she started to talk again. She described a morning in a two-room apartment over a garage in Manchester, New Hampshire. 'I was standing in front of a mirror as if I'd never really seen my own face before.' You had to lean down close to hear. 'I felt strange. I knew something had happened, but I didn't know what.'

She drifted off. Her eyes were half-open but you could see she was looking somewhere else. The bedroom window was filling with light.

'Dad,' she said. 'What are you doing here?'

'Mom?'

She was silent for a time and then, suddenly, her eyes

were wide open. Her grip relaxed. 'The pain is going away,' she said.

You said that was good. The light seemed to have entered the room all at once.

'Are you still holding my hand?' she asked.

'Yes. I am.'

'Good,' she said. 'Don't let go.'

HOW IT'S GOING

The apartment has become very small. Michael snores on the couch. Your head is pounding with voices of confession and revelation. You followed the rails of white powder across the mirror in pursuit of a point of convergence where everything was cross-referenced according to a master code. For a second, you felt terrific. You were coming to grips. Then the coke ran out; as you hoovered the last line, you saw yourself hideously close up with a rolled twenty sticking out of your nose. The goal is receding. Whatever it was. You can't get everything straight in one night. You are too excited to think any more and too exhausted to sleep. If you lie down you are afraid you will die.

The phone goes off like a shrill alarm. You catch it on the second ring. Through the noise and cryptic epigrams you gather that it is Tad, that he wants you to meet him at Odeon. There is a party. Your presence is requested. You tell him you'll be there in ten minutes.

You throw a blanket over Michael and a jacket on

yourself; check your nearly empty wallet, then close and lock the door. When you hit the street you begin to jog. At the door of the Sheridan Square all-hours bank office you insert the plastic card which a sign tells you is your passport to banking convenience. When the buzzer sounds, you pull the door open and step into a room the color of an illuminated swimming pool. A specimen in camouflage combat gear stands at the cash-machine as if he were playing a video game, body English in his every motion. If he doesn't hurry up, you think, I will have to kill him.

Finally he turns to you and throws up his hands. 'Fucking computers. They ain't gonna take over the world at this rate. This goddamned Citibank unit—it couldn't take Staten Island on a Sunday morning. Go ahead, try your luck.' This neo-guerrilla sports a button which reads: I'M NOT AS THINK AS YOU STONED I AM.

Not at all confident that your fellow late-night Citi-banker is capable of operating the equipment, you pre-serve the hope of imminent cash. You step up and read the message on the screen which welcomes you in Span-ish and English and asks you which language you prefer to do your banking in. You decide on English; nothing happens. You press the button again. Eventually you try all of the buttons on the console, which keeps flashing the same hearty greeting. You are not the kind of person who beats on recalcitrant vending machines. Neverthe-less, just this once, you would like to put your fist through the video screen. You jam the buttons down into their sockets, raise your foot and uselessly kick the wall. Words vile and violent pass your lips. You hate banks. You hate machines. You hate the idiots outside on the sidewalk.

With your last five you stake yourself to a cab. You begin to feel better once you're in motion.

As you pull up to Odeon, Tad is coming out the door with his friend Jimmy Q from Memphis. Luckily, Jimmy has a limo. You climb in. Jimmy gives the driver an address. The Caddy floats over the downtown streets. You can tell you are moving only by the passage of lights across the tinted windows. Some of the lights have dim halos and others spill crystalline shards into the night.

The car stops in front of a warehouse. You hear the party throbbing like a helicopter above the deserted street. You can't wait to get up there. You drum your fingers on the doorframe as you wait for the elevator.

'Take it easy,' Tad says. 'You're wired to detonate.'

You ask whose party it is. Tad provides a name he claims belongs to the heir of a fast-food fortune.

The elevator door opens directly into the loft, which is roughly the size of a Midwestern state and at least as populous. There are windows on three sides and mirrors on the fourth. A bar and buffet is set up at one end. The dance floor is down at the other end, somewhere near New Jersey.

At the bar, Tad introduces you to a woman, Stevie, who wears a slinky black gown with a scalloped hemline. She is very tall. Long blonde hair, tasseled white silk scarf wrapped around her neck. Stevie says, 'Do you dance?'

'You bet.'

You take Stevie's hand and make for the dance floor, where you add yourselves to the confusion. Elvis Costello says pump it up when you don't really need it. Stevie carves sinuous figures between the beat. You do your patented New York Torque. The music is just about loud enough to drive everything between your ears down through the spinal column into your bones, and possibly you can shake it out via your fingertips, femurs and toes.

Stevie puts her arms on your shoulders and kisses you. When she says she has to go to the Ladies', you head for the bar to get drinks.

Tad awaits you. 'Have you seen our friend?'

'Which friend?'

'Your formerly deceased not-yet-ex wife.'

You look up from the bottles and scan the immediate vicinity. 'Amanda?'

'Sure enough. The face that launched a thousand trips to Bloomingdale's.'

'Where?'

Tad puts his hand behind your head and directs your gaze to a group near the elevator. She is standing in profile, not twenty feet away. At first you think this is just a close resemblance, then she lifts her hand to her shoulder and begins to twirl a strand of hair between the tips of her fingers. Her agent used to tell her she'd ruin her hair that way. There is no doubt.

Not now, you think.

She's wearing toreador pants and a silver flak jacket. Beside her, a Mediterranean hulk in a white silk shirt emanates a proprietary air. As you watch he smiles at something Amanda has said, and reaches over to squeeze her ass.

Au contraire, Pierre. Sexual Abandonment in spades.

The man looks like he was carved by Praxiteles in 350 B.C. and touched up by Paramount in 1947. You wonder if the physique is functional or cosmetic. How well would he respond if you ripped his ears off?

166

'Who's the greaseball?' Tad says.

You reach down for a bottle and pour yourself a large drink. 'Must be lucky Pierre.'

'I've seen him somewhere.'

'Gentlemen's Quarterly.'

'No. I've seen him around. I know it.' Tad nods his head up and down, as if trying to dislodge a memory. 'I saw him at a party. Note the coke spoon dangling betwixt his hairy pecs.'

'I don't want to hear about it.'

'He wasn't with Amanda. Some other bimbo.'

Stevie returns from the bathroom. 'Here's the dancing fool,' she says.

'I don't need to dance to be foolish.'

Tad says, 'Batten down the hatches, Coach. She's coming at you.'

Sure enough, here's Amanda.

She says, *'Ciao, bello,'* and before you can react she kisses your cheek.

Is she out of her mind? Doesn't she know that you desist from strangling her only through the exercise of heroic restraint?

She kisses Tad with the same formal benevolence. Tad introduces Stevie to Amanda. You can't even believe this is happening. Shouldn't someone say what a nice party this is?

'Is that your Italian stallion?' Tad says, nodding in the direction from which Amanda has come. 'Or your Greek peak? Your French mensch? Or some other species of wetback?'

'That's Odysseus,' Amanda says. 'My fiancé.'

'Odysseus,' Tad says. 'Odysseus. Right, the Greek.' You wish Tad would shut up.

Amanda smiles at you as if you were an acquaintance whose name she is eager to remember. Won't she at least berate you for trying to trash her fashion show?

'So, how's it going?' she says. You stare at her, craving a glimmer of irony or shame in her big blue eyes.

'How's it going?' You start to laugh. She laughs too. You slap your thigh. She wants to know how it's going. A very funny question. Hilarious. Amanda is a riot. You are laughing so hard that you choke. Stevie slaps your back. As soon as you catch your breath you start laughing even harder. Amanda looks alarmed. She doesn't know how funny she can be. You want to tell her she's a barrel of monkeys but you can't speak. You are laughing. People are pounding your back. It's funny. People are funny. Everything's so funny you could die laughing. You can't breathe. You can't even see.

'Drink,' Tad says. He is holding you up with one arm and holding a plastic cup with the other. 'Let there be space,' Tad says to the faces around you. You don't see Amanda's.

'What's the matter?' Stevie asks.

'He's epileptic,' Tad says. 'I know how to handle this.' She retreats, understandably.

'I'm not epileptic,' you say.

'No, just an emotional quadriplegic.'

'I couldn't believe it,' you say. '*How's it going?* Can you believe she said that?' You start to laugh again.

'Take a breather, Coach.' Tad deposits you in a Mies van der Rohe chair. 'You think *that's* funny,' Tad says, 'wait till you hear this.'

'What?'

'Odysseus, right? You remember who he is?'

'How could I forget?'

'I finally figured out where I saw him before.'

'With his hand on Amanda's ass.'

'No. Listen to this. I have this account at the agency. No need to name names. But there's this old babe in Atlanta who runs a company and comes up to New York two or three times a year for a face lift and free meals on the agency's expense account. Naturally, she expects company for the evenings. So we provide this service through a little outfit called 'Dial a Hunk.' Male escort service, very top drawer. And when I say *escort* I am being uncharacteristically discreet. Anyway, about a year ago we dialed a hunk and *voilà* Odysseus.'

'Don't try to cheer me up.'

'It's true. I had to go out with these freaks two nights running, and needless to say the Allagash Express was derailed. The agency paid for his services, which definitely did not include witty conversation.'

When you start to laugh, Tad says, 'Careful.' But it's under control.

'Dial a Hunk.'

'That's it.'

'Dial a Fucking Hunk.'

'Now *that*,' Tad says, 'is funny. The wily Odysseus.'

'Amanda's finally got the right number,' you say, wishing you found it funnier. You wish this laughter could lift you out of your heavy body and carry you beyond this place, out through an open window and up over the city until all this ugliness and pain were reduced to a twinkling of faraway lights.

'I don't know,' you say. 'Actually, it's not that funny. It's just pathetic.'

'Don't pour good sympathy after bad,' Tad says.

'Where's Stevie?'

'That's another sob story. You want to steer clear of that, Coach.'

'Why?'

'Stevie, aka Steve, had his third operation a few weeks ago. Convincing, isn't he?'

'You expect me to believe that?' You replay images of Stevie in your mind. 'Bullshit.'

'Would I lie? Ask Jimmy Q if you don't believe me. What do you think the scarf around the neck is for? You can't remove an Adam's apple.'

You have no idea whether Tad is serious or not, having been taken in by him on numerous occasions. Your curiosity about Stevie's chromosomes is by now exhausted. It is too late in the night to care.

'I was going to tell you.'

'Thanks.' You stand up.

'Take it easy, Coach.' He puts his arm around your shoulders.

'I just realized something.'

'What's that?'

'You and Amanda would make a terrific couple.'

'I suppose that means that you get Odysseus all to yourself.'

'Later, Tad.'

A set of bedrooms is tucked away in a corner of the loft. The first two rooms are full of coke fiends and earnest conversers. The third is free, and a phone sits on a table beside the bed. You find the number in your wallet.

'What time is it?' Vicky says after you identify yourself. 'Where are you?'

'It's late. I'm in New York. I just wanted to talk.'

'Let me guess; you're with Tad.'

'I *was* with Tad.'

'It's a little late for a chat. Is something wrong?'

'I just wanted to tell you my mom died.' You hadn't meant to be so abrupt. You are moving too fast.

'Oh, God,' Vicky says. 'I'm sorry. I didn't know she was . . . when?'

'A year ago.' The Missing Person.

'A *year* ago?'

'I didn't tell you before so I wanted to tell you now. It seemed important.'

'I'm sorry.'

'It's all right. It's not so bad. I mean, it was.' You can't manage to say what you mean. 'I wish you could've met her. You would've hit it off. She had hair like yours. Not just that.'

'I'm not sure what to say.'

'There's something else I didn't tell you. I got married. Bad mistake, but it's all over. I wanted you to know, in case it makes a difference. I'm drunk. Do you think I should hang up?'

In the ensuing pause you can hear the faint hum of the long-distance wire. 'Don't hang up,' Vicky says. 'I can't think of anything to say right now, but I'm here. I'm a little confused.'

'I tried to block her out of my mind. But I think I owe it to her to remember.'

'Wait. *Who*?'

'My mother. Forget my wife. I'm talking about my mother. I was thinking today, after she found out she had cancer, she was talking to Michael and me . . .'

'Michael?'

'That's my brother. She made us promise that if the

pain became unbearable we'd help her, you know, end it all. We had this prescription for morphine so there was this option. But then it got really bad. I asked her and she said that when you were dying you had a responsibility to the living. I was amazed she said that, the way she felt. And I was just thinking that we have a responsibility to the dead—the living, I mean. Does this make any sense?'

'Maybe. I can't tell, really,' Vicky says.

'Can I call tomorrow?'

'Yes, tomorrow. Are you sure you're all right?'

Your brain feels like it is trying to find a way out of your skull. And you are afraid of almost everything. 'I'm fine.'

'Get some sleep. Call me if you can't.'

The first light of the morning outlines the towers of the World Trade Center at the tip of the island. You turn in the other direction and start uptown. There are cobbles on the street where the asphalt has worn through. You think of the wooden shoes of the first Dutch settlers on these same stones. Before that, Algonquin braves stalking game along silent trails.

You're not sure exactly where you are going. You don't feel you have the strength to walk home. You walk faster. If the sunlight catches you on the streets, you will undergo some terrible chemical change.

After a few minutes you notice the blood on your fingers. You hold your hand up to your face. There is blood on your shirt, too. You find a Kleenex in your jacket pocket and hold it to your nose. You advance with your head tilted back against your shoulders.

By the time you reach Canal Street, you think that

you will never make it home. You look for taxis. A bum is sleeping under the awning of a shuttered shop. As you pass he raises his head and says, 'God bless you and forgive your sins.' You wait for the cadge but it doesn't come. You wish he hadn't said anything.

As you turn, what is left of your olfactory equipment sends a message to your brain: fresh bread. Somewhere they are baking bread. You can smell it, even through the nose-bleed. You see bakery trucks loading in front of a building on the next block. You watch as bags of rolls are carried out onto the loading dock by a man with tattooed forearms. This man is already at work so that normal people can have fresh bread for their morning tables. The righteous people who sleep at night and eat eggs for breakfast. It is Sunday morning and you haven't eaten since . . . when? Friday night. As you approach, the smell of bread washes over you like a gentle rain. You inhale deeply, filling your lungs. Tears come to your eyes, and you feel such a rush of tenderness and pity that you stop beside a lamppost and hang on for support.

The smell of bread recalls you to another morning. You arrived home from college after driving half the night; you just felt like coming home. When you walked in, the kitchen was steeped in this same aroma. Your mother asked what the occasion was, and you said a whim. You asked if she was baking. 'Learning to draw inferences at college, are we?' you remember her asking. She said she had to find some way to keep herself busy now that her sons were taking off. You said that you hadn't left, not really. You sat down at the kitchen table to talk, and the bread soon started to burn. She had made bread only two other times that you could recall. Both times it had burned. You remember being proud of your mother then for never having submitted to the tyranny of the kitchen, for having other things on her mind. She cut you two thick slices of bread anyway. They were charred on the outside but warm and moist inside.

You approach the tattooed man on the loading dock. He stops working and watches you. There is something wrong with the way your legs are moving. You wonder if your nose is still bleeding.

'Bread.' This is what you say to him, although you meant to say something more.

'What was your first clue?' he says. He is a man who has served his country, you think, a man with a family somewhere outside the city.

'Could I have some? A roll or something?'

'Get outa here.'

'I'll trade you my sunglasses,' you say. You take off your shades and hand them up to him. 'Ray-Bans. I lost the case.' He tries them on, shakes his head a few times and then takes them off. He folds the glasses and puts them in his shirt pocket.

'You're crazy,' he says. Then he looks back into the warehouse. He picks up a bag of hard rolls and throws it at your feet.

You get down on your knees and tear open the bag. The smell of warm dough envelops you. The first bite sticks in your throat and you almost gag. You will have to go slowly. You will have to learn everything all over again.

A NOTE ON THE AUTHOR

Jay McInerney is also the author of the novels *Ransom, Story of My Life, Brightness Falls, The Last of the Savages, Model Behaviour* and *The Good Life*, one story collection, *How It Ended*, and two works of non-fiction, *Bacchus and Me* and *A Hedonist in the Cellar*. He lives in New York and Nashville.

BRIGHTNESS FALLS

Before *The Good Life* came *Brightness Falls*, which captures lives-in-the-making: men and women confronting their sudden middle-age with wit and low behaviour, fear and confusion, and, just occasionally, a little honesty and decency. Corrine Calloway is a young stockbroker on Wall Street, her husband Russell an underpaid but ambitious publishing editor. The couple head into New York's 1980s gold rush where prospects and money seem to be flying everywhere. But the Calloways soon find out that what goes up must come crashing down, both on Wall Street and at home.

'A funny, self-mocking, sometimes brilliant portrait of
Manhattan's young literary and Wall Street crowd'
TIME

'Smart, funny and brilliant'
INDEPENDENT

✳

ISBN 978 0 7475 8485 8   PAPERBACK   £7.99

THE LAST OF THE SAVAGES

When Patrick Keane arrives at an exclusive New England prep school in the 60s he meets his roommate, the radical Will Savage. The last in the line of a privileged white family from the Mississippi Delta, Will disavows his father's expectations and embraces the searing anthems of black soul music. From wildly different backgrounds Patrick and Will form an unlikely friendship that is to span three decades, from the turbulent sixties to the nineties. *The Last of the Savages* is a dazzling exploration of interracial love, music, family, and enduring friendship.

'Offers nothing less than three decades of Stateside history, in which the changing image of America is embodied in the existential shape-shifting of the main characters'
INDEPENDENT

'Gives Scott Fitzgerald's fictional world a modern make-over'
SUNDAY TIMES

✳

ISBN 978 1 4088 0095 9   PAPERBACK   £7.99

B L O O M S B U R Y

HOW IT ENDED

Discover a world of sex, excess and urban paranoia where worlds collide, relationships fragment and the dark underbelly of the American dream is exposed. A transsexual prostitute accidentally propositions his own father. A senator's serial infidelities leave him in hot water. And two young lovers spend Christmas together high on different drugs. McInerney's characters struggle together in a shifting world where old certainties dissolve and nobody can be sure of where they stand.

'Jay McInerney is the type of American novelist to whom English readers instinctively warm ... *How It Ended* is the work of a fine writer on the top of his form'
SUNDAY TELEGRAPH

'Sharp, spare, exquisitely observed writing'
DAILY MAIL

*

ISBN 978 0 7475 8520 6 PAPERBACK £7.99

MODEL BEHAVIOUR

Connor McNab's girlfriend is off to California, allegedly on a fashion shoot, but he doesn't know where she is staying and a sinking feeling tells him that she might never come back. Connor's friend Jeremy is no help: he is a writer with an imminent publication date and some people holding his dog to ransom. Connor's sister Brook is too busy anguishing over Rwanda and Bosnia. His editor at *Ciao Bella* is only concerned about the suddenly elusive celebrity of the month. Thanks goodness for Pallas, a knock-out table dancer with a heart of gold.

'A fast-paced, funny tale of true love gone wrong, full of McInerney's wit and style'
COSMOPOLITAN

'A comedy of dysfunction ... Yet, beneath its running gags and scathing one-liners, there lies a more urgent critique of America's vainglory'
DAILY EXPRESS

*

ISBN 978 0 7475 8521 3 PAPERBACK £7.99

B L O O M S B U R Y

THE GOOD LIFE

Ten years on from *Brightness Falls*, Russell Calloway is still a literary editor although in a diminished capacity; his wife, Corrine, has sacrificed her career to watch anxiously over their children. Across town Luke McGavock, a wealthy ex-investment banker, is taking a sabbatical from making money, struggling to reconnect with his socially resplendent wife, Sasha, and their angst-ridden teenage daughter, Ashley. These two Manhattan families are teetering on the brink of change when 9/11 happens. *The Good Life* explores through the lens of catastrophe that territory between hope and despair, love and loss, regret and fulfilment.

'Tender and moving ... of all the 9/11 books this is possibly the only one that will pass the test of time'
ARENA

❖

ISBN 978 0 7475 8581 7   PAPERBACK   £7.99

THE LAST BACHELOR

In true McInerney style, this new collection of stories examines post 9/11 America in all its dark and morally complex glory. From the streets of downtown New York during the 2003 anti-war march and the lavish hotel rooms of the wealthy social elite, to a husband and wife who share a marital bed with a pot-bellied pig, the people in these stories search for meaning while struggling against each other.

'Welcome to the weird world of Jay McInerney where anything and anyone comes and goes ... a dirty dozen of cautionary tales. The results are funny, shocking and moving'
DAILY EXPRESS

❖

ISBN 978 1 4088 0071 3   PAPERBACK   £7.99

ORDER YOUR COPY: BY PHONE +44 (0)1256 302 699; BY EMAIL: DIRECT@MACMILLAN.CO.UK
DELIVERY IS USUALLY 3–5 WORKING DAYS. FREE POSTAGE AND PACKAGING FOR ORDERS OVER £20.
ONLINE: WWW.BLOOMSBURY.COM/BOOKSHOP
PRICES AND AVAILABILITY SUBJECT TO CHANGE WITHOUT NOTICE.
WWW.BLOOMSBURY.COM/JAYMCINERNEY

BLOOMSBURY